THE MISSIOLOGICAL SPIRIT

Christian Mission Theology
in the Third Millennium Global Context

Amos Yong

CASCADE *Books* · Eugene, Oregon

Cascade Book
An Imprint of Wipf and Stock Publishers
199 W. 8th Ave., Suite 3
Eugene, OR 97401

www.wipfandstock.com

ISBN 13: 978-1-62564-670-5

Cataloguing-in-Publication Data

Yong, Amos.

The missiological spirit : Christian mission theology in the third millennium global context / Amos Yong.

xvi + 276 p. ; 23 cm. Includes bibliographical references and indexes.

ISBN 13: 978-1-62564-670-5

1. Missions—Theory. 2. Pentecostalism. 3. Christianity and other religions. 4. Holy Spirit. I. Title.

BV2063 .Y65 2014

Manufactured in the U.S.A.   11/10/2014

To
Julie and Wonsuk Ma,
and to Scott Sunquist,
exemplary models of the missiological spirit

Contents

Preface

THIS BOOK IS CLOSE on the heels of and intended to be a companion to my *The Dialogical Spirit: Christian Reason and Theological Method for the Third Millennium* (Cascade Books, 2014). I am grateful to Robin Parry, Rodney Clapp, and the editorial team at Cascade Books for seeing their value, especially since these two volumes consist, by and large, of essays and articles written for and published separately in other venues. Christian Amondson, Matthew Wimer, and Laura Poncy, among others at Wipf and Stock, have also been helpful in bringing the project from separate pieces into a coherent whole.

All of the twelve chapters in the four parts of this book have been written since the turn of the third Christian millennium (2001 and after). Each chapter includes acknowledgments (usually in the initial or final footnote) that document my gratitude at the time of writing. They have been reprinted here largely without alteration—except that any clarifications or additions are inserted in bracketed footnotes—so that readers can trace the progression of my thinking on this important and interrelated set of topics. The introduction and the conclusion are newly written for this volume, and the former explains more about the motivations for each chapter and how they combine to hold together the book's central argument and overarching rationale.

Over the last decade plus during which the pieces of this book have been written, my wife, Alma, has been faithfully by my side, extending her loving companionship, which stretches back almost thirty years now since we first met. She keeps reminding me to think hard about why I do what I do, oftentimes because I get distracted and sometimes attempt to run in multiple directions. As she gives me pause on these various moments on our journey together, she helps me reconnect with the vocation that is not just mine but ours: to bear witness to the gospel of Jesus Christ. This is how we attempt to faithfully live out the Christian mission, which theological dimensions this book explicates.

Enoch Charles, my graduate assistant at Regent University, helped in formatting the text according to Cascade guidelines and creating the bibliography, among so many other tasks that he did for me and others in the School of Divinity. He is a product of Christian missions (from American to India) and committed to thinking further about mission theology (from India to the world) going forward. Ryan Seow, my current graduate assistant at Fuller Seminary, helped with the indexing. May the missiological spirit flourish for him, and for Enoch and his wife Steffi, along this unpredictable path.

I dedicate this book to my dear friends Julie and Wonsuk Ma, and Scott Sunquist. Scott was instrumental in wooing me away from Regent University to join the Fuller Seminary School of Intercultural Studies (SIS) faculty in the spring of 2014. He has been an exemplary model of the Christian scholar-missionary, producing substantive historical work and bringing those important insights to bear on the Christian mission. I already feel as if I have known Scott for a lifetime, even during our short time of working together. He has convinced me that he as a historian and I as a theologian can indeed join in common cause in leading the Fuller SIS into the next chapter of its already prestigious history. Providentially, I had already submitted the manuscript of this volume to Cascade Books when the invitation came, and so I could legitimately say that I had written at least one book on Christian mission theology that would qualify to underwrite my missiological credentials. I am looking forward to many years of working both with SIS faculty, staff, and students as the director of both Fuller's Center for Missiological Research and SIS's PhD program in intercultural studies.

I first seriously engaged the Mas' work when I read Julie's published PhD thesis, and this resulted in a lengthy review essay (now published as chapter 1 of this book). Over the years, our paths have crossed professionally and personally on many occasions. Not only have both of them written for books I have edited, but I have also edited a book—with Chandler Im, titled *Global Diasporas and Mission* (2014)— for the Edinburgh Centenary Series in mission studies, over which Wonsuk serves as general editor (published by Regnum International). More importantly, they have devoted their lives to many different facets of the Christian mission in our present global context, and have also published extensively on Christian theology of mission. They are exemplary Christian missionaries (even if they do not always fit the classical missionary mold) for our post-Christian, post-Western, postcolonial, and postsecular world, while I am just a theologian who has spent some time thinking about Christian mission in a pluralistic world of many faiths (one of the primary subjects of this book). Although they can improve on much of what appears, even as they would be in better position than almost anyone I know to distinguish the wheat from the chaff in the pages to come, this dedication is made because if I were to ever grow up to become a missionary, I pray such will follow the path that they have charted, as they have followed Jesus Christ.

Amos Yong
September 2014
Pasadena, California

Acknowledgments

ALL OF THE CHAPTERS in this book either have been previously published or were written for publication in other venues. I am grateful to the editors and publishers (listed first, if not clearly identifiable in the citation) for permission to reuse the following material for this volume, and have in some specific cases appended their own requested acknowledgments:

1. Brill: "Going Where the Spirit Goes. . . : Engaging the Spirit(s) in J. C. Ma's Pneumatological Missiology," *Journal of Pentecostal Theology* 10:2 (April 2002) 110–28.

2. World Council of Churches and Wiley-Blackwell: "'As the Spirit Gives Utterance. . . ': Pentecost, Intra-Christian Ecumenism, and the Wider *Oekumene*," *International Review of Mission* 92:366 (July 2003) 299–314.

3. The American Society of Missiology and Sage Publications: "A P(new)matological Paradigm for Christian Mission in a Religiously Plural World," *Missiology: An International Review* 33:2 (2005) 175–91.

4. The American Society of Missiology and Sage Publications: "The Spirit of Hospitality: Pentecostal Perspectives toward a Performative Theology of the Interreligious Encounter," *Missiology: An International Review* 35:1 (2007) 55–73.

5. The Regents of the University of California: "Missiology and the Interreligious Encounter" (coauthored with Tony Richie), in Allan Anderson, Michael Bergunder, André Droogers, and Cornelis van der Laan, eds., *Studying Global Pentecostalism: Theories and Methods* (Berkeley, CA: University of California Press, 2010), 245–67.

6. Emeth Press: "From Demonization to Kin-domization: The Witness of the Spirit and the Renewal of Missions in a Pluralistic World," in Amos Yong and Clifton Clarke, eds., *Global Renewal, Religious Pluralism,*

and the Great Commission: Toward a Renewal Theology of Mission and Interreligious Encounter, Asbury Theological Seminary Series in World Christian Revitalization Movements in Pentecostal/Charismatic Studies 4 (Lexington, KY: Emeth, 2011), 157–74.

7. Wipf and Stock Publishers: "The Missiology of Jamestown: 1607–2007 and Beyond—Toward a Postcolonial Theology of Mission in North America," in Amos Yong and Barbara Brown Zikmund, eds., *Remembering Jamestown: Hard Questions about Christian Mission* (Eugene: Pickwick, 2010), 157–67.

8. Steiner Verlag: "The Buddhist-Christian Encounter in the USA: Reflections on Christian Practices," in Ulrich van der Heyden and Andreas Feldtkeller, eds., *Border Crossings: Explorations of an Interdisciplinary Historian—Festschrift for Irving Hexham*, Missionsgeschichtliches Archiv 12 (Stuttgart: Franz Steiner Verlag, 2008), 457–72.

9. Peter Lang Publishers: "The Church and Mission Theology in a Post-Constantinian Era: Soundings from the Anglo-American Frontier," in Akintunde E. Akinade, ed., *A New Day: Essays on World Christianity in Honor of Lamin Sanneh* (New York: Peter Lang, 2010), 49–61.

10. World Council of Churches and Wiley-Blackwell: "Primed for the Spirit: Creation, Redemption, and the *Missio Spiritus*," *International Review of Mission* 100:2 (November 2011) 355–66.

11. "Christological Constants in Shifting Contexts: Jesus Christ and the *Missio Spiritus* in a Pluralistic World"—a slightly revised version will be published as "Christological Constants in Shifting Contexts: Jesus Christ, Prophetic Dialogue, and the *Missio Spiritus* in a Pluralistic World," in Steve Bevans and Cathy Ross, eds., *Mission as Prophetic Dialogue: Contemporary Theological Reflections on Christian Mission* (London: SCM Press, 2015).

12. "God, Christ, Spirit: Christian Pluralism and Evangelical Mission in the 21st Century," was originally intended for and will be published later in Armin Triebel, ed., *Roswith Gerloff—Auf Grenzen: Ein Leben im Dazwischen von Kulturen / On the Border: Living between Cultures* (Berlin: Weissensee-Verlag, forthcoming).

Introduction

THE LAST TWO TO three decades have seen a renaissance in the field of missiology, the discipline that researches and studies the field of Christian mission, its history, development, methods, and theology. If, fifty years ago, pundits were thinking that the forces of secularization would not only stifle religion in general, not to mention the Christian religion particularly, but also gradually strangle the impulses of religious mission, the explosion of religion since that time has precipitated a frantic search for a new paradigm for researching and understanding Christian expansion and its concomitant advancement activities. David Bosch's magisterial *Transforming Mission* became a classic almost overnight after its publication in 1991,[1] both because it captured the missional enterprise undergirding Christianity's vitality as a world religion and because it provide articulation for its theological substructure—the more specific tasks of *theology of mission*—that were in need of rethinking given the global dynamics.

This book enters at least in part into the theology of mission arena charted by Bosch but works intentionally in the direction of what might be called *mission theology*. If the former theology of mission focuses on the theological dimensions of the Christian mission—its rationale, justification, methods, and relationship to other theological loci—the latter mission theology accentuates how the Christian theological enterprise as a whole can be understood in missiological perspective. As a systematic theologian, I hope to contribute to the discussion of theology of mission not only by thinking about the Christian mission from a theological angle but also by reversing the emphasis and reconsidering Christian theology from a missiological or missional perspective. The four parts of this book thus work from more explicitly missiological concerns toward reconsiderations of aspects of the systematic and dogmatic theological landscape.

1. Bosch, *Transforming Mission*.

1

However, my work in Christian mission theology has also unfolded over the last fifteen years in sustained interaction with the realities of religious pluralism in our time. In this venue, a multiplicity of conversations are intertwined: in theologies of religions, theologies of interfaith encounter, theologies of interreligious dialogue, comparative theology, theologies of the unevangelized, theologies of pluralism, etc. Further, much of the developments at these various junctures are interwoven with theological engagements with the following, among many other topics: the legacy of the Enlightenment and its universalizing epistemology, globalization and its economic transformations, colonialism and the postcolonial reaction, secularization and the postsecular, and the postmodern condition (characterized also as our post-Western, post-European, and post-Christendom situation). A number of excellent missiologies have emerged in this context.[2] My own contribution is marked specifically by the pentecostal experience and perspective I bring, both informed by the explosion of contemporary scholarship on global pentecostalism.[3] The thesis of this volume, one that has emerged over the course of in my work in this arena, is that the missiological compulsion of the present twenty-first-century global and pluralistic context can be invigorated by a pneumatological imagination derived from the Day of Pentecost narrative, and as such can not only inspire more faithful Christian witness but also be a resource for Christian theology of mission and mission theology for the third millennium.

This book provides a more-or-less autobiographical perspective on these matters by following out the thread of my thinking about pentecostal faith and Christian mission in a pluralistic world. The four part titles of the book reflect aspects of my own journey, beginning with the sense of needing to establish my credentials as a systematic theologian rather than in the area that pentecostal scholars had been much more known for (missiology); moving into a more explicit attempt to reconsider pentecostal missiology in light of the challenges of religious pluralism and advances in theologies of interfaith encounter; then providing North American case studies of how such a pentecostally-inspired missiological posture—what I call in this book the pneumato-missiological imagination—might have something to contribute to the present discussion; and concluding by coming full circle to systematic questions and concerns, now illuminated by such a pneumato-logically formulated missiology. The genre and structure of the volume thus presumes there is a biographical and narrative dimension to the theological

2. Besides Bosch, see Muck and Adeney, *Christianity Encountering World Religions*, and Tennent, *Invitation to World Missions*.

3. Including, but not limited to Hollenweger, *Pentecostalism*; Vondey, *Beyond Pentecostalism*; and Anderson, *Ends of the Earth*.

task and therefore seeks to not only depict, but conduct theological—in this case, missiological—inquiry in such a mode.[4] The following identifies the animating (autobiographical) concerns behind each of the chapters even while situating them vis-à-vis the volume's overarching issues.

RELUCTANT MISSIOLOGY: CHRISTIAN MISSION'S IRREPRESSIBILITY

Pentecostal theology as a scholarly enterprise began in the late 1980s and was sustained in its first decade primarily by contributions in theology of spirituality and theology of mission because, among other reasons, pentecostalism was considered more a spirituality and a missionary movement than a theological tradition. So while books had begun to appear on *pentecostal missiology* or *pentecostal spirituality* in the 1980s and early 1990s,[5] the notion of a *pentecostal theology* was still somewhat of an oxymoron at the time when I opted for graduate training in theological studies in the early and mid-1990s.[6] Perhaps I might be forgiven, then, when my training in systematic theology led me to embrace a professorial vocation as a systematician rather than as a missiologist. The problem was that pentecostal systematic theology had yet to emerge on its own terms (being reliant on categories, frameworks, and resources derived from other Christian traditions, sometimes to its own detriment),[7] so I labored to discern what that might look like and how I might make a contribution to such a task.

My response then, and now, remains that pentecostal spirituality and experience generates a distinctive hermeneutic, method, and imagination revolving around encountering the living God of Jesus Christ through the Holy Spirit, and this spirituality of encounter has the potential to revitalize

---

4. Narrativity is central to the pentecostal tradition that informs my thinking; see Cartledge, *Testimony in the Spirit*, esp. 15–18. For more on the biographical dimension of Christian theology, see McClendon Jr., *Biography as Theology*; cf. my *Dialogical Spirit*.

5. I describe the emergence of pentecostal scholarship in my essay, "Pentecostalism and the Theological Academy." One of the most important pentecostal theological contributions in that first decade (with ongoing influence) was arguably in the area of spiritual theology: Land, *Pentecostal Spirituality*. Indicators of the emerging pentecostal contribution in missiology include Dempster et al., *Called and Empowered*, and Jongeneel, *Pentecost, Mission, Ecumenism*.

6. Even after the turn of the third millennium, the long history of pentecostal anti-intellectualism has perpetuated the oxymoronic reputation of *pentecostal theology*; this is documented by Nañez, *Full Gospel, Fractured Minds?*

7. For such an assessment, see Macchia, "Revitalizing Theological Categories"; cf. also my essay, "Whither Systematic Theology?"

and renew Christian theology for the third millennium.[8] When starting out as a graduate student, however, my concerns were not merely to formulate such an expansive theological vision but to address what I felt were some of the most pressing concerns for Christian theology as a whole (including systematic theology) as we faced (then) the twenty-first century: that regarding the Christian encounter with other faiths. My early work was dominated by this horizon of theological reflection: how to make sense of the Christian tradition in light of religious pluralism, including the many theological (and other) claims made by adherents of other traditions. Again, my response then, as now, is that a distinctively pneumatological imagination had the capacity to enable both Christian interaction with others on their terms and Christian witness to others based on our commitments. My arguments at that early phase, however, were driven first and foremost by discussions in theology of religions, theology of interreligious dialogue, and comparative theological issues, all intended to make contributions to the rethinking of Christian systematic theology in a pluralistic world, and *not* by theology of mission concerns.[9] After all, my goal was to further the discussion as a systematician, not as a missiologist.

This desire to avoid being tabbed as another pentecostal motivated by missiological matters no doubt led me to approach the pentecostal missiology of Julie Ma as I did (chapter 1 below). I was invited then by John Christopher Thomas, the editor of the *Journal of Pentecostal Theology*, to review Ma's published thesis, and rather than interact with it missiologically, I donned the religious studies hat fitted during my doctoral course of study and reviewed it in light of those concerns. Readers of this book can surmise given later developments in my thinking how, if I were to review Ma's *When the Spirit Meets the Spirits* today, a more explicitly missiological perspective would note different emphases and make other connections. Yet while the disciplinary or analytical lens might shift, let me highlight a number of themes explicitly denoted in my initial assessment that I believe remain important for present thinking in missiology and missiological theology. First, the question of Christian mission, discipleship, and maturation across the majority of the world *after* globalization will remain with us going forward;

8. See Warrington, *Pentecostal Theology*, although the notion of "encounter" functions more rhetorically than technically in his treatment. My most comprehensive articulation of this so far is a one-volume systematic theology that is going to press simultaneously with this book, written with Jonathan A. Anderson: *Renewing Christian Theology*; cf. also my *Spirit of Love*.

9. Two of my first three books were in this vein: *Discerning the Spirit(s)* and *Beyond the Impasse*. I returned a few years later to develop these ideas in *Hospitality and the Other*, which remains the most succinct and mature articulation of my thinking along these lines.

there will be both theological and missiological dimensions to these matters, with the former being more unequivocally detailed in my thinking with Ma about what it means for the church, and theology, to be reformed and always being reformed (or renewed and always being renewed). Second, my identification of four horizons of intersection will persist for Christian theology and mission (see the final subsection, "Theological Methodology: A Genuinely Interreligious and Interdisciplinary Dialogue," in chapter 1); those coming from perspectives other than a pentecostal one and those working with people other than Ma's Kankana-ey Christians will nevertheless need to factor in those horizonal dynamics. Last but not least, at the heart of Christian theology and mission are the perennial questions related to the gospel-culture interface; my deliberations with Julie Ma from a religious studies perspective surely ought to be complemented by those of other vantage points, but they will not be displaced on this side of the eschaton, or so long as the religious and cultural dimensions of human life remain distinct but yet intertwined in anticipation of the coming reign of God.

It should now be clearer why I entitled this part of this book "Reluctant Missiology": I considered my work in this earlier period demarcated primarily by the fields of religious studies and systematic theology, rather than by that of missiology. Yet even as I struggled to establish my bona fides in the field of systematics, the missiological character of the Christian theological task would not be easily marginalized.[10] Chapters 2 and 3 of this book provide glimpses into how my theological imagination kept getting interrupted by missiological interventions. Both articles reflect my realization, even then, that the most pressing issues raised by my initial monographs on theology of religions and interfaith encounter and dialogue were both theological and missiological, together. "As the Spirit Gives Utterance" (chapter 2) grappled with both fronts in the wake of the publication of my doctoral dissertation, *Discerning the Spirit(s)* (2000). On the theological register, I wrestled with how to make universal claims for Christian faith in a postmodern and even post-Christian world. This challenge turned fundamentally on the issue of how to talk both about Christian particularity (related to the scandal of incarnation and crucifixion, for instance) and universality. As a pentecostal theologian, it also pressed for me the question of pentecostal specificity and Christian catholicity. That one could err on either side on this matter (the former risking ecumenical relevance, the latter ignoring the gifts of the modern pentecostal movement) illuminated how one could also err on either side in the twenty-first-century context of

10. I tell more about this—now in hindsight, productive—struggle in my "Spirit, Vocation, and the Life of the Mind."

the Christian encounter with other faiths. Thus did the theological register traverse both with and against the missiological axis: in a post-Western and postcolonial global context, how can Christians avoid an imperialism either of domesticating other faiths for Christian purposes or of muffling, twisting, or silencing the testimonies of religious others altogether? Hence I suggested then, and continue to defend, the idea that the biblical account of the Day of Pentecost event provides resources for both theological and missiological tasks, enabling distinctiveness of witness both within the Christian ecumenical field and across the wider interfaith spectrum.

It was my second book on comparative theology and the interfaith encounter, *Beyond the Impasse* (2003), which generated a more substantive response.[11] "A P(new)matological Paradigm for Christian Mission in a Religiously Plural World" was written specifically to address the acute questions raised by the theological program sketched in this early work. While a few of my critics rightly noted the importance of what I identified as the "christological impasse" for the overall thesis being argued, most missed that what was to be avoided was the missiological rather than christological scandal of particularity. I have always realized that any proclamation of Christ, the hope of Christian faith, would always be scandalous, as indeed already declared by St. Paul (e.g., Gal 5:11, 1 Cor 1:23); but that did not mean that Christian theology in the third millennium could ignore other faiths or could not gain from considering their claims, and it surely did not mean that Christian approaches to those in other faiths ought to be intentionally scandalous. More recently, evangelical theologians across the spectrum are realizing that Christian proclamation and mission can—in fact, should— proceed in respectful dialogue and encounter with others,[12] and I see my own proposals as providing a pentecostal and pneumatological justification for such undertakings. The point is not to urge an untenable universalism or a naïve syncretism of Christianity and other faiths, but to think theologically through the fact of religious plurality and its implications for Christian self-understanding and mission. Yet while I was thinking and writing principally as a systematician, I was realizing—however reluctantly—that I could not evade the missional dimension of Christian faith and theology.

11. Largely because of the Baker Academic imprint, I surmise (with seventeen published scholarly/critical reviews that have come to my attention), in contrast to my doctoral thesis, which was published in the *Journal of Pentecostal Theology* Supplement series, and as such did not catch the attention of the broader theological academy as much (reviewed ten times).

12. E.g., McDermott, *Can Evangelicals Learn?*; Tiessen, *Who Can Be Saved?*; and Metzger, *Connecting Christ*.

PENTECOSTAL MISSIOLOGY: MISSIOLOGICAL PRAXIS

The three chapters in this part of the book reflect my thinking specifically about Christian missiology from a pentecostal perspective. By the time I wrote what is now chapter 4 in 2006, not only was I a bit more secure as a systematic theologian—I had just published my fourth book and finished a draft of a fifth manuscript[13]—but I had also relocated to working in the PhD program in Renewal Studies at Regent University. The latter invited me to live more explicitly into my pentecostal and renewal identity,[14] and I realized that this included the opportunity to embrace more intentionally the mission emphasis in pentecostal churches and traditions. Chapters 4–6 therefore together reflect my efforts to achieve a number of overarching theological objectives once I realized I no longer needed to be a reluctant missiologist.

First, I had to come to grips with the fact that there is a missiological aspect to, if not character shaping, all theological reflection. As a pentecostal scholar working in theology of religions, then, I had to ask both about the missional aspect of the Christian encounter with other faiths in a pluralistic world and about how pentecostal perspectives might inform, if not advance, such a discussion, especially at the theological level. Second, then, my systematic theological work in relationship to the religions could also be brought to bear on pentecostal theology. Whereas heretofore pentecostal scholarly work had been otherwise more practically focused on theologies of mission, I saw the opportunity to develop such both more systematically (read: more pneumatologically and more Trinitarianly) and dogmatically (read: in conversation with the historic and ecumenical theological tradition), with greater attention to the contemporary Christian encounter with other faiths (read: in light of actual mission practices and also in view of advances on the comparative theological landscape). Third, if all Christian theology is missionally-related in some respect, then all Christian missiology is also fundamentally theological. As a pentecostal theologian of the religions, then, I had the opportunity to speak into existing discussions in theology of mission both from a pentecostal standpoint and in view of practical and theoretical developments in Christian interfaces with other religions in the present time. It began to dawn of me that while these three

13. Yong, *Spirit Poured Out on All Flesh*, and, the later book, *Theology and Down Syndrome*.

14. "Renewal" at Regent includes pentecostal, charismatic, and other related movements stretching back through the historic Christian tradition and across the full scope of the contemporary ecumenical, including Roman Catholic and Orthodox, spectrum; see my article, "Poured Out on All Flesh."

goals could be distinguished, they were also unavoidably intertwined, even as it would be difficult to prioritize them.

The fourth chapter, "The Spirit of Hospitality," was written in response to the invitation to provide a plenary address at the 2006 annual meeting of the distinguished American Society of Missiology. The theme of the conference was devoted to the implications for Christian missiology of the growth and expansion of pentecostalism globally, so I took this opportunity to suggest how pentecostal perspectives might inform a more pneumatologically-oriented theology of interreligious encounter. Three themes are noteworthy in this context. First, a pentecostal and pneumatological approach would be concerned not only with abstract theological formulations but with more concrete practical explications, consistent with the modern pentecostal affinity with the New Testament Acts of the Apostles, which highlighted how the disciples of Christ carried out the Christian mission as empowered by the Holy Spirit. Hence, I suggested what I then, and still now, call a *performative* theology of interfaith encounter, an approach to the interreligious arena that emphasizes the missional work of the Holy Spirit in enabling relationships between people of any (or no) faith. Second, such a performative (rather than descriptive) approach to Christian mission in a pluralistic world would essentially involve being both hosts of and guests to those in other faiths. Such a performative theology of interfaith hospitality is profoundly pneumatological (in terms of the Spirit's outpouring on all flesh; Acts 2:17), christological (in terms of Christ's incarnation and reception into the world), and Trinitarian (in terms of God's creating [making space for] and reconciling [inviting fellowship of] the world to himself through the Word and Spirit), even as it could potentially invigorate Christian witness in a postcolonial and postmodern milieu.[15] Last but not least, I developed this pneumatological theology and missiology of interfaith hospitality from the Lukan (Luke-Acts) portions of the apostolic witness. This not only develops my prior work on biblical theology in the various constructive sections of *The Spirit Poured Out on All Flesh* (2005), but also contributes at least thematically and from a pentecostal perspective to ongoing scholarship on Lukan materials.

Chapter 5 is coauthored with Tony Richie, a longtime sojourner with me on the otherwise oftentimes lonely roads where pentecostal theology transects with theology of religions and comparative theology.[16] Unlike detractors who could little appreciate, much less understand, me either because they have failed to conduct a thorough reading of my work related to

15. The seeds sown in this article germinated in my *Hospitality and the Other*.
16. See also my foreword to Richie, *Speaking by the Spirit*, xi–xii.

these matters or because their interpretive perspective is uninformed by the wider theological conversation (in the case of some pentecostal opponents) or is unsympathetic to pentecostal sensibilities and commitments (in the case of other evangelical, and non-pentecostal, critics), Tony has been a dialogue partner, theological editor, and thoughtful sounding board since we first exchanged emails in 2002 and then met personally in 2003. Our "Missiology and the Interreligious Encounter," written as a methodological primer for the study of contemporary pentecostalism, provides in summary form the basic thrusts of the pentecostal and pneumatological theology of religions informing much of my work and situates these squarely amidst the ongoing discussion of pentecostal missiology. If I were to ever write afresh a book at the juncture of these topics, I would return to this chapter for the basic outline. The argument therein reflects most explicitly my recognition that pentecostal and Christian theology of religions has a missiological facet and pentecostal and Christian theology of mission also has to include consideration of the contemporary pluralistic and global context.

I wrote chapter 6 initially to respond to and conclude a collection of essays triangulating around the themes of global pentecostal and renewal Christianity, Christian mission, and religious pluralism.[17] On the one hand, "From Demonization to Kin-domization" addresses one of the practical realities of popular pentecostal mission endeavors that is contested in the pluralistic public square, the demonization of other faiths and their adherents; on the other hand, the essay persists in developing a pentecostal and pneumatological approach to the interfaith encounter out of sustained engagement with the apostolic experience in the book of Acts. If the Acts narrative is central to pentecostal theology and spirituality more generally, here (again) I foreground its potential for inspiring missiological reflection in a pluralistic world.[18]

---

17. The book was published as Yong and Clarke, eds., *Global Renewal, Religious Pluralism, Great Commission*.

18. I have continued my exploration of Luke-Acts in a few of my books—e. g., *Hospitality and the Other* (2008), *In the Days of Caesar* (2010), and *Who is the Holy Spirit?* (2011)—and this cumulative work has led pentecostal biblical scholar Martin Mittelstadt to suggest: "Yong not only demonstrates ongoing Pentecostal persistence to embody the Lukan story, but stands as one of the most influential Pentecostal voices to bring this confidence to the current generation . . ." and "biblical scholars will soon come to regard him as the most influential contemporary Pentecostal scholar of the Lukan corpus"; ("Reimagining Luke-Acts," 26, 29).

NORTH AMERICAN MISSIOLOGY: MISSION POST-CHRISTENDOM

The chapters gathered in parts II and III of this volume were originally written over a similar period of time. In fact, there is a wider span for those in the second part (from 2005–2010) compared to those in the third (from 2007–2009). However, I have gathered them under their respective headings to separate out the more specifically pentecostal thinking of the former from the more focused contextuality of the latter. If the preceding triad of essays is more globally oriented by virtue of my taking up the issues as a pentecostal and renewal theologian, those of part III have their locus in the North American setting. This reflects in part my own diasporic identity as what some call a 1.5 generation Asian American theologian, born and raised in part in Malaysia but educated since my middle school days in the North American West.[19] Hence while the global horizon is continuously a part of my theological work, I have also been attentive to the peculiar opportunities and challenges for theology and mission in North America.[20]

Perhaps at the popular level, many do not think of the Christian mission in relationship to the North American scene. But of course if mission is no more or less than the church's witness to the gospel, then this ought to be of global, not least North American, pertinence. Rather than being ordered sequentially according to the time of their original publication (one of the structuring guidelines for the rest of this book), the three chapters gathered here are organized in relationship to their historical content. I begin with "The Missiology of Jamestown"—written second, in 2009—because it deals with issues that stretch back further in North American mission history: the encounter between European missionaries and the native population. Although written and published first, in 2007 and 2008 respectively, "The Buddhist-Christian Encounter in the USA" follows because it unfolds such across its twentieth-century North American history. We conclude with "The Church and Mission Theology in a Post-Constantinian Era," which emerged out of the research and writing of my book on political theology in 2008–2009,[21] since it deals with the nature of mission in a contemporary

19. See my book *Future of Evangelical Theology*, especially its introductory chapter that documents my journey as an Asian American.

20. See my essay, "Between Local and Global"; cf. also part I of *The Dialogical Spirit*, which takes up the task of doing theology in a postfoundationalist epistemological era in conversation with thinkers in the tradition of North American philosophical pragmatism.

21. Chapter 9 of this book provides a parallel line of thinking to Yong, *In the Days of Caesar*, ch. 5, which sketches a pentecostal theology of cultural engagement.

America that is paradoxically both postsecular and post-Christian simultaneously. In each case, however, Christian mission theory begs for practical explication and Christian mission praxis invites clarification of the underlying theological justification, for better or worse.

Chapters 7 and 8 deal with the post-Western, post-Enlightenment, and postcolonial realities as played out specifically in North America. The former revisits these matters in light of the history of the Christian mission to Native America, while the latter takes up similar issues against the North American Christian-Buddhist encounter. Yet thinking about Christian mission in conversation with Native Americans across the continent highlights not only the atrocities committed to indigenous cultures by more-or-less sincere Christians but also unearths the various theological warrants depended upon for such endeavors. Part of the vision that justified the triumphalism manifest in North American mission history rests between the lines of the seventh chapter rather than being unequivocally detailed, and it concerns the theological supersessionism that marginalized the Jewish character of Christian faith in order to assert a Euro-American version of the gospel, which had little capacity to tolerate, much less receive the contribution of, the voices and perspectives of indigenous and other non-Western cultures.[22] The point is that if Christian mission *after* Jamestown—as symbolizing the entirety of the Christian missionary encounter with Native America—has to find a way to be receptive to the indigenous contribution to Christian identity, self-understanding, and mission, then it also has to find a way to overcome the historical racism that infects at least some strands of modern Western Christianity. To be sure, lessons learned in this conversation are applicable across the majority of the world in light of the interwoven fortunes of the colonial and missionary enterprises.

The eighth chapter of this book deals with many of the same issues opened up by its predecessor but comes at them from another set of interconnected vantage points: the history of Asian migration to America, the globalization processes, and the phenomenon of the so-called reverse mission. While this last matter has in recent missiological literature referred to how majority world migration to Europe and North America has also invigorated missionary activities intended to renew Christianity in the Western hemisphere, the history of Buddhism in the USA also unveils the

---

22. This opens up to discussions on how modern Western theology depends on an unarticulated understanding of race that minimizes nonwhite racial, ethnic, and cultural perspectives. For explication, see Carter, *Race*, and Jennings, *Christian Imagination*. For pentecostal and renewalist conversations with the Carter and Jennings thesis, see the theme issue "Race and Global Renewal" of *Pneuma: The Journal of the Society for Pentecostal Studies* 36:3 (2014).

Buddhist missionary enterprise on American shores. This has involved both Buddhists drawing from Christian missionary ideas and practices on the one hand and Christians learning from Buddhists on the other hand. What emerges from a missiological perspective are how beliefs and practices are entangled, so much so that effective mission practices need more precise theological articulation even as some theological formulations ought to be jettisoned in view of what is happening on the ground with the Christian-Buddhist and wider interfaith encounters. While providing a performative missiological entry point to my work in this arena that spans the last two decades,[23] "The Buddhist-Christian Encounter in the USA" impresses especially the import of thinking about Christian mission in the West *beyond* the dichotomy of West and East (in our globalizing world), and also *after* the disintegration of Christian hegemony in the Western public square.

If the Christian missions to Native America and American Buddhists cross cultural, racial, and religious lines, then chapter 9's "The Church and Mission Theology in a Post-Constantinian Era" picks up where the other two leave off. The opportunities opened up for Christian missionary engagements with those in other faiths (Native Americans and Buddhists included) in the present time are challenged by the postmodern and post-Christian condition within which we all live. On the one hand, postmodernity insists on the plurality of perspectives, even religious ones, so that no one can simply assert its superiority; on the other hand, our post-Christian political situation, rather than leveling the playing field between all religionists—which is what affirmative action, applied to religion, would insist on—actually puts believers in Jesus as Messiah in a more subordinate position given its dominance through at least much of the twentieth century. This final chapter of part III thus unpacks both the opportunities and challenges in what I thus call our post-Constantinian era, one in which Christianity is no longer the politically governing and privileged faith in the North American public square. On the one hand, such a post-Constantinian environment is pluralistic, democratic, and secular, presuming freedom of religion and no church-state coalition; on the other hand, it is also postsecular in that many see any segregation of religion and public life to be not only arbitrary but also antireligious and thus contrary to any purported advocacy of religious freedom. In such a vortex, Christian theology of mission has the opportunity to reengage its task not from the "Constantinian center," but from the cruciform margins. Such an approach will be postcolonial and post-Western in a pluralistic arena but also postmodern and postsecular

---

23. For highlights of my sojourn at the crossroads of where Christianity has met Buddhism, see the preface to Yong, *Pneumatology and Christian-Buddhist Dialogue,* xi–xvi.

in insisting that those in all faiths ought to be able to speak into the public domain from out of the deepest resources of their religious traditions. The question is whether North American Christianity can—or even should?!—relearn what it means to be a countercultural and minority tradition while it maintains a majority demographic.[24]

SYSTEMATIC MISSIOLOGY: TOWARD A MISSIOLOGICAL THEOLOGY

The case studies in part III clarify the major issues that any plausible Christian theology of mission for the twenty-first century will need to engage. So the concreteness and particularity of the North American case studies have to be read in tandem—or back and forth—with the last three chapters of this book, which return to take up, at a more abstract level of theological discussion, the salient themes reaching back across the volume. The shift here, however, is from the missiological and theology of mission concerns of before to the bigger-picture questions related to Christian mission theology. As a systematician, I have come to appreciate how any Christian theological articulation has a mission-related aspect.[25] This book, among some of my other more recent writings,[26] makes clear that Christian thinking about mission ought also to impact systematic theological reflection, and vice versa.

Chapters 10–12 sketch, at least rudimentarily, both sides of this mission-systematics thoroughfare. The first provides a pneumatological theology of mission framed by the classical history of salvation Christian narrative; the second explicates a pneumatological Christology of mission in our pluralistic context; and the last steps back toward a more Trinitarian vision of contemporary global mission. Hence together, the three chapters provide both a more diachronically oriented approach to Christian mission theology on the one hand, and a more synchronically, or systematically, structured theological framework for Christian missiology on the other hand. Further, Christian mission theology can only be Trinitarian and christological if it is robustly pneumatological on the one side, and Trinitarian theology can only be comprehensively pneumatological if it is missiological on the other side. Last but not least, a final set of commitments is registered

24. A parallel argument is presented in Yong, "Many Tongues, Many Practices."

25. Already indicated, in more implicit form, in my argument in *Spirit-Word-Community*, esp. ch. 6, that all theology has a pragmatic and performative dimension.

26. Yong, *Spirit of Love*, and, with Jonathan A. Anderson, *Renewing Christian Theology*.

across these chapters: that the mission of the Spirit—the *missio Spiritus*—is also the mission of God and the mission of Jesus Christ, and that this involves the world as created by God, as the habitation of the incarnation of the Word, and as the receptor of the outpouring upon all flesh of the Spirit by Jesus from the right hand of the Father.

"Primed for the Spirit" not only unpacks the salvation historical structure of the Trinitarian *missio Dei* but also accentuates its eschatological horizon. The goal is not to generate any false or naïve optimism about God's saving the world.[27] Yet the eschatological architectonic of this volume follows out the foundational character of the divine self-revelation as hospitable creator, incarnate Son, and Pentecostal (in the Acts 2 sense) Spirit to reconcile the world to God. Each moment of this cosmic drama—of primordial creation, historical incarnation, and eschatological culmination—is fully Trinitarian. This means not only that God's salvation history has missiological implications but also that it cannot be fully elucidated apart from the triune—one and yet three—mission of Father-Son-Spirit.

"Christological Constants in Shifting Contexts" provides one of the most extended responses especially to criticisms of my earlier work that my view of the *missio Spiritus* as distinct from yet related to the mission of the Son bifurcated the divine mission.[28] The argument there both secures the distinction and yet relatedness of the Spirit and the Son and connects pneumatology and Christology to missiology and mission praxis, and vice versa. In other words, the performative dimensions of pneumatological, christological, and Trinitarian theology are unfolded in relationship to the Christian witness while contemporary mission practices and engagements with especially those in other faiths are given further theological (read: Trinitarian, and pneumato-christological) grounding.

"God, Christ, Spirit" returns to develop a Trinitarian mission theology. This both provides a theological undergirding for Christian witness

---

27. Any soteriological universalism will not be able to honor the freedom of creatures given by God, even as the latter exists as a fundamental intuition of the Wesleyan-Arminian theological framework that has informed my thinking since my seminary studies at Western Evangelical Seminary (now George Fox Evangelical Seminary). For the Wesleyan features of my theological work, see *Spirit Poured Out on All Flesh* and *The Dialogical Spirit*, ch. 3, among other articles and essays including: "Wesley and Fletcher—Dayton and Wood"; "Sanctification, Science, and the Spirit"; and "Heart Strangely Warmed."

28. See the opening paragraphs in ch. 11 within; I will say here only that my evangelical critics have formulated their criticisms based on an incomplete reading of my work even as they appear incapable of appreciating how my pentecostal and pneumatological approach is helpful for sustaining Christian mission in a postmodern, postcolonial, and postsecular world.

in the twenty-first-century global and pluralistic context and suggests how contemporary Christian theology can and should be missionally shaped. The movement is from Spirit to Trinity and mission, on the one hand, and from mission praxis to Trinitarian theology on the other hand. Again, the performative dimension of pneumatological and Trinitarian theology is explicated both from theory to practice and vice versa. The Spirit's outpouring upon all flesh (Acts 2:17) is understood not only (if not less) as a descriptive comment about what happened on the Day of Pentecost but (perhaps more so) as anticipating Christian response to and empowering messianic participation in the *missio Spiritus* to bear witness to the God of Jesus Christ to the ends of the earth and the end of the age.

Three subthemes coalesce around one major argument in the following pages. First, with regard to theology of mission, Christian mission practice is performatively multifaceted; in this book, I suggest viewing mission as kerygmatic or proclamatory, as shalomic or socially transformational, and as relational or mutually dialogical vis-à-vis the world. Second, with regard to the missiological framework more generally, Christian mission unfolds contextually; in the twenty-first century such mission will be attentive to local particularities (and their opportunities and challenges) as they interface with global dynamics (related to our postmodern, postcolonial, and postsecular world) in a pluralistic world (in regard at least to cultural, ethnic, and religious pluralism). Third, Christian mission praxis must be fundamentally theological in order to avoid being coopted by the ideologies of any era; the goal of Christian mission is the reconciliation of the world in all of its complexity to God through Jesus Christ by the power of the Holy Spirit.

The central thesis and major argument of this book, then, is that only a pneumatological imagination can secure the Trinitarian vision that empowers missional performance amidst the many tongues of the many missionary contexts. The concluding chapter of the volume will present a synoptic articulation of this pneumatologically shaped mission theology. The previous twelve chapters orient us toward that end.

PART I

Reluctant Missiology

Indirect Missiological Reflection

CHAPTER 1

Going Where the Spirit Goes . . .

Engaging the Spirit(s) in J. C. Ma's Pneumatological Missiology

PENTECOSTALS HAVE ALWAYS BEEN missions-minded people. This certainly flows from the centrality of Acts 1:8 to the pentecostal *Weltanschauung*. Pentecostal missiology, however, has developed in theoretical sophistication over the course of the twentieth century. It is fitting that the dawn of a new millennium in pentecostal missions should be marked by the publication of a Korean Assembly of God missiologist's reflections that bring together historical and anthropological approaches to religion, biblical, and ethnic theology, and mission theory.[1] As a pentecostal, I am happy to see the direction that this volume charts for pentecostal missiological reflection. As one whose academic training is in religious studies and theology, I welcome the fact that pentecostal missiologists are seeing the necessity of engaging these disciplines with greater depth and rigor than ever before. The following reflections will therefore highlight these religious and theological components of the volume under consideration, and focus on the missiological motifs only as they arise in the discussion.[2] My goal is to pay tribute to the author of this book by engaging with her proposals within the context of the larger conversation underway among the current generation of scholars

---

1. Ma, *When the Spirit Meets the Spirits*; all page references to this work will be noted parenthetically in the body of the text.

2. I am confident that missiologists who review this book will highlight the aspects of the volume that I consciously marginalize.

who work in both religious studies and theology. Before doing so, however, a brief overview of the volume under review is in order.

OVERVIEW OF THE BOOK

Julie Ma has served with her husband as missionary to the Philippines for more than fifteen years, with at least half of that time spent among the Kankana-ey tribe of the northern Luzon area. Her book is divided into four parts. Part I sets the sociopolitical and historical context of the Christian mission to the *Cordilleran* "mountain people" (Spanish, *Igorot*) of the northern Luzon. Against the background of the sociopolitical developments in this region during the twentieth century, Ma introduces the Catholic, Episcopal, United Church of Christ (in the Philippines), and Southern Baptist missionary ventures. This allows her to identify the similarities and differences between these non-pentecostal mission endeavors and that of the pentecostal Assemblies of God. The story of the Assemblies of God features the heroic efforts of the single female missionary Elva Vanderbout (d. 1990), as well as brief overviews of the founding and development of various churches in the area by others, including nationally trained ministers.

Part II consists of a single, lengthy chapter detailing indigenous Kankana-ey religious beliefs and practices. Using James Spradley's anthropological categories, Ma introduces and provides data analyses of three aspects of Kankana-ey religion: its pantheon of spirit beings, the roles of priests, and its thanksgiving and ritual practices.[3] "Domain analysis" enables identification of the types of entities under the category of spirit beings, the kinds of religious professionals under the category of priests, and the kinds of ritual activities that Kankana-ey people practice. Following these same categories, "taxonomic analysis" and "componential analysis" sort out the arenas of involvement of the various spirit beings, the religious functions of the various priests, and the end results correlative with the various ritual performances. Finally, "theme analysis" pulls together in a succinct statement the central components that spirit beings, priests, and rituals play in the Kankana-ey world view. The exposition is lucid, the ethnographic details rich and thick, and the overall picture is superbly depicted. Ma's skills as a missionary observer are clearly evident here.

In Part III, Ma switches to strictly pentecostal discourse on themes central to the pentecostal missiological enterprise among the Kankana-ey. She focuses on the notions of "power encounters," "truth encounters," and "allegiance encounters" made prominent by individuals associated with the

---

3. Ma references Spradley, *Participant Observation*.

School of World Mission at Fuller Theological Seminary.[4] Ma's use of these categories, however, is dynamic, emphasizing the movement from power encounters (producing spiritual and religious conversion) to truth encounters (producing intellectual or world view conversion) to allegiance encounters (producing moral, affective and volitional conversions).[5] She emphasizes the importance of seeing these encounters as integrating and interworking, and provides, in a separate chapter, an extensive overview of "power encounters" drawn from the Hebrew Bible, the Synoptic Gospels and the Pauline literature.

The concluding part of this volume consists of three chapters. The first is an ethnological analysis of Kankana-ey Christianity derived from responses to a detailed questionnaire regarding how Christian conversion has transformed beliefs about divine connections with blessings and curses, sickness and healing, the revelation of omens and dreams, and the cosmological and afterlife conceptions of the spirit world. The second is a comparative assessment of indigenous Kankana-ey, practical pentecostal, and Kankana-ey pentecostal theologies.[6] Ma concludes her book with suggestive missiological recommendations that await a new generation of pentecostal missionaries for implementation.

4. Ma's book is a revision of her PhD dissertation completed at Fuller under missiologists Paul Pierson, Charles Kraft, and Charles van Engen. The influence of Kraft's well-known work, *Christianity and Culture*, is evident in Ma's book, as is the work of others associated with the School of World Mission such as John Wimber and Kevin Springer (their *Power Points* is referenced while themes from their *Power Evangelism* and *Power Healing* are not far beneath the surface). In this connection, it is somewhat disappointing that the insights and strategies of others associated with the School of World Mission—such as that found in Woodberry, van Engen, and Elliston, *Missiological Education for the Twenty-First Century*—are conspicuously absent in Ma's book. I return to this point in sections II and III later.

5. The parenthetical remarks are my own categorical constructs appended to Ma's. Here, I introduce the dynamics of conversion drawn primarily from Bernard Lonergan and Donald Gelpi (see Gelpi, *Conversion Experience*), which I not only consider to be consonant with what Ma is saying, but which I think better get at the religious and theological issues that feature prominently in the next two sections of this review.

6. By "practical Pentecostal," Ma refers to that theology that "is lived by Pentecostal Christians in their everyday affairs" (213). I'm not sure that there is a formal difference between what Ma refers to as "practical Pentecostal" and "Kankana-ey Pentecostal" theologies since it seems to me that as presented, the latter is simply a regional (read: northern Filipino) specification of more abstractly stated life attitudes. I will return to this point later as well.

RELIGIOUS STUDIES PERSPECTIVES

My own critical reflections will bring primarily religious studies and theological perspectives to bear on Parts II–IV of this book. In this section, I anticipate questions from phenomenological and anthropological approaches to the study of religion, and then make some observations on the phenomenon of syncretism, also from the angle of religious studies. Let me begin by engaging Ma's summary of Kankana-ey Christian theology as emergent from the questionnaire she administered.

Kankana-ey Christianity from the Perspective of Religious Studies

Ma asked a group of 660 Kankana-ey pentecostals ages twenty and up eight questions. These focused on eliciting their responses to specific situations fraught with religious significance, such as what they would do if their crops were destroyed by a typhoon, if a family member fell ill, or if they had an omen or dream forewarning disaster. The results of this survey seem to confirm the radical nature of pentecostal conversion from the Kankana-ey animist world view. While this does not appear to be part of Ma's explicit agenda, it is certainly evident as an empirical conclusion. That the results of the survey are detailed without critical or alternative interpretations of the data seems to imply that Ma is in basic agreement with the contrasts as presented. One of the issues I want to probe as a scholar of religion is whether the contrasts are as stark as Kankana-ey Christians (and Ma?) envision them to be.

Take, for example, the question concerning the failure of crops and plants in farming. Kankana-ey Christians were asked two questions: what they would have done prior to their conversion to Christianity and what they would do now. Tabulating the results of the survey, the responses are as follows:

Pre-Christian responses	Perform ritual	Curse ancestors	Experience stress or depression	Get drunk	Borrow money to begin another business venture
Number of respondents	261	30	174	50	138
Percentage of respondents	39.5	4.5	26.4	7.6	20.9

Table 1: Responses to the question, What would you have done given crop or farm failure prior to becoming a Christian?[7]

Christian responses	Pray and put one's faith in God	Remain thankful to God	Remain peaceful and joyous	See the experience as a trial or test from God	Borrow money to begin another business venture
Number of respondents	422	30	52	105	47
Percentage of respondents	64	4.5	7.9	15.9	7.1

Table 2: Responses to the question, What would you do given crop or farm failure now that you are a Christian?[8]

From the perspective of Christian spiritual formation, a number of items stand out. First, the Christian leadership among the Kankana-ey pentecostals should be applauded for the educational work they are doing among the native converts. None of the Kankana-ey Christians even so much as intimated that they would be tempted to return to the indigenous priests for ritual performances. This contrasts with the practices of those in sub-Saharan African independent or Spirit Churches and rural Latin American

7. I did not include in this table seven who indicated they would seek advice from friends or relatives. The total number of responses recorded is therefore 653 instead of 660.

8. There is a discrepancy in the totals of 660 preconversion responses and 656 responses as Christians. It appears that four persons who answered about what they would have done as animists did not answer about what they would do now as Christians.

pentecostals who might continue to consult their local shaman, especially if they felt that their prayers were not being answered.

Second, whereas 38.5 percent thought that prior to their becoming Christians they would have experienced stress and depression as well as curse their ancestors or get drunk, 32.3 percent now believed that they would remain at peace, be thankful toward God, or see this as a trial and opportunity to learn and grow. This is a sign of the growing maturity of Kankana-ey pentecostals.[9]

Finally, it is startling that while 39.5 percent indicated they would previously have consulted a priest in order to perform the appropriate ritual, a whopping 64 percent now believed that the solution lies in trusting God who answers prayer. On the surface of things, then, it would certainly appear that Christian conversion has brought about a drastic change in the attitudes, world view, and behavior of the Kankana-ey people.

From the perspective of *Religionswissenschaft*, however, two counter-observations may be made. First, on the very practical level of what should be done about crop failure, 7.1 percent of Kankana-ey pentecostals still believed that borrowing money to begin anew is appropriate. While it would have been interesting to determine if there is an overlap between those who indicated they would have borrowed money prior to conversion to Christianity and those who approved of borrowing money as Christians, that information is neither included in Ma's presentation of the data nor is it crucial for our purposes. The point is that belief in God does not preclude taking practical steps toward reestablishing one's financial situation.

Second and more important is the contrast implied in distinguishing between the performance of ritual and Christian prayer. I should add that I do not mention in my tabulation of the data above how Kankana-ey pentecostals understand prayer and Bible study to go together. From the perspective of phenomenology of religion, however, is not either activity taken separately or both taken together a form of Christian ritual practice?[10] In other words, on the practical level, the performance of ritual is a crucial

---

9. The study of religion aside, however, psychological states such as the feelings of peace and joy or even the experience of depression are inconclusive for at least two reasons. First, from a biblical perspective, one can certainly experience a false sense of security given that Satan is a deceptive angel of light. Further, one can also feel what the Psalmist calls the "heavy hand of the Lord" upon oneself (Ps 32:4; cf. the experiences of Jeremiah [20:7ff.] and Amos [as a "burden bearer," the meaning of his name]). Second, while experience is essential to theologizing, we should resist overemphasizing experiential criteria in theological argument, since to do so runs the risk of reducing theology to pragmatism. I will say more about this later.

10. Pentecostals are now beginning to see that this is, indeed, the case; see Albrecht, *Rites in the Spirit*.

response to crop and farm failure. Prior to conversion to Christianity, native Kankana-ey presented sacrificial offerings to spirit beings through the local priests. After conversion, they offered up prayers to God, oftentimes calling upon their local pastors and other church members to do the same on their behalf.

To push the analysis further, how do religious rituals work? Ma wants to emphasize that pentecostal prayer consists of a newly developed relationship with a personal God. This is meant to contrast starkly with the native Kankana-ey ritual approaches, characterized perhaps as magical transactions with potentially arbitrary spirit beings. The logic of native Kankana-ey ritual can be expressed as a variation on the following formula: if you sacrifice enough cows and/or fulfill your ancestral obligations, then the ancestor spirits will answer your petition. From a phenomenological perspective, however, pentecostal prayer functions similarly. Its logic, as believed by Kankana-ey pentecostals and summarized by Ma, goes like this:

> The Kankana-ey Pentecostal Christians expect the regular working of the Holy Spirit in their lives. They believe that the Holy Spirit readily works when people of God urgently beseech him. The Kankana-ey Pentecostals, when a family member gets sick, intensely pray for the intervention of the Holy Spirit. It is believed that, when the Holy Spirit is present, healing will take place (224).

Pentecostal ritual logic, in short, is predicated upon the assumption that if you pray sincerely enough and/or hard and long enough, God will hear your prayer.

On both indigenous and Christian accounts, one persists in one's ritual performance if the desired results are not quickly forthcoming. Native Kankana-ey ritual emphasizes increasing the number of sacrificial animals to appease the spirit beings until the situation is rectified. Pentecostal ritual emphasizes intensification of prayer, as well as waiting and persevering in faith and trust for the blessing of God (218). On this point, then, Ma appears to exaggerate the discontinuities between traditional Kankana-ey beliefs and traditions and pentecostalism in concluding that the converted Filipino tribespersons "seem to deal with crises in *totally* new ways" (210; my emphasis). While this might be arguable at one level, it is not true from specifically anthropological and phenomenological approaches to religiousness.

"Syncretism" as a Religious Phenomenon

I wonder then about Ma's apparently unqualified endorsement of the discontinuities between indigenous Kankana-ey religiosity and Kankana-ey pentecostalism. I suspect that part of what motivates this strategy may be the concern to avoid syncretism. Evidence for this can be found at the close of her book when Ma writes that the Assemblies of God's "radical appeal to the power of God precluded the possibility of syncretism from the very beginning" (239). By this, Ma is referring to the world view transformation that has taken place in the hearts and minds of the Kankana-ey people when they have converted to pentecostal Christianity. Certainly, Ma understands syncretism as an evil to be avoided.[11] For various reasons, however, this seems to betray more of a Western, specifically North American, reading of the situation than not.

First, claims that syncretism has been completely avoided seem too simplistic since all inculturation is a dialectic between continuity and discontinuity, between similarity and difference.[12] From a cultural analysis of the modern West, we have come to realize that to emphasize one side to the exclusion of the other either distorts the facts or signifies an imperialistic imposition of foreign categories upon "the other." This betrays the West's hegemonic intentions as sustained by a polarized symbolic discourse. All that is good, true, and beautiful is represented by the light of the West, while all that is bad, false, and ugly is represented by the darkness of the non-Western world. One of the accomplishments of Ma's book is that by highlighting the emergence of an indigenous pentecostalism in the Philippines, it dismantles this Western/non-Western dichotomy. Yet I am unsure if Ma understands this to extend to the concept of syncretism.

From a religious studies perspective, syncretism is a polyvalent notion.[13] On the one side, syncretism connotes the inappropriate fusion of beliefs, symbols, and practices from two distinct traditions to form a third religious system that compromises the essential components of the original

---

11. It may be the case that Ma's experience as a Korean pentecostal has alerted her to the potential problems of inculturating pentecostalism in Asian contexts. Given the well-known charges that Korean pentecostalism is actually a syncretistic phenomenon of pentecostal-type Christianity and indigenous Korean shamanistic practices (see Boo-Woong Yoo, "Response to Korean Shamanism"; Cox, *Fire from Heaven*, 213–41; and Tai, "A Study of Spirituality of Korean Christians"), Ma's hesitation on this score is understandable.

12. My use of "inculturation" in this paper is synonymous with contextualization, indigenization, assimilation, translation, incorporation, and acculturation (see Kaplan, "Africanization of Missionary Christianity").

13. On this, see, e.g., Gort et al., *Dialogue and Syncretism*.

religions. It is clear that this is the kind of syncretism that Ma not only opposes, but believes Kankana-ey pentecostals have managed to avoid. On the other side, syncretism is understood to refer to the various processes set in motion when two (or more) cultures, civilizations, or religious traditions meet and interact with each other. Insofar as this encounter is genuine and sustained, what emerges is considered to be, to a greater or lesser degree but unavoidably so, syncretism. It is for this reason that individuals like Walter Hollenweger have called for Christians to exercise a "theologically responsible syncretism" in inculturating Christianity in the non-Western world.[14]

Now Ma clearly realizes that true inculturation requires a much more intentionally dialogical approach whereby missionaries "should learn the culture and customs of the Kankana-ey tribal people in order to develop more effective approaches with the gospel" (242). It is possible but improbable that Ma thinks this is simply a statement about learning about Kankana-ey culture rather than about the religio-cultural matrix of the Kankana-ey people. Given that it is impossible to completely disentangle religious from cultural elements of any people group, this means, then, that one has to learn about a people group's religious beliefs and practices, as well as the interpretations and meanings that these beliefs and practices intend, evoke, and nurture. That Ma calls Part IV of her book "an ethnotheological analysis" (27) confirms that an ethnic or contextualized theology underlies her quest. In order to pursue this objective, however, one needs to push beyond anthropological and phenomenological analyses toward a mutually informing and transforming dialogue between Kankana-ey and pentecostalism[15]

THEOLOGICAL ANALYSES

I want to engage Ma's quest for an ethnic Kankana-ey theology along two fronts. First, why is such an effort imperative and why it is characterized by ongoing struggle? Second, what kind of theological methodology does such an authentically indigenous theology require?

14. See Hollenweger, *Pentecostalism*, 132–41.

15. On this, see Schreiter, *Constructing Local Theologies*; Schreiter, *New Catholicity*; and Cobb Jr., *Beyond Dialogue*.

The Necessary Struggle toward an Indigenous Kankana-ey Theology

I fully endorse as valid the current missiological strategy in effect in the Philippines as it is engaging the present social, political, historical, and economic context of the area. Ma is convincing in her argument that the success of Assemblies of God missionary efforts in contrast to non-pentecostal enterprises can be explained by the central beliefs in spiritual beings and spiritual power in both pentecostal and Kankana-ey world views. Pentecostal cosmology, for example, allows for a reinterpretation of Kankana-ey spirit beings, whereas non-pentecostal Christian cosmologies either downplay the existence of spirit beings or evacuate them of power and hence of reality. Further, the pentecostal belief in the healing power of the Holy Spirit answers to the deepest needs and circumstances of the Kankana-ey people. Finally, as Ma points out, the theological immanentism of the pentecostal *Weltanschauung* provides for continuity with the traditional Kankana-ey world view in that both see the mundane affairs of human beings as intricately connected with the reality of the spiritual realm; what is discontinuous, of course, is how the spiritual realm is understood. All this combines with other factors to explain the success of pentecostal missions in the northern Luzon.

The question, however, is what this means for an indigenous Kankana-ey theology. At present, for example, Kankana-ey pentecostals have redefined their cosmology. Whereas previously they believed that spirit beings were departed ancestors or gods of various types, now they believe that what was actually perceived by them prior to their becoming Christians were instead demonic spirits (211). Is this, however, the only valid alternative to understanding ancestor spirits? I would like to suggest that while such a theological position is legitimate in this historical context, in the long term, ethnic Kankana-ey theology needs to be reformed and continually reforming for two related reasons.

To begin with, pentecostals of all people should be sensitive to the postmodernist critique. We have begun to realize that the onset of postmodernity provides us with the space necessary to theologize according to our experiences, our categories, and our values.[16] No longer do we have to acquiesce to foreign interpretations of our experience, whether such be evangelical, liberal, secular, or otherwise. In fact, part of the growth and maturity of pentecostalism is evidenced by the fact that the pentecostal voice and perspective has come to be increasingly appreciated and evaluated on its

16. See, e.g., Johns, "Partners in Scandal."

own terms in the public square. At the same time, of course, the conditions of postmodernity are such that local voices, local discourses, local epistemic processes, and local systems of knowledge are recognized as legitimate alternatives to the dominant modern Western paradigm.

This postmodern condition, however, means that ethnic theologies need to emerge from an ongoing dialectical conversation between the local and the global. To simply "demonize" the spirit beings of the Kankana-ey cosmology may be, at worst, only a rhetorical ploy derived from the ideology of the Enlightenment. On the other hand, to affirm uncritically the indigenous Kankana-ey cosmology is to succumb to postmodernist relativism. Certainly this relativism should be guarded against. At the same time, we should refrain from indiscriminately reading foreign categories—including pentecostal ones—onto the Kankana-ey experience.[17] The kind of syncretism that Ma fears—as when pentecostal categories are subsumed under Kankana-ey ones—is also susceptible to a reverse development that appears to have occurred. In this case, however, it is the Kankana-ey categories that appear to have been muted by pentecostal ones. The important point is that if the central and important categories inherent to either side are disregarded, a truly indigenous Kankana-ey Christian (pentecostal) theology will never be reached. What we need is a critical correlation between Kankana-ey and pentecostal categories that is mutually transformative but which does not compromise their essential insights. This kind of theology, however, can only emerge out of a prolonged struggle by Kankana-ey pentecostals to understand God, self, and world within their specific intercultural and interfaith context.

Before saying more about how such an encounter should proceed, let me provide another related reason as further incentive against being satisfied with the current state of Kankana-ey theology in general and demonology more specifically. Now the notion of ancestor spirits as demons is part and parcel of a pentecostal cosmology that features the Holy Spirit as the divine power opposed to the demonic realm. Ma notes that one of the main reasons why the Kankana-ey people are attracted to pentecostalism is that the Holy Spirit is, in their perspective, a "Miracle Worker" (224). This is especially crucial given their socioeconomic context, one lacking many of the basic sanitary, medical, and provisionary necessities of life (225). The question that arises is this: what will happen to pentecostal Kankana-ey cosmology during the generations after such provisions are made available? What happens when medical supplies are accessible, or when the socioeconomic

17. I address below the possible pentecostal rejoinder that to "demonize" Kankana-ey spirit beings is not to commit pentecostal imperialism but to truthfully interpret the reality of the world according to biblical categories.

conditions of the Kankana-ey people are transformed such that disease is no longer as problematic?[18]

My point is that when we depend on pragmatic criteria to undergird our power-pneumatology, we run the risk of theological irrelevance once power is obtained through other sources. Ma describes such a trend already developing among Kankana-ey pentecostals (236–37). She astutely observes that with the onset of modernity among the Kankana-ey and the exposure of civilization to its peoples, "the 'golden hour' for evangelism may soon come to an end" (242–43). Can this be read as an unverbalized fear that "power encounter" strategies will soon be obsolete among the Kankana-ey? If that is the case, so will be the attending cosmology and theology. Rather than admit that, I suggest that it is far better to continuously rethink one's cosmology and theology of power. This is why I insist that Kankana-ey theology should be reformed and always reforming.

Pentecostal concerns, however, include the fear that intellectualism robs the Christian of "pentecostal power." Ma does suggest the possibility that the decline of what she calls "power ministry" might be due, at least in part, to the increase of a more intellectualized form of Bible study as well as theological training (237). The implication is that prevalent among many pentecostals: that advanced theological training saps the individual and the community of faith of the experience of spiritual power. Alternatively, my hypothesis is that the dynamic nature of human "being in the world" means that we exist progressively in different stages of life wherein we encounter different contexts that necessitate different strategies of engagement with the world. To return to the Kankana-ey experience, a preindustrial and pretechnological (or, animist, in Ma's terms) society provides an environment of religiosity that nurtures and cultivates "power encounters." Technological advance, however, brings with it an increased rationalization of the world, as Weber puts it. This leads to the abandonment of "power encounters" *only if* one assumes a certain nonnegotiable definition of "power" and a specific form of "encounter" as normative. If, on the other hand, we are authorized to understand "power encounters" in alternative ways, then the replacement of an animist society by a technological one will not threaten the pneumatological orientation valued by (Kankana-ey) pentecostals.

In the same way, it is my conviction that pentecostals need to find ways of preserving their insights into the spiritual nature of reality not by returning to a premodern mentality about ghosts and spirits, but by

---

18. In another connection, Ma notes that the local Jehovah's Witnesses' response to the growth of pentecostalism was, "Your God is bigger than ours because your church building is bigger than ours" (235). But what happens when the size of church buildings no longer matter?

reconceptualizing "spiritual power" within the context of a post-Einsteinian cosmology. Failure to do so is to rely on purely pragmatic considerations in determining theological truth. Sure, pragmatism needs to be one of the perspectives and criterion applied to determining truth in theology. Similarly, anthropological and phenomenological approaches to the study of religion have their place. The ethnographic work of Ma the cultural anthropologist opens up a wonderful window into indigenous Kankana-ey religiosity. On its own, however, such provides only descriptive analyses favorable to pragmatic interpretations—as in how the Kankana-ey uses rituals symbolically to attain desired ends. This leaves untouched ontological or metaphysical assessments of Kankana-ey cosmology. The latter can be accomplished only by a theology that is reformed and always being reformed.

Theological Methodology: A Genuinely Interreligious and Interdisciplinary Dialogue

How then is such a theology developed? My conviction is that this requires a truly interreligious and interdisciplinary conversation, much like the one jump-started for us in *When the Spirit Meets the Spirits*. So, to push the conversation forward, let me put the questions this way: what can pentecostals learn from Kankana-ey, and how can what is learned be understood against the context of the biblical and the contemporary world? In other words, my thesis is that a Kankana-ey pentecostal theology requires an interreligious and interdisciplinary interchange that involves at least the four horizons of pentecostal convictions, Kankana-ey insights into reality, biblical scholarship and the Christian tradition, and the contemporary global public.[19]

19. I need to say, however, that these are listed in symbolic order that does not betray either methodological or ontological commitments. Thus, as will be seen, I do not proceed in this order. While I do begin with pentecostal experience and the biblical and Christian tradition, that does not mean that I privilege either. Rather I begin with pentecostal experience because we all begin where we are located—and my location is informed first and foremost by my pentecostal heritage. Moving secondly toward the biblical horizon is simply a heuristic strategy conveying my desire to be submitted to the Christian norm. It does not mean that we can simply impose the Christian norm on our experience of the world since, for starters, my reading of the Bible can never be purely objective but is rather informed by my pentecostal "being-in-the-world." Thus, I am convinced that the biblical and the contemporary horizons interpret each other— are mutually correlative, according to David Tracy (see *The Analogical Imagination*). In short, the encounters between the four horizons are actually genuinely dialectical, reflecting the to-and-fro movement of mutual engagement and appropriate transformation. The discerning reader will also note that the matrix I have sketched is a reformulation of the Wesleyan quadrilateral—Scripture, tradition, reason, and experience—in the context of indigenous theologizing in the northern Luzon; for a defense of

Let us begin with the current understanding of Kankana-ey pentecostals who have replaced their beliefs in ancestor spirits with beliefs in evil (demonic) spirits. In reflecting on how to interpret a dream featuring a deceased father warning of impending disaster, Kankana-ey pentecostals now warn that "it takes time to instruct the [new Kankana-ey] believer disturbed by the above dream that the 'father' is not one's own father, but rather is a disguised evil spirit trying to intimidate the family" (228). How might we aver this theological interpretation and yet remain open to its continuous reformulation?

To begin with, it is important to reaffirm, as Ma does, the common pentecostal conviction regarding the media of divine revelation through dreams and visions (227–28; cf. Acts 2:17). From the pentecostal point of view, dreams are not to be ignored. Rather, the appropriate pentecostal response is to interpret and discern each dream on its own terms. It may be that particular dreams are insignificant, derived from demonic sources, or genuinely from God. But those should be conclusions arrived at after discerning consideration, not a priori attitudes with which we approach dreams.

From this starting point, space is created to discern Kankana-ey interpretations of dreams. Various dream theories can be brought to bear in forging a Kankana-ey theology of dreams. First, it should certainly be admitted that some dreams are of demonic origins, especially those that induce fear and incapacitate the dreamer and his or her family. Second, and by way of contrast, however, a Christian theological perspective would not necessarily attribute all dreams that contain fearful elements to demonic sources. In fact, certain dreams of this nature could be divinely ordained, as the examples of Pharaoh's and Nebuchadnezzar's dreams reveal (cf. Gen 41:1–8; Dan 2:1ff., 4:4ff.). But what about the indigenous Kankana-ey insistence that the personages in their dreams are the spirits of deceased ancestors? A third interpretive scheme might draw on psychoanalytic theory whereby an individual's being disturbed by images of deceased family members is symptomatic either of unresolved issues between the dreamer and the departed member or of attachments that have remained through the grieving process. From a Christian theological perspective, such dreams may indicate the need for the living (whether as individual or as a family community, depending on the circumstances surrounding the death) to grant forgiveness of various sorts to the dead in order to make their peace. Alternatively, personal obligations may need to be fulfilled in accordance with communal standards and practices.

---

the quadrilateral, see my "Demise of Foundationalism," 579–87.

Such a move puts us as pentecostals at the heart of an important conversation currently engaging the larger Christian theological community. I have in mind recent efforts by recognized theologians like Jürgen Moltmann, Harry Sawyerr, and others to reformulate a theology of ancestor spirits in the African and African American indigenous contexts.[20] For Moltmann, for example, the animistic notion of ancestor spirits needs to be retrieved in order to invigorate Christian theological reflection that has neglected the intergenerational connections of human life. I think this is an important point that pentecostals in general (and Kankana-ey pentecostals more specifically) need to recognize. We are biologically, environmentally, socioeconomically, traditionally, culturally, and even spiritually connected with those who have preceded us and with those who follow after us. While such connectedness does not mean we worship ancestor spirits or offer ritual sacrifices to them, it does mean that the biblical injunctions to honor our parents and to recognize the "great cloud of witnesses" (Heb. 12:1) that have preceded us are not simply pietistic attitudes or respectful emotive states. Rather, these are affective mechanisms that orient us toward both our ancestors and our descendants in ways that support environmental, socioeconomic, and cultural consciousness and responsibility.

My point is that an a priori and uncritical demonization of ancestor spirits imposes a needless construct on the Kankana-ey that dismisses their fundamental intuitions into the generational interdependence of human life. In fact, I hazard to guess that such pentecostal rhetoric may more so reflect the remaining fears of Kankana-ey pentecostals themselves than articulate either cosmological or theological truth. Pentecostals need to be reminded that not too long ago, their glossolalic utterances were attributed to demonic frenzies by those who are now considered to be fellow Christians! A more nuanced assessment should therefore be available in this newly emerging Kankana-ey pentecostal theological context, one that dispenses neither with the category of the demonic nor with the import of dreams for regulating (both Christian and non-Christian) Kankana-ey life. In this way, pentecostals can affirm the central Kankana-ey insight into the nature of dreams and their crucial function in Kankana-ey society.

This "demythologization" of the Kankana-ey cosmology opens up further space for additional theological reformation. By this, I mean that Bultmann's program should be pushed from modernity into postmodernity such that the mid-twentieth-century positivistic and materialistic

20. See Moltmann, *Coming of God,* 104–10, and Sawyerr, *Practice of Presence,* 43–55; see also Fasholé-Luke, "Ancestor Veneration and Communion of Saints." I attempt something similar in a pentecostal dialogue with Umbanda, an Afro-Brazilian religious tradition; see my *Discerning the Spirit(s),* ch. 8.

assumptions underlying existentialist demythologization are discarded in favor of the postmodern convictions about the world's enchantment—convictions that move us far beyond a literalistic premodernist reading of reality.[21] Thus, rather than demonizing the Kankana-ey pantheon, we should attempt to develop a post-animistic Kankana-ey theology that reinterprets, in genuine dialogue with these people, the spirits beings of the Kankana-ey cosmology. Take, for example, the spirits of the underworld: *Pinad-eng* (forest spirits), *Tinmongao* (mountain spirits), *Penten* (water spirits), *Butat-tew* and *Ampasit* (cave spirits), as well as other spirit beings (229; cf. 106). These are beings that in all probability have been named as a result of the Kankana-ey experience of unfortunate and tragic incidents, usually deaths, occurring in the inhospitable mountain and river regions far from the safer tribal environments. Is it not the case then that these spirits accurately identify dangerous realms and activities that Kankana-ey persons should either avoid or, if approach is unavoidable, engage with extra caution? And in the latter case, does not such caution include physical, mental, and even spiritual preparation such that one negotiates one's way through the mountainous forests in daylight instead of at night, or avoids rapid waters, or traffics away from cliffs, or travels cognitively alert rather than drunk, and so on? Insofar as these cautions have been ignored resulting in tragedy and loss of life, the causes are, in those respects, appropriately understood by the Kankana-ey as dangerous spirits and by pentecostal Christians as demonic ones. My concern is that we avoid reification of these categories and instead work together—within this specific interreligious context—toward a more sophisticated theological framework by which to understand the nature of spiritual reality.

But having begun to deconstruct the Kankana-ey cosmology, are we not also under obligation—and this continuously so, I maintain—to do the same with the pentecostal one? In other words, as pentecostals, should we not be continuously asking if our own experiences and ideological blinders have led us to eisegete the biblical text, resulting, in this case, in the reification of demons and spirits? I am thinking specifically, for example, of Ma's treatment of the powers (145–48). This is a fairly traditional Christian reading through pentecostal lenses, even as Ma draws from the work

---

21. On the "re-enchantment of the world" motif, see Griffin, *Reenchantment of Science*. I disagree with the process theism underlying Griffin's agenda, but believe that the fundamental intuitions presented by him and the contributors to this volume are compatible with pentecostal assumptions about the self and the world.

[For more recent attempts to defend a pentecostal-process theological vision that does not depend on Griffin's dipolar theism, see the recent work of pentecostal theologian Joshua D. Reichard, "Toward a Pentecostal Theology of Concursus," "Of Miracles and Metaphysics," and "Relational Empowerment."]

of theologians and scholars like James Cobble, Walter Wink, Henry Chadwick, and Josh McDowell and Don Stewart.[22] Because of the central role of "power encounters" in Ma's book, however, I am curious about her use of Wink's work specifically. Wink's basic thesis, argued over a series of works, is that the biblical language of power calls attention to the inner dynamics of all things.[23] Reality, in Wink's cosmology, consists of both outer, concrete actualities, as well as inner, spiritual dispositions. Thus, we encounter and engage institutions, organizations, groups, networks, persons, etc. Each of these have their inner dimension thus making it appropriate to speak of the spirit or power of an institution, an organization, a group, a network, a person, etc.[24] While Ma does not mention any of these aspects of Wink's biblical theology, I submit that this way of reconceptualizing the biblical notions of "spirit" and "the demonic" are congruent with contemporary theological efforts to understand "power" in terms of fields of force, laws, habits, tendencies, and dispositions.[25]

There are a number of reasons why this kind of reconceptualization is advantageous, of which I will enumerate four in no particular order. First, it allows us to continue seeing the relevance of the biblical categories and how they illuminate a much more sophisticated understanding of power in our postmodern world. Second, it does not compromise fundamental

22. The pentecostal lenses I am referring to are Ma's own, shaped as they are by the charismatic readings of power promulgated by those associated with the School of World Mission at Fuller (see note 4). I could not find Ma's reference to Chadwick in the bibliography. Cobble's book *Church and the Powers* is more a practical ecclesiology than a demonology or theology of the powers, while McDowell and Stewart's *Understanding the Occult* is a popular-level discussion of new religious movements in the North American context.

23. Ma references in passing only the first volume of Wink's *The Powers* trilogy, *Naming the Powers*. Nowhere does she take up his basic thesis, later developed in two other books: *Unmasking the Powers* and *Engaging the Powers*.

24. Here, Wink's work extends the thesis previously submitted by other biblical scholars and theologians like Berkhof, *Christ and the Powers*; Caird, *Principalities and Powers*, esp. 31–53; and Yoder, *Politics of Jesus*.

25. For the notion of "spirit" or "power" as force fields, I have in mind Pannenberg, *Systematic Theology*, 1:382–84; Moltmann, *Spirit of Life*, 195–97; Welker, *God the Spirit*; and Snook, *What in the World?*. For "spirit" as laws, habits, or vectors, see Gelpi, *Divine Mother*. My interpretation of "spirit" as dispositions is drawn from Jonathan Edwards's dispositional ontology and theology; on this, see Lee, *Philosophical Theology of Jonathan Edwards*, and Boyd, *Trinity and Process*. I develop these notions of "power" further in my *Discerning the Spirit(s)*, ch. 4, and "Spiritual Discernment: A Biblical-Theological Reconsideration."

[See also my *Spirit of Creation*, ch. 6; *In the Days of Caesar*, ch. 4; and *The Cosmic Breath*, ch. 2, for updates on my thinking in this area. I am now more reluctant to use the language of force fields except as understood in a distantly analogical manner.]

pentecostal and Kankana-ey insights regarding the interconnectedness of spiritual and material reality, the sacred and the profane, the spiritual and bodily form and culture. Third, it deconstructs Enlightenment dualisms and introduces holistic perspectives that enable us to fully engage our world. Such engagement, however, cannot be dominated by any one party, whether (in this case) Kankana-ey, pentecostals, biblical scholars, or others; by definition, holistic understandings can only be accessed from multiple perspectives, approaches, assumptions, and disciplines. Finally, this will drive a truly dialogical Kankana-ey–pentecostal conversation, resulting in a truly contextualized and indigenous Kankana-ey theology. In short, Ma's book invites us to listen in on and participate in the meeting between the spirits—the Holy Spirit and the Kankana-ey spirits—in a truly interreligious, interdisciplinary, and dialogical sense. And, it is precisely this kind of encounter that will need to run its course in order for an authentic and indigenous Kankana-ey pentecostal theology to emerge that is relevant to the spiritual environment of the Northern Luzon.[26]

I am genuinely encouraged by what I see in *When the Spirit Meets the Spirits*. This book points the way forward for this generation of pentecostal missiologists and theologians. The success of any missionary endeavor is the emergence of an indigenous church, including, as Ma insists, its own indigenous theology. At this past meeting of the Society for Pentecostal Studies, David Bundy suggested that the creative potential, energy, and vitality of Christian theology in this new century belong to pentecostalism.[27] The work currently being done all over the world by pentecostals like Julie Ma may indicate that Bundy is more of a prophet than he is a historian. I, for one, hope that to be the case.[28]

---

26. I think that the difference between what is found is Ma's book and what I am proposing may be explicable as the difference between a first-generation indigenous pentecostal Kankana-ey theology and a more developed pentecostal theology open to engagement with the global pentecostal public and the full breadth and depth of the Christian tradition. This difference has also been characterized as that between theologies propounded in non-Western contexts primarily for their pragmatic relevance by indigenous Christians, and theologies proffered in these same places for their wider ecumenical significance by more socially established thinkers, perhaps with Western training. Birgit Meyer has distinguished between indigenous theologies emergent from nationals and theologies promoted by theologians affiliated with mainline churches working among animist peoples thusly ("Beyond Syncretism," esp. 59–60). I think that we as pentecostals are primed to bridge this gap insofar as we are globally situated, are actively engaged "spiritually" in just these areas, and continue to listen to and learn from each other.

27. Bundy, "Problems and Promises."

28. I am grateful to Chris Thomas [then editor of *Journal of Pentecostal Theology*] for inviting my response to this important book.

CHAPTER 2

"As the Spirit Gives Utterance . . . "

Pentecost, Intra-Christian Ecumenism, and the Wider *Oekumene*

RATHER THAN BREAKING NEW ground, my goal in this paper is to explore the question of what may happen if three distinct topics of current theological discussion were to converge. I refer to work that is presently being done on the doctrine of the Holy Spirit (pneumatology), the theology of mission and evangelization, and the reality of religious pluralism (*theologia religionum*). In order to lay the groundwork for the deliberations that follow, let me briefly comment on the state of the discussion in each of these areas.

During the past generation, theological reflection on the Holy Spirit, long thought to be the silent or shy member of the Trinity and referred to as the orphan doctrine of Christian theology, has begun to emerge. Arguably, Henry Pitt van Dusen's *Spirit, Son and Father: Christian Faith in the Light of the Holy Spirit* (1958) signaled the dawn of this new age in Christian thinking. Since van Dusen's richly suggestive work, theologians have been working hard to retrieve the doctrine of the Spirit from the back burner where it has sat for centuries. The result has been an increasing number of monographs not only on pneumatology, but also a reframing of other theological loci in pneumatological perspective.[1] In each case, distinctively pneumatological resources and approaches have reopened questions long

---

1. For a recent summary of the contemporary discussion, see Kärkkäinen, *Pneumatology*.

thought to have been either answered or unanswerable, and charted new ground for ongoing exploration.

Theological reflection on the Christian mission has also intensified and taken new turns as we have entered into what some have called the postmodern world. The magnum opus of the late David Bosch suggests that what may be called a postmodern missiological paradigm would include at least the following elements: a rethinking of the nature of the church (ecclesiology and ecumenism); a reconsideration of the doctrine of salvation (soteriology); the quest for justice and liberation; more sophisticated theories of knowledge (epistemology) and of culture, along with more precise notions of contextualization and inculturation; the role of the laity in particular and of the whole people of God in general for the Christian mission; continued exploration of the idea of "eschatological missiology"; and, directly related to our topic today, the tension between dialogue and evangelization vis-à-vis people of other faiths.[2]

Christian reflection on other faiths has also traversed a variety of routes since the Parliament of Religions over a century ago (1893). The traditional exclusivist, inclusivist, and pluralist models for understanding other religious traditions is now seen to have been motivated primarily by Christian soteriological concerns and assumptions rather than by serious consideration of these traditions on their own terms. This acknowledgment of the need for a more robust theology of religions (rather than a theology of the unevangelized), however, has also recognized the danger of slipping into purely descriptive modes of discourse. After applying historical, phenomenological, sociocultural, and other methodological tools toward understanding these religious others, the persistent Christian theological questions remain: what is the relationship between Christianity and other religious traditions? What is the truth about salvation and other religious doctrines? How should Christians relate to members of the non-Christian faiths?[3]

It is certainly the case that connections between these topics have already begun to be explored. The idea of a pneumatological missiology has been discussed,[4] as has that of a pneumatological approach to a theology

---

2. See Bosch, *Transforming Mission*, Part 3.

3. For my previous work in this arena in general and on some of these questions particularly, see Yong, *Discerning the Spirit(s)* and *Beyond the Impasse.*

4. Previous attempts to develop a pneumatological theology of mission include Gordon, *Holy Spirit in Missions*; Allen, "Pentecost and the World"; Boer, *Pentecost and Missions*; Taylor, *Go-Between God*; Pomerville, *Third Force in Missions*; Penney, *Missionary Emphasis of Lukan Pneumatology*; McConnell, ed., *Holy Spirit and Mission Dynamics*; and, most recently, Bevans, "God Inside Out." See also the entire issue of

of religions.[5] And, the ecumenical movement has long debated the means and ends of the Christian mission in light of the emerging consciousness of the vitality of the non-Christian faiths.[6] What has yet to receive attention is how a triadic convergence of these topics—pneumatology, missiology, and religious pluralism—might be mutually illuminating. To my knowledge, no sustained deliberation has been given to the implications of a pneumatological understanding of mission and evangelization in a religiously plural world.[7]

In what follows, I wish to take up this question in a very preliminary way. To do so, my own pentecostal background and formation leads me intuitively to the Pentecost narrative in Acts 2. The main body of this paper (section II) will attempt to unearth Pentecostal and pneumatological resources for rethinking the Christian encounter with other faiths. The concluding section (III) will present theses for a pneumatological theology of mission and evangelism in a religiously plural world.

PENTECOST, CHRISTIAN MISSION, AND THE NON-CHRISTIAN FAITHS

The thesis I wish to explore is the following: The Holy Spirit is the ground of a) human encounter; b) identity in diversity and unity in plurality; and c) the arriving eschatological kingdom of God. How does the Pentecost narrative specifically and Luke's pneumatology in the book of Acts generally support this tripartite thesis, and how does it inform the quest for a pneumatological theology of mission and evangelization in a religiously plural world?

International Review of Mission 80:317 (1991), which was devoted to the missiological implications of the WCC Canberra conference, the theme of which was "Come Holy Spirit—Renew the Whole Creation." See especially the editorial introduction of Duraisingh, "Mission and the Holy Spirit."

5. Besides my own work (see note 3), see the exploratory but undeveloped proposals of Khodr, "Christianity in a Pluralistic World"; Samartha, "Holy Spirit and People of Various Faiths," ch. 5 of his *Courage for Dialogue*; and Knitter, "A New Pentecost?"

6. Discussion of religious pluralism has become standard in missiologies published during the past generation. For an introduction to issues for Christian mission in a religiously plural world, see the essays in section one of Anderson and Stransky, eds., *Faith Meets Faith*.

7. Some initial thoughts can be found in Pinnock, "Evangelism and Other Living Faiths," and Kärkkäinen, *Toward a Pneumatological Theology*, ch. 17.

The Holy Spirit is the Ground of Human Encounter

Pentecostal theologian Jean-Jacques Suurmond has previously called attention to seeing the Pentecostal outpouring of the Holy Spirit "upon all flesh" (Acts 2:17) as signaling "a decisive new change in the relationship between God and the world and thus also in relationship between human beings." More specifically, Suurmond suggests that the coming of the Spirit into the world on the Day of Pentecost released charismatic gifts that enable human beings to encounter each other authentically other rather than as projections of and for the self. And, of decisive importance, this possibility of new modes of relationship extends beyond what Christians experience with other Christians to what Christians experience with those outside the church.[8]

How can this be argued from the Pentecost narrative? The clue, I suggest, is derived from a phenomenological reading of the Acts 2:

> When the day of Pentecost had come, they were all together in one place. And suddenly from heaven there came a sound like the rush of a violent wind, and it filled the entire house where they were sitting. Divided tongues, as of fire, appeared among them, and a tongue rested on each of them. All of them were filled with the Holy Spirit and began to speak in other languages, as the Spirit gave them ability. Now there were devout Jews from every nation under heaven living in Jerusalem. And at this sound the crowd gathered and was bewildered, because each one heard them speaking in the native language of each. Amazed and astonished, they asked, "Are not all these who are speaking Galileans? And how is it that we hear, each of us, in our own native language? Parthians, Medes, Elamites, and residents of Mesopotamia, Judea and Cappadocia, Pontus and Asia, Phrygia and Pamphylia, Egypt and the parts of Libya belonging to Cyrene, and visitors from Rome, both Jews and proselytes, Cretans and Arabs—in our own languages we hear them speaking about God's deeds of power." All were amazed and perplexed, saying to one another, "What does this mean?" But others sneered and said, "They are filled with new wine." (Acts 2:1–13)

Among the many miracles of Pentecost, the most important for our purposes is that it made possible the encounter of human beings with each other that, left to themselves, would not have entered into relationship. Whether such was a miracle of speech or of hearing is not of concern here. The crucial issue is that understanding occurred across linguistic lines: "in our own

8. Suurmond, *Word and Spirit at Play*, 198–203; quote from 201.

languages we hear them speaking about God's deeds of power." More specifically, in this case, Galileans who spoke Aramaic were able to communicate with those from around the Mediterranean world, Luke's identification of native languages being a nonexhaustive listing of the visitors present in Jerusalem on that day. On this point, then, one of the miracles of Pentecost was to reconcile a human race divided by language since the Tower of Babel, only that the uniting tongue was not of merely human provenance, but spoken as the Spirit gave utterance.

Yet I suggest that the encounter made possible here goes beyond linguistic lines toward what we might call intercultural or cross-cultural communication. Certainly, those present at Jerusalem were identified as "devout Jews" (v. 5) and to that extent, were not "culturally" other than the 120 who descended from the Upper Room. But it needs to be noted here that to identify Jews only as a cultural category during the first century is problematic for at least two reasons. First, it would imply the anachronistic distinction between "cultural Jews" and "religious Jews" that derives more from the modern period than from the Second Temple period. Diaspora Jews during the Second Temple period were certainly ethnically distinct, but less certainly culturally demarcated.[9] Second, and more importantly, Jewishness also functioned during the first century as an ethical and a political marker, and as such, complexifies the cultural and linguistic distinction.

In addition, however, to assume that no Gentiles were present in Jerusalem because Luke explicitly identifies devout Jews at the scene is to overlook other exegetical clues. First, Luke qualifies his description of these Jews by noting their derivation "from every nation under heaven" (v. 5). Second, they also heard the 120 speaking "in the native language of each" (v. 6). Finally, and most revealing, is the presence of proselytes—Gentile converts to Judaism—on the scene at hand (v. 10). While most commentators read Luke straightforwardly and see these proselytes as hailing only from Rome, it is also (at least grammatically) possible that Jews and proselytes "does not refer to any specific national group with its own language . . . , but covers *all* the preceding groups with respect to religious affiliation."[10]

In any case, what we have here is the presence of both the Jewish diaspora and Gentile converts to Judaism.[11] The Jews present had remained devout worshippers of God in spite of their dispersion abroad, and had visibly set themselves apart through various practices—e.g., their observances

9. See the discussion in Barclay, *Jews in Mediterranean Diaspora*, esp. 402–12.

10. Haenchen, *Acts of the Apostles*, 171; italics orig.

11. On the Jewish diaspora, see, e.g., Collins, *Between Athens and Jerusalem*, and Rajak, *Jewish Dialogue with Greece and Rome*. On proselytes, see Levinskaya, *Book of Acts*, esp. chs. 2–3.

at mealtime, of male circumcision, and of the Sabbath. Yet having been removed from their "homeland" for generations if not centuries, they had certainly grown up in other places, learned other languages that were now native to them, and been shaped by these languages and the cultures within which they flourished. In the case of the Gentile converts to Judaism, the situation is even more complex. Some proselytes stopped short of circumcision, even while adhering to Jewish law. Is it also possible that others were not pure monotheists, or perhaps had not severed ties with the pagan communities from which they came?[12] The fact that there were degrees of conversion to Judaism should caution us against homogenizing the "proselytes" Luke identifies as eyewitnesses on the Day of Pentecost. This group of persons undoubtedly had fused (or were in the process of fusing) a variety of practices, values, customs, and traditions into their Jewish identity.

In either case (of devout Jew or Gentile proselyte), whereas previous generations may have overlooked the interconnectedness between language and culture, no longer can we responsibly do so. To speak a language fluently because one has grown up with it is significantly different from taking on a second language. The former includes the socialization that language provides. That those present in Jerusalem were natives of places as disparate as Asia (Minor), Mesopotamia, and North Africa, among others, means that their experience of the one God had been similarly shaped by the particularities of their linguistic, sociohistorical, and cultural backgrounds. The Pentecost narrative therefore portrays an intercultural encounter of wide magnitude.

To make the association between language and culture, however, raises a further connection: that between language, culture, and religion. Current scholarship in religious studies continues to debate the links between religion and language, and religion and culture. Can religion be clearly demarcated from language and culture? Is it possible to understand religion in its purity, apart from cultural considerations? What would religion abstracted from language and culture sound or look like? On the other side, are there purely linguistic, cultural or cultural-linguistic phenomena apart from religion? In these various disciplines there are arguments made about the interdependence of language and religion and of culture and religion. While

12. I pose this as a question since such was clearly the case with the "God-fearers" who become prominent later in the book of Acts (e.g., 10:1–2 and passim; cf. Collins, *Between Athens and Jerusalem*, 270). Did proselytes to Judaism differ from God-fearing Gentiles who resisted conversion to Judaism precisely on these points? Yet it is also the case that the God-fearers were very close to Judaism in various ways, many being practically adherents of local synagogues even if they did not take out formal membership. Regardless, the difficulty of the category of "proselyte" should be evident, which is my main point.

language, culture, and religion are certainly distinguishable for purposes of communication and reflection, in reality, however, they overlap and are deeply interconnected. The boundaries between these domains of human experience, if existing at all, are seriously contested. These questions, along with that of whether one is more primordial than the other two, and if so, which one, are beyond the scope of this paper.[13]

I need to be clear that I am not suggesting Luke intended his account of the Day of Pentecost to be anything other than an account regarding the miracle of communication, either of speech or of hearing. Whether or not Luke understood Pentecost as a intercultural or interreligious event will not be decided exegetically. The line of exploration I am raising is first and foremost theological. Yet I am suggesting that implicit in the Pentecost narrative are significant and heretofore untapped resources for the intercultural and interreligious engagement.

The Holy Spirit is the Ground of Identity in Diversity and of Unity in Plurality

In order to pursue this theological line of thought, I turn to the second thesis. Here again, I want to suggest that a pneumatological grounding of identity in diversity, and of unity in plurality, is implicit in the Pentecost narrative. This point has been argued most powerfully by a non-pentecostal theologian who has served as a suggestive dialogue partner for pentecostals: Michael Welker.[14]

Welker's pneumatology is actually self-characterized as a "realistic biblical theology" that pays as much attention to the diversity as to the unity of the biblical narratives and traditions.[15] In his excellent chapter on the Spirit on the Day of Pentecost and in the book of Acts, Welker suggests that the miracle of Pentecost "lies not in what is difficult to understand or incomprehensible, but in a totally unexpected comprehensibility and in an unbelievable, universal capacity to understand"; to be more precise, "this difference between the experience of plural inaccessibility to each other and of enduring foreignness, and unfamiliarity, on the one hand, and of utter

13. I would suggest that religion, language, and culture be seen as equi-primordially informing the human condition. For succinct overviews of the pertinent issues, see the articles especially in sections III and V on "Religious Languages and Scripts" and "Beliefs and Language," in Sawyer et al., *Concise Encyclopedia of Language and Religion.*

14. I rely primarily on Welker, *God the Spirit*, esp. ch. 5, on the Spirit in Acts. This book spawned a fruitful exchange with the pentecostal theologian Frank Macchia: see Macchia, "Discerning the Spirit in Life," and Welker, "Spirit Topics."

15. Welker, *God the Spirit*, x–xi.

commonality of the capacity to understand, on the other hand—this is what is truly and shocking about the Pentecostal event. . . . An astounding, indeed frightening clarity in the midst of the received complexity and variety, a dismaying familiarity in the midst of the received inaccessibility and unfamiliarity—this is what is miraculous and wonderful about the revelation at Pentecost. The Pentecost event connects intense experiences of individuality with a new experience of community."[16]

Notice that Welker's account calls attention to the radical pluralism implicit in the Pentecost account. Yet this pluralism, rather than being erased or sublated by the universal outpouring of the Spirit on all flesh, is that which actually constitutes the powerful universality of the pentecostal gift. The result is what Welker calls an "overcomprehensibility" that both amazes and perplexes the onlooking spectators.[17] Therefore, the response "What does this mean?" (v. 12) was not a request for explanation of what was spoken, but was an expression of the bewilderment that the crowd felt in being able to understand the testimony of the 120 about "God's deeds of power" (v. 11). Read in this light, then, the Pentecostal event signifies nothing less than that "God effects a world-encompassing, multilingual, polyindividual testimony to Godself."[18]

This unity-in-diversity theme of the Day of Pentecost should not be underestimated. The first *ekklesia* (2:37–47) emerged precisely out of those who congregated that day on the streets of Jerusalem. Notice again some of the regions represented from around the Mediterranean. There were devout Jews, and possibly Gentile proselytes, from Egypt, perhaps denoting what is now called the African continent and thereby including the black race. (Even if this is only implicit in Acts 2, that the book of Acts includes the African in the congregation of the Lord is undisputed given the account of Philip and the Ethiopian eunuch in ch. 8). Further, there is reference to Jewish, and possibly Gentile, Cretans, of who it was alleged were all "liars, vicious brutes, [and] lazy gluttons" (cf. Titus 1:12). While this stereotype remains as a challenge to the church regarding how she views "foreigners" or those "outside" her walls, it also served as an ongoing reminder of the radical diversity—understood both positively and negatively—within her ranks. Translated theologically and colloquially, the church of Jesus Christ consists of none other than sinners saved by grace. Last (but not least) for our purposes, what about the Jewish, and possibly Gentile, Arabs present, and perhaps even constitutive of the 3,000 baptized that day? Might the

16. Ibid., 230–31 and 233.

17. Ibid., 232.

18. Ibid., 235.

history of the Middle East have been any different if Jews and Arabs would have developed sustained relationships by the power of the Spirit from that pentecostal experience?

This theme of unity in diversity—neither being subordinated to the other, and both mutually informing the other—has far-reaching ecclesiological implications. In his essay, "The Ephesian Moment," Andrew Walls suggests that the present Gentile-dominated church has for too long taken for granted the Gentile identity of the people of God and neglected the revealed mystery that astounded even the angels: that in Christ, God has accomplished a new, reconciled humanity from that which was formerly antagonistically set off as Jew and Gentile, and that it was precisely the goal of the unity of the Spirit to produce an eschatological unity of faith according to the full measure of Christ.[19] Walls further suggests that reread in this way, the letter to the Ephesians reveals how the early church struggled with deep theological issues as the presence of Gentiles in the community of faith grew. Rather than retrenching into the secure confines of its Jewish identity, however, the church creatively incorporated Gentile (read: pagan) elements into its language and liturgy; the adoption of the Greek *Kyrios*, used by Gentiles for their cult divinities, as a christological title; and the cosmic interpretation of Jesus' significance.

The point I wish to emphasize, however, is that the unity of the newly established body of Christ preserves rather than cancels out the diversity of its members. This ecclesiological reading of the Pentecost narrative can illuminate the structure of personal identity as well. In my own case, I was born in the country of Malaysia to Chinese parents replete with Confucian values (even while retaining some Confucian practices), and grew up speaking three languages (English, Cantonese, and Malay). Our family moved to California, USA when I was ten. I am married to a Hispanic (Mexican) American, and we have lived in the radically individualistic Pacific Northwest, in an Italian community in New England, and now in what may be called the "New Scandinavia" of the Upper Midwest region of the USA. While raised in a typical pentecostal home—in the Assemblies of God, with whom I remain affiliated as a credentialed minister—with an undergraduate degree from a pentecostal Bible college, I have also attended Holiness and Methodist seminaries, and currently teach in a pietist Baptist liberal arts environment. I carry memberships in academic societies as diverse as the Society for Pentecostal Studies, the Evangelical Theological Society, and the American Academy of Religion, among others. Furthermore, having spent the last ten-plus years studying the Buddhist tradition in some depth has led

19. See Walls, "Ephesian Moment," ch. 2 of his *The Cross-Cultural Process.*

me into the circles of the Society for Buddhist-Christian Studies. This past year, I got a chance to revisit Malaysia for the first time, during which I not only reconnected with extended family members (most of who continue to live there), but rediscovered ethnic, cultural, and social aspects of my own personal identity that had long been submerged due to my emigration. Along the way, I have lost fluency in the non-English languages I grew up with, but have picked up some Spanish, French, and German, not to mention a bit of biblical Hebrew and Greek—even while I am far from having mastered any of these—along the way.

When I look back over my own personal journey, it is no wonder (at least to me) why I oftentimes feel confused about my own identity. Yet this confusion, while potentially debilitating, has never actually been so. Rather, as I have discovered, such "confusion" can also be understood as a sign of "richness," evidence of the diversity of traditions, narratives, and stories which combine in my life history. Are we not the experiences that have shaped and formed us? If so, then to greater or lesser degrees and to be developed in some ways and neglected in others, I am (in no particular order) pentecostal, evangelical, pietist Baptist, Chinese, American, Malaysian, Confucian, Buddhist—the meanings of each and every one of these constructed categories subject to extensive debate—and, perhaps even a Christian. As such, this plurality and diversity serves to provide a wide pool of resources from which I can draw as needed in life's situations.[20] In and through all of this, then, I am an individual constituted by plurality. And how is this possible? Explicating from the Pentecost narrative, the answer is analogous to how the church is the one body of Christ constituted by a diversity of members: by and through the gift of the spirit of God.

The Holy Spirit is the Dynamic Ground of the Arriving Eschatological Kingdom of God

My third thesis flows forth from the first two, emphasizing and preserving the otherness and the diversity of the other who the Holy Spirit enables us to encounter. I am thinking here, for example, of the imagery in the Apocalypse regarding the pluralism of nations bringing their honor and glory into the New Jerusalem (Rev 21:24–26; cf. also the many peoples, tribes,

---

20. From reading the personal reflections of other Asian-born immigrants to the US, I learned how not being centered in any one community while belonging to and being constituted by many narratives and traditions could be empowering rather than incapacitating; see Phan and Lee, *Journeys at Margins*. See also Yong, "Review of *Journeys at Margins*."

tongues, and nations standing before the throne of the Lamb and rejoic-
ing in the salvation provided by him in Rev 7:9–10).[21] Put in Lukan terms,
I want to briefly explore several aspects of this thesis that the Pentecostal
Spirit dynamically grounds and anticipates the arrival of the eschatological
kingdom of God.[22]

To begin, note that Peter himself identifies the Pentecost experience as
an eschatological event. In response to the confusion of the crowd, he refers
to the prophecy of Joel that "in the last days it will be, God declares, that I
will pour out my Spirit upon all flesh" (Acts 2:17; cf. Joel 2:28). "This is that
which was prophesied," Peter in effect proclaims. As such, the Pentecostal
outpouring of the Spirit also inaugurated the "last days" of the world. Leaving to one side the question of the *terminus ad quem* of these "last days"
(the Christian Testament itself notes this issue—cf. 2 Pet. 3:3–4), what is
more germane to our present discussion is the eschatological nature of the
Pentecost experience.

But what is it that identifies or distinguishes Pentecost as an eschatological event? I suggest, building on the previous theses, that it is the
reconciliation of humankind in all its diversity as a new people of God,
temporarily in the church of Jesus Christ in anticipation of the arrival of
the kingdom of God. Note that the eschatological outpouring of the Spirit
recognizes no ethnic, racial, gender, age, or even socioeconomic barriers, to
put it in today's politically correct terms. Sons and daughters will prophesy;
young and old will see visions and dream dreams; slaves and free persons
will receive the gift of the Spirit (cf. Acts 2:17–18). And I have already commented on the likelihood that the first 3,000 who were baptized included
Jews and proselytes from every nation under heaven. As such, the Pentecost
event serves as a microcosmic lens through which to view and anticipate
the "universal restoration that God announced long ago through his holy
prophets" (Acts 3:21). It is also a foretaste of the results of the Spirit's empowering work so that the gospel can go from Jerusalem through Judea and
(even!) Samaria, to the ends of the earth (Acts 1:8), to include the Gentiles
with whom it was unlawful for Jews to associate (cf. Acts 10:28). This would
simply be a fulfillment of the promise made to Abraham, that "in your descendants all the families of the earth shall be blessed" (Acts 3:25; cf. Gen
12:3 and 22:18). In Luke's terms, "God shows no partiality, but in every nation anyone who fears him and does what is right is acceptable to him" (Acts

21. And the key, as Kobus de Smidt points out, is that it is the Spirit leads the church
to bear witness to Christ precisely because the Spirit is sent from the throne of God into
the world; see Smidt, "Hermeneutical Perspectives," esp. 37–39.

22. Bilaniuk, *Theology and Economy of Holy Spirit*, talks about "The Mystery of the
Eschatological Fulfillment as the Definitive Pentecost" (ch. 10).

10:34–35). More specifically, both "*everyone* who calls on the name of the Lord" (Acts 2:21) and "*everyone* whom the Lord ... God calls to" (Acts 2:39) shall be saved (italics mine).

But it is also important, especially in any discussion of religious pluralism, to emphasize that what Christians hasten and yearn for is the arrival not just of any kingdom, but that of the kingdom of God. The Pentecostal Spirit is not any spirit, but the Holy Spirit poured out upon all flesh by Jesus according to the promise of the Father (cf. Acts 2:32). Entrance into the kingdom involves (at least in this dispensation) repentance (before God), baptism in Jesus' name for the forgiveness of sins, and reception of the Holy Spirit (Acts 2:38). In short, the Spirit is but the spirit of Jesus Christ and the spirit of God, and any pneumatological theology, rather than being a "monism of the Spirit," is an opening toward the triune God.[23]

From this, the Christian mission that is empowered by the Spirit and directed to the kingdom of the Father through Jesus Christ demands our full immersion into the liberating and reconciling work of the spirit of God in all spheres of life. If the work of the kingdom is to redeem the fallen dimensions of human existence, then it is the mission of the Spirit to heal and reconcile the social, economic, political, etc., divisions and fragmentations of our world.[24] This is consistent with the Lukan theological vision whereby the Pentecostal outpouring (in Acts) is simply the completion of the redemptive work of God accomplished in the life and death of Jesus (in Luke), and as such, an invitation to human beings to participate in the life of Christ and to do the things that Jesus did.[25] And, of course, Jesus recognized his own mission as being anointed by the Holy Spirit to "bring good news to the poor ... , to proclaim release to the captives and recovery of sight to the blind, to let the oppressed go free, [and] to proclaim the year of the Lord's favor" (Luke 4:18–19).[26]

The question I have is why would this reconciling work of the Spirit (and of Christ) not include the redemption of the religious sphere of human life?[27] This reconciliatory work is especially important since the religions, no less than other dimensions of human experience, are fallen and in need

23. On this point see Newbigin, *Trinitarian Faith in Today's Mission*, esp. 75–76.

24. See Potter, "Mission as Reconciliation."

25. This is one of the emphases in the splendid and detailed work of Anderson, *A Vatican II Pneumatology of Paschal Mystery*, esp. 277–94.

26. And Maurice Hobbs notes that Jesus accomplished his mission in part by meeting people at their point of need; see Hobbs, "Our Lord's Approach to People of Other Cultures."

27. On this "reconciliation with people of other faiths," see Clapsis, "What Does the Spirit Say?," esp. 337–38.

of redemption.[28] Yet while Christians have been open to considering the redemption and appropriation of the cultural, social, economic, and even political dimensions of life, some have been much more resistant when the religions have been brought into the equation. My own sense is that Christians have traditionally drawn a line in the sand on this point because the choice had been between Christian *faith* and non-Christian *religions*. In this way, an absolute dualism has been established between these two kinds of realities.

Today, however, we can no longer define Christianity and the other *faiths* in such dualistic or essentialistic terms. And if religion, language, and culture are not so easily distinguishable, neither are religion, society, politics, gender issues, etc. This does not make all religious ways of life equally appropriate, or all religious claims to truth commensurate. If we can affirm that the Spirit's outpouring upon all flesh does not necessarily lead to universalism, then we can also affirm that the Spirit's presence and activity in national, cultural, socioeconomic, political, and even religious spheres of human life does not necessarily mean that every aspect of each dimension must be uncritically accepted or that every spirit be seen as divinely inspired.[29] To determine what is what, discernment has to proceed cautiously, on a case-by-case basis. Making this affirmation of the Spirit's presence and activity in the religions, however, does require Christians to rethink what it means to embrace the reconciling work of the Spirit directed toward the kingdom of God.

More specifically, if the radical particularity of otherness is preserved in and through the pentecostal experience as a foretaste of the kingdom, I wonder about the particularities of religious otherness that we are more alert to than ever today. Herein lies the rationale of extending the insights of Pentecost for intra-Christian ecumenism toward the wider *oekumene*.[30] David Bosch has called attention to how the evolution of themes in World Council of Churches (WCC) conferences devoted to the relationship of

28. This is the important qualification I would add to John Taylor's suggestion that all religions are traditions of response, even if of unequal value, to the Spirit of the triune God (*Go-Between God*, ch. 9, "The Universal Spirit and the Meeting of Faiths"). Because of this fallen character of religiosity, I follow Barth in rejecting any religious tradition, as such, even Christianity, as salvific. Only God saves.

29. This importance of not confusing the Holy Spirit and other spirits in the religions and cultures of the world was sounded clearly by evangelical and Orthodox participants at Canberra; see Kerr, "Come Holy Spirit," esp. 101–3.

30. See the discussion of this ecumenical development in the editor's introduction, Phan, ed., *Christianity and Wider Ecumenism*, esp. ix–x. Here, I am applying Frank Macchia's ecumenical strategy—in Macchia, "Tongues of Pentecost"—toward the interreligious encounter.

Christianity and other faiths has reflected the progression of Christian consciousness on exactly this point (my emphases in what follows):

- Commission for World Mission and Evangelism meeting in Mexico City (1963): "The Witness of Christians *to* Men of Other Faiths" (one-way monologue, although others are recognized as being of faith rather than not)

- East Asia Christian Conference in Bangkok (1964): "The *Christian Encounter* with Men of Other Beliefs" (Christian initiative)

- Ditto (1967): "*Christians in Dialogue with* Men of Other Faiths" (still a Christian enterprise and concern)

- Ajaltoun (Lebanon) (1970): "Dialogue *between* Men of *Living* Faiths" (otherness affirmed positively and others seen as equal dialogue partners)

- Chiang Mai (Thailand) (1977): "Dialogue *in Community*" (fully egalitarian—i.e., non-gendered—attitudes assumed)[31]

Now again, I reject the kind of conservatism that sees this development as leading down the slippery slope to relativism. Rather, I believe a Lukan, Pentecostal, and pneumatological orientation to the interreligious encounter enables us to ask not "Why should I choose Jesus rather than the Buddha, etc.?" but rather, "How does my Buddhist, etc., identity inform my commitment to Christ and my Christian confession in anticipation of the impending kingdom of God?"[32] In this way, we would not need to deny the particular experiences of women and men, young and old, the poor and the affluent, oriental and occidental, Jew and Greek, red and yellow or black and white, those who speak and those who sign, and even the Muslim, the Hindu, the Buddhist, the Confucian, etc. Rather, each of these can be seen to give particular testimony to the nature of humankind and of humanity's relationship to God (theological anthropology) in anticipation of the full reconciliation to be accomplished in the kingdom.[33]

---

31. Bosch, *Transforming Mission*, 484.

32. My putting the questions this way was assisted by Lee, "A Response to: Why Jesus?," esp. 90.

33. Assuming, here, Calvin's conviction of the interrelatedness between self-knowledge and the knowledge of God elaborated in chapter one of his *Institutes of the Christian Religion*. [The particularity of these "witnesses" are certainly partial and even fallible, although for these reasons no less true; yet from a Christian faith perspective, these testimonies are completed, fulfilled, and vindicated finally, if at all, in the light of the coming Christ.]

THESES FOR A PNEUMATOLOGICAL THEOLOGY OF MISSION AND EVANGELIZATION IN A RELIGIOUSLY PLURAL WORLD

Let me conclude with five theses and a set of practical suggestions emergent from the preceding reflections.

Thesis #1: A viable contemporary theology of mission and evangelization is necessarily pneumatological. While the connection between the Holy Spirit and evangelism has long been recognized,[34] the fundamental and irreducible relationship between the Holy Spirit and the Christian mission as a whole has slowly been rediscovered. A generation ago, Harry Boer called attention to the New Testament emphasis on Pentecost, not the Great Commission, as the central axiom from which emanates the missionary dynamic of Christian faith.[35] As such, any theology of mission and evangelization has to be nothing less than pneumatologically founded, framed, and delineated.

Thesis #2: A viable contemporary theology of interreligious ecumenism can be understood in part as an outgrowth of a pneumatological theology of intra-Christian ecumenism. Just as the ecumenical implications of the doctrine of the Holy Spirit are now widely recognized,[36] so I am suggesting that Christians begin to rethink the interfaith encounter from within a pneumatological framework. I have sketched aspects of such a perspective from the Pentecost narrative. Much more biblical and theological work can and should be done in this area. Part and parcel of what will continue to emerge is what ecumenical statesman Albert Outler calls a "pneumatological or ecumenical hermeneutics," a method of reading texts and interpreting religious experiences that is increasingly dialogical in taking into account the perspectives of others.[37] I would suggest that so long as we proceed with proper caution and discernment, there is no reason why such an ecumenical hermeneutic should not be informed by the interreligious encounter.

Thesis #3: A pneumatological theology of mission and evangelization in an interreligious context is able to safeguard the perennial tension which exists between dialogue and proclamation. On the one hand, as Lawrence Folkemer put it some time ago, "Interfaith dialogue must be seen increasingly

34. Keener, "Spirit Empowers Us for Evangelism," ch. 3 in his *Gift and Giver.*

35. Boer, *Pentecost and Missions*, chs. 1–2.

36. Raiser, "Holy Spirit in Modern Ecumenical Thought," overviews the place of pneumatology in the history of the WCC.

37. Outler, "Pneumatology as Ecumenical Frontier," esp. 370. Cf. also Thomas Oden's call for a "consensual theological method" in *After Modernity*, 160–64. For more on a pneumatologically informed, ecumenical, and consensually hermeneutic and theological method, see my *Spirit-Word-Community*, esp. Part III.

as an arena for the working of the Holy Spirit."[38] The Holy Spirit is the one who has not only sent the church into the world, but also gone before the church into this same world. As such, the Spirit meets us in and through the image of God etched in the faces of religious others and their communities, and provides the common ground—the common humanity or meeting point—of the Christian encounter with them. If this is the case, then there needs to be a genuinely dialogical encounter between Christians and those in other faiths. One of the marks of whether authentic dialogue is occurring is whether or not Christians are willing to subject their faith assumptions, claims, and criteriologies to the criticism of their dialogue partners.[39] So long as Christians are unwilling to test the viability of their beliefs across the spectrum of human life, they betray a fideistic attitude that hinders veritable encounters with non-Christians.

On the other hand, the Holy Spirit is the spirit of Jesus, sent to turn the world to Jesus and to remind the world of his words and deeds. As Roland Allen notes, the Acts account shows that neither the monotheism of the Jews nor the philosophy of the Greeks were sufficient apart from the *evangelion* of Jesus Christ.[40] Apart from the Christian witness to Jesus the Christ, no authentic representation of the Christian faith would occur, and in this case, the dialogue would once again slip into a monologue, this time from the religious other to the Christian. Genuine dialogue requires the presence of Christian conviction and testimony. Christian mission is thereby necessarily marked by both dialogue and proclamation, openness and responsiveness, sensitivity and activity, and humility and boldness[41] (here, I do not mean to imply that the latter elements of the preceding pairs has priority over the former). I am proposing that a pneumatologically informed approach to the wider ecumenism can protect both moments as essential to genuine encounters and engagement.

Thesis #4: A pneumatological theology of mission and evangelization will also enable a truly crucicentric and, hence, liberative solidarity to emerge in the interreligious encounter. Given that the Holy Spirit is the spirit of Jesus, a robustly pneumatological theology of religions will be, as previously mentioned, a Trinitarian theology of religions, and, as such, also a christocentric theology of religions. With regard to the latter, the Spirit not only witnesses

38. Folkemer, "Dialogue and Proclamation," esp. 429–31; quote from 430.

39. This is the thesis of Chapman, "Phenomenological Method of Post-Dialogue."

40. See Allen, *The Ministry of the Spirit*, 37.

41. Here, I resonate with Henry E. Lie's "open particularism" proposal, forged in the Asian religious context, which is christocentric, biblically committed, evangelistically motivated, soteriologically inclusive, and yet dialogically open, even to the point of learning from religious others; see Lie, "Open Particularism."

to Christ and enables confession of Jesus as Lord, but also is the anointing who empowers the ministry of Jesus the Christ, leads him to and through the passion of the cross, and culminates with raising him from the dead. This enables the understanding that "the cross as clue to the suffering of God is at the heart" of the confession of Jesus Christ in a world of religious pluralism.[42]

Following from this, however, the life and death of Christ binds him together with a suffering humanity. It is precisely through the solidarity of Jesus with the poor, the downtrodden, the oppressed, etc., that the redemption of humankind from sin and from the bonds of the devil is accomplished. Extended toward the interreligious encounter, then, a pneumatological theology of mission and evangelization is shaped by this cruciform event to empower the words and deeds of human beings—both Christians and their interfaith dialogue partners—in liberating suffering humanity in every sphere, in seeking for and establishing justice and peace in the world, and in truly declaring and hastening the healing and reconciling Day of the Lord.

Finally, *Thesis #5: On a practical level, a pneumatological theology of mission and evangelization in a religiously plural world will need to be especially alert for what the Spirit is saying and doing in and through the churches, be sensitive to the presence and activities of religious others, and be discerning about the broader context of the Christian ministry.* Life in the Spirit is necessarily thoroughly contextual, attentive to the specifics of the situation at hand. Why should a pneumatological approach to mission and evangelization in a religiously plural environment be any less so? There can therefore be no hard and fast rule of action that should dictate Christian approaches to engaging with religious others motivated by following after the Spirit.

In this case, then, what can and should we do? Among other things, Christians in the past have

- established denominational offices and organizations to facilitate congregational awareness of and engagement with non-Christian faiths

- strategized about how and when overt evangelism should proceed from their churches, thereby requiring discussions of what conversion means, how Christian initiation occurs, the issues regarding proselytism, the nature of interreligious relationship and dialogue, etc.

- developed formal intercongregational and interreligious events in order to foster better relationship, understanding, and mutual respect

---

42. Thomsen, "Confessing Jesus Christ." For an in-depth argument regarding the Spirit who raises Jesus from the dead, the impossible possibility which is suggestive of what might be called a "pneumatology of the cross," see Dabney, *"Pneumatologia Crucis."*

- nurtured community solidarity and development across faith lines[43]

Why should Christians not continue to do all this and more? By so doing, as John Taylor has suggested, other religious traditions receive "blood transfusions" from Christ and the Christian faith.[44] As a result, they are re-formed precisely through the interreligious encounter with Christians by the Spirit. Further, however, authentic interreligious encounter transforms Christians as well. If deeper commitments to Christ and to our neighbors—the brothers and sisters of Jesus who are hungry, thirsty, sick, in prison, etc.—result, is this not also the work of the Holy Spirit in our midst?[45]

43. The preceding derives from Neely, "Religious Pluralism," esp. 39–42. Cf. also Hooker and Lamb, *Love the Stranger*.

44. Taylor, *Go-Between God*, 194–97.

45. This paper was originally presented to the North American Academy of Ecumenists, Washington, DC, September 27–29, 2002, under the title, "Pneumatology, Mission and Evangelization in a Religiously Plural World." My thanks to Jeff Gros, FSC, of the Secretariat for Ecumenical and Interreligious Affairs, United States Conference of Catholic Bishops, not only for recommending my participation in this meeting, but also for providing critical feedback on an earlier draft of this paper. Needless to say, the faults that remain are my own.

CHAPTER 3

A P(new)matological Paradigm for Christian Mission in a Religiously Plural World

IN THIS ESSAY, I wish to summarize recent work at the intersection of pneumatological theology and theology of religions, proceed to explore that convergence for help in rethinking Christian mission in the twenty-first century, and conclude with some brief reflections on other important theological matters related to these topics. Our guiding question throughout is this: how might recent developments in the doctrine of the Holy Spirit (pneumatology) illuminate perennial challenges in Christian reflection about the plurality of religions (theology of religions) and inform the increasingly complex task of Christian mission in a religious plural world (missiology)? While I apologize up front for the many references that follow to my previous work, I am also happy to say that what I have done has not only extended previous thinking on these matters but also continued to provoke further discussion. As such, especially in the final section of this essay, I will take up the most pressing questions critics have posed for this new pneumatological paradigm for Christian mission in our contemporary religiously plural world.

ELEMENTS OF A PNEUMATOLOGICAL THEOLOGY OF RELIGIOUS PLURALISM

The turn toward a pneumatological approach in Christian theological reflections on the plurality of religions has been a recent development in response to what I have called the christological impasse.[1] In brief, christo-logical categories at the center of thinking about theology of religions has led to asking if other faiths are (a) opposed to Christ, and hence false (or demonic—the traditional "exclusivistic" position); (b) fulfilled in some way by Christ (hence pointing to Christ as the Old Testament points toward the New—the traditional "inclusivistic" position); or (c) testify in their own ways to the same truth as that which Christ represents (hence there being diverse testimonies to the truth, in which case "many roads" lead to the same final destination—the traditional "pluralist" position). The problem with (c) is that it both assumes a metaposition (which is unavailable to historical creatures like human beings) from which to gauge all religious traditions and it does not take seriously the specific claims of the various religious traditions. The problem with (b) is that is assumes a superiority of Christian faith over that of other religions in an arbitrary way, leading to the impasse because other traditions also assume their superiority to Christian-ity in turn. The problem with (a) is either that demonizing other religion-ists is politically and ethically inappropriate, or that such demonization or denunciation is generally done without much attempt to understand those in other traditions on their own terms. Taken together, these difficult ques-tions raise the following dilemma: *either* define other religious traditions on Christian terms but thereby preserve the centrality of Christ in theological reflection on the religions, *or* engage theologically with other religious tra-ditions on their terms but thereby lose the centrality of Christ in Christian reflection on the religions.

But what if Christian theology of religions were to proceed within a more pneumatological (and hence Trinitarian) framework instead? Follow-ing in the footsteps of others who have sketched the possibility of such a pneumatological theology of religions—e.g., Georges Khodr (Orthodox), Paul Knitter and Jacques Dupuis (Roman Catholic), and Stanley Samartha and Clark Pinnock (Protestant)—I have attempted to develop this idea into a full-fledged model that not only helps with our understanding of religious pluralism (the theological or theoretical dimension) but also en-ables our engagement with religious otherness (the practical or intersubjec-tive dimension).[2] In brief, a pneumatological theology of religions begins with the doctrine of the Holy Spirit as the universal presence and activity of God, and attempts to understand the world of the religions within that universal framework. Allow me to elaborate on three basic elements of such

1. For details, see my *Discerning the Spirit(s)*, esp. ch. 2.

2. Begun in *Discerning the Spirit(s)* and continued in my *Beyond the Impasse*. For my overviews of the work of others who have explored and attempted to develop the pneumatological path, see *Beyond the Impasse*, chs. 4 and 5.

a pneumatological approach to religious pluralism: its "grounding" in the Pentecost narrative of Acts 2; its furnishing dynamic categories for comprehending the phenomena of religion and religiosity; and its providing a dialogical and intersubjective means of adjudicating multiple religious truth claims.

Pneumatology and the "Ground" of Religious Pluralism—First, a pneumatological theology of religions proceeds at least in part from the Pentecost narrative of the spirit of God being poured out "upon all flesh" (Acts 2:17). This involves understanding "all flesh" to have universal application on the one hand, and to include the world of the religions on the other. With regard to the former point, my reading "all flesh" as having a universal reference is supported *both* by the immediate context of this claim, which includes sons and daughters, young and old, and slave and free, *and* by the broader context of the Pentecostal outpouring of the Spirit upon the many who were gathered on the streets of Jerusalem from around the known (Mediterranean) world.[3] While at one (exegetical) level it might be argued that "all flesh" is limited to the class of Christians drawn from the categories of sons, daughters, etc., at another (theological) level, the sons, daughters, etc., are Christians precisely because they are those upon whom the Spirit is poured out. In this latter reading, "all flesh" would not be qualified by "Christians." Further, while some might argue that "all flesh" is limited to Jews and proselytes to Judaism derived from the Jewish diaspora, this overlooks three more universalistic trajectories embedded in this text: (a) that proselytes are not full converts: rather, being at different stages of their spiritual journeys, they embody in their lives multiple traditions and cultures in various degrees; (b) that the summary list of regions and languages present in Jerusalem symbolize (weaker) or represent (stronger) the breadth of the known first-century world; and (c) that Luke's own narrative is guided by a universalistic vision whereby "all flesh" includes those from Jerusalem, Judea, Samaria, and "the ends of the earth" (Acts 1:8).[4]

From this universalistic reading of the Pentecost narrative, it is but a short series of steps to understanding the world of the religions in pneumatological perspective. First, it is undeniable that this Pentecost narrative should be read against the narrative of the Tower of Babel (Gen 11) when human beings were dispersed across the earth through the confusion of their languages. Against this background, the outpouring of the Spirit redeems the diversity of languages, enabling each tongue to become a vehicle

---

3. I presented this argument initially in my essay, "As the Spirit Gives Utterance," esp. 301–3. [See ch. 2 in this book, above pp. 40–50.]

4. I develop (b) and (c) in my *Spirit Poured Out on All Flesh*, §4.3.3.

to communicate the wondrous works of God. Building on this, the diversity of languages is also correlated with the diversity of cultures (or, nations, tribes, and peoples, to use first-century Mediterranean categories; cf. Rev 7:9 and passim). This is the theological basis for not only accepting but also valuing the plurality of cultures, and is the missiological basis for methods that emphasize the inculturation, indigenization, and contextualization of the gospel. This connection between language and culture is then extended to include the religious dimension of human life. Because the phenomena of language and culture cannot be arbitrarily separated from that of religion, the principle of linguistic and cultural diversity necessarily includes that of religious diversity. Hence, the Pentecost narrative can be understood to redeem not only human languages and cultures, but also human religiosity. However, just as this does not mean that all human words and all aspects of human culture are holy without qualification, so also does it not mean that all human religiousness is sanctified. Language, culture, and religion must all be discerned, even as each is potentially a vehicle for mediating the grace of God. But acceptance of this possibility establishes the Day of Pentecost as the narrative "ground" for understanding the world of the religions in pneumatological perspective.

Pneumatology and the Dynamism of Religion—The second basic element of a pneumatological approach to religious pluralism is that pneumatology furnishes dynamic categories for comprehending the phenomena of religion and religiosity.[5] Let me explicate this dynamism in terms of a few fundamental religious concepts: conversion, tradition, and praxis. *Conversion* in pneumatological perspective emphasizes the process of salvation in its various dimensions. This understanding complements the classical theological tradition's understanding of conversion as occurring at a point in time. The strength of a pneumatological theology of conversion is precisely its capacity to recognize crisis moments in the spiritual journey without abstracting these from the entire life process. Whereas the classical understanding resulted in asking questions like whether or not "once saved, always saved," a pneumatological viewpoint emphasizes Christian conversion—i.e., conversion to Christ—as a lifelong path toward being made into the image of Jesus wherein the various dimensions of an individual life (e.g., intellectual, aesthetic, moral, social, and religious[6]) are engaged and transformed over time. Put in theological terms, salvation hence includes the interrelated processes of repentance, justification, sanctification, and glorification. Put

5. I argue this idea of a pneumatological dynamic from exegetical, theological, and philosophical perspectives in my *Spirit-Word-Community*, 43–48, and passim.

6. See Gelpi, *Conversion Experience*.

in existential terms, "I was saved, I am being saved, and I will be saved." Put in religious terms, spiritual life is dynamic rather than static, and religious beliefs and practices are similarly flexible in the ways they operate in the lives of devotees to bring about religious transformation. In short, a pneumatological approach to theology of religions would be better sensitized to the unfinished and dynamic character of religiosity (orientations and dispositions), religiousness (states of piety and devotion), and religious life (ritual and praxis), and how each contributes to the religious shaping of human souls.

Tradition is similarly dynamic in pneumatological perspective because it emphasizes how the institutional carriers of religion are themselves continuously in flux. This also complements the classical theological understanding wherein "tradition" was that which was given once and for all (e.g., as an unchanging deposit of revelatory truth). The strength of a pneumatological theology of tradition is precisely its capacity to recognize the givenness and facticity of divine revelation without absolutizing any particular interpretation or expression for all time. So whereas the classical understanding resulted in questions like whether or not the Bible or the patristic fathers *are* normative for Christian theology, a pneumatological viewpoint explores *how* the Bible or patristic fathers, etc., are normative for those in other places and times. Whereas the classical understanding defined the church in static terms, a pneumatological ecclesiology emphasizes the institution of the church as the "fellowship of the Holy Spirit." In this pneumatological framework, the Christian tradition and church not only *exist*, but are also *becoming*, because the tradition and church are the concrete expressions of human responses to and participation in the Spirit's outpouring upon—presence and activity in—the world. Similarly this pneumatological perspective would more naturally enable recognition of the dynamic character of other religious traditions. In the same way as the Christian tradition can be discerned only through its continually changing empirical manifestations—to see if the Spirit's presence and activity can be detected or if the Spirit is absent in some respect—so also are the traditions of Judaism, Islam, Buddhism, Hinduism, etc., discernible through their ever-changing manifestations. A pneumatological theology of religions would be better equipped to recognize "religions" and "religious traditions" not as nouns, but verbs: they are formed by the processes of human "traditioning"[7] and thereby shaped by the various human activities in relation and responses to realities considered transcendent.

---

7. See Irvin, *Christian Histories, Christian Traditioning.*

Last (for our purposes) but not least (for the point under consideration), religious *praxis* obviously calls attention to the dynamic character of religiosity. In pneumatological perspective, however, praxis becomes just as, if not more, important than beliefs (doctrines) precisely because pneumatology calls attention to divine activity rather than divine being. This complements the classical understanding wherein "praxis" was secondary to "doctrine" in defining a religious tradition. The strength of a pneumatological theology of tradition is precisely its capacity to recognize the interrelatedness of praxis and doctrine without subordinating either to the other. Rather, praxis is understood to be guided by doctrine even as praxis shapes doctrinal formulations. A pneumatological viewpoint both acknowledges and is able to provide a theological account for the interrelatedness between praxis and doctrine. Hence a pneumatologically informed theology of religions is better able to comprehend religious otherness not only in terms of the category of doctrine but also in terms of other dynamic praxis categories like ritual, piety, devotion, morality, and the like. Unlike previous theologies of religions with their almost exclusive focus on the beliefs of religious others, a pneumatological *theologia religionum* is much better able to account for the diversity of beliefs that are linked to and shaped by different social, moral, and religious practices.[8]

Together, these brief discussions of conversion, tradition, and praxis are suggestive of how a pneumatological approach inculcates a more dynamic understanding of the phenomenon of religion. In the same way as pneumatology points to eschatology (the doctrine of things related to the end), so also a pneumatological theology of religions recognizes the open-endedness and unfinished character of religious traditions and human religiousness. Certainly, scholars of religion have long been advocates of this more dynamic understanding of human religiosity.[9] The contribution of a pneumatological perspective is a specifically theological (rather than philosophical or empirical) rationale for this kind of dynamic interpretation of religion.

Pneumatology, Truth, and the Religions—This leads to the third basic element of a pneumatological approach to religious pluralism: its capacity to provide an intersubjective mode of engaging religious truth.[10] Previous approaches to religious doctrines have noticed and, often, emphasized their contradictory quality when explicated in terms of the correspondence

8. On the intrinsic relationship between Christian beliefs and practices, see Mc-Clendon Jr., *Systematic Theology*; Hütter, *Suffering Divine Things*; and Volf and Bass, *Practicing Theology*.

9. Going back to Smith, *Meaning and End of Religion*.

10. The following is a synopsis of my "Spirit Bears Witness."

theory of truth. So Buddhists believe that death leads either to reincarnation or Nirvana, while Christians believe that death leads either to heaven or hell—in which case, either Buddhists or Christians are right (and the other wrong) since both sets of claims cannot be simultaneously true. The problem here is that claims regarding reincarnation, Nirvana, heaven, or hell are either transcendental or eschatological, resulting in Buddhist and Christian claims and counterclaims without any means of adjudicating the apparent contradictions.

More recent developments seek to emphasize how any particular doctrinal (hence: truth) claim is nested semiotically within a larger web of interlocking doctrines and religious practices, thereby requiring explication in terms of the coherence theory of truth. In this case, Buddhist or Christian claims only make sense within Buddhist or Christian frameworks since doctrines function with regard to religious traditions in ways similar to how grammars function with regard to languages.[11] The problem here is twofold: *either* religious frameworks are incommensurable—based as they are on different semiotic and praxis systems—and hence apparently contrary claims are essentially nonadjudicable; *or* any attempt to adjudicate religious (doctrinal or truth) claims requires that one not only learns about or observes from a distance another tradition but also that one enters into and participates in its semiotic system. The former results in religious relativism: what is true for the Buddhist is not true for the Christian and vice versa. With regard to the latter option, students of religion recognize the challenges of risking scholarly objectivity when one moves from being an "outsider" to being an "insider" of a religious way of life,[12] even as Christian theologians struggle with how one retains one's Christian identity in the process of entering into the beliefs and practices of another faith. Is it then possible to adjudge between contrary claims to truth among the religions?

The pneumatological approach to this dilemma provides a specifically theological (rather than philosophical or politically correct) rationale for holding both correspondence and coherentist theories of truth and methods for their resolution in tension. Let me explicate this claim in three steps. First, going back to the Pentecost narrative, the outpouring of the Spirit enables each one to give witness to the wondrous works of God (Acts 2:11) in and through the diversity of languages. Now insofar as language can only be arbitrarily divorced from culture and religion, to the same extent, then, cultures and religions are potentially vehicles for mediating the grace and

11. E.g., Lindbeck, *Nature of Doctrine*, builds on the work of Wittgenstein.

12. E.g., McCutcheon, ed., *Insider/Outsider Problem*, and Arweck and Stringer, eds., *Theorizing Faith*.

truth of God. More specifically, the Spirit who gives the capacity to speak in a foreign language also can enable, by extension, participation in a foreign culture and even a foreign religion, so that one can experience those realities to some degree "from within." From a Christian perspective, this is confirmed by the acknowledgment that "outsiders" can understand Christian faith only when they enter, by the Holy Spirit, into that faith experience at some level and "taste and see that the Lord is good" (Ps 34:8). On the other side, of course, those in other faiths also claim that their truth claims are comprehensible only when we enter into their beliefs and practices at some level. May I suggest that the same Spirit whose outpouring on the Day of Pentecost enabled the speaking in foreign tongues today also enables genuine crossover into and return from other faiths so as to engage in their claims to truth?

But, second, the Spirit not only enables testimony to be given to the wondrous works of God, but also explicitly to Jesus Christ. This christomorphic aspect is therefore not accidental but essential to the identity of the Holy Spirit. With this, of course, we confront once again the "stumbling block" of Christian tradition. The pneumatological perspective adopted here, however, does not allow the christological norm to act as a conversation terminator. Rather, because a robust pneumatology is *both* christological and Trinitarian, a robust pneumatological theology *both* points to the particularity of Jesus Christ on the one hand and to the eschatological horizon of the kingdom of God on the other. In faith, Christians believe these two realities are not contradictory. However, in their details, Christians have to wrestle with how they are continuous. The advantage of a pneumatological approach is that it grants *theological* (read: Trinitarian) warrant for holding together the tensions between the historical Jesus and the eschatological Christ, between the outpouring of the Pentecostal Spirit and the in-breaking of the divine kingdom.

This means, third, a pneumatological approach to the phenomenon of religion empowers a robustly dialogical and intersubjective approach to religious truth. On the one hand (from the Christian perspective), the Spirit graciously enables our entrance into, inhabitation of, and testimony to faith in Jesus Christ. On the other hand (from the theology of religions perspective), this same Spirit also graciously grants understanding of, guides participation in, and empowers engagement with other languages, cultures, and even religious traditions. This dialogical relationship thus means that we engage our own and other religious traditions both as "insiders" and as "outsiders." We are "outsiders" even to our own Christian tradition insofar as we are still not fully converted to the image of Christ (on this side of the eschaton), and we are "insiders" even to other faiths insofar as the Spirit enables our crossover into those traditions. Hence we engage our own and other traditions neither merely "objectively" (as "outsiders") nor merely "subjectively" (as "insiders"), but intersubjectively—e.g., both within and without each tradition, as individuals and as members of (both) communities, in terms of both beliefs (doctrines) and practices (participation and inhabitation, in some respect), in historical reality and yet anticipating eschatological consummation. This dialogical and intersubjective engagement with religious truth therefore neglects neither the criteria of coherence nor of correspondence, but highlights the processes of adjudication as involving the mutual transformation of religious persons and traditions by the power of the eschatological Spirit.

TOWARD A PNEUMATOLOGICAL MISSIOLOGY OF INTERFAITH ENCOUNTER

In the preceding section, I have outlined three basic elements of the pneumatological approach to Christian theology of religions: its "grounding" in the Pentecost narrative, its dynamic categorical scheme, and its intersubjective mode of engaging religious truth. In the process, we have already begun to touch on themes related to Christian mission in the twenty-first century. In this section, I wish to make explicit the implications of this (relatively) new theological framework for Christian mission in a religiously plural world. Forgoing any attempt to be exhaustive, let me elaborate briefly on three of the most important missiological implications of a pneumatological theology of religions: that related to interfaith dialogue; that related to interreligious conversion; and that related to cross religious fertilization.

The Spirit, the Religions, and the Interreligious Dialogue—The classical missionary strategy emphasized evangelization and proclamation. A pneumatological approach to the religions provides theological (and not just pragmatic, missionary, or strategic) justification for engaging in *both* dialogue and proclamation together.[13]

The spirit of God who gives the gift of communication enables dialogue to occur. Authentic dialogue involves genuine interpersonal engagement. In a dialogical relationship, both sides listen and are listened to. Further, both sides take the other side seriously on the other's own terms. This involves the genuine effort to set aside one's biases and perspectives in order to hear out and then enter into the perspective of the other. Finally, in the interreligious dialogue, both sides take seriously the beliefs (doctrines) of the other. This does not mean uncritically accepting the testimony of the other as true,

---

13. E.g., Burrows, ed., *Redemption and Dialogue*.

but rather making an honest intersubjective effort to understand the other's doctrines from the other's perspective.

At the same time, the spirit of God enables dialogue to occur in part through empowering religious proclamation (witness and testimony). Authentic dialogue involves not only listening but also speaking. If only one side were listening all the time, this would be a monologue. As important, however, is that religious proclamation be sincere and honest. If religious matters are about matters of ultimate concern, then both sides should be given space and encouraged (even demanded) to speak apologetically and even urgently. An authentic dialogue will involve moments of proclamation whereby challenges are issued by one side and received and engaged by the other. Only the genuine give and take of proclamation can sustain any dialogue, including the dialogue of religions.

We have seen above that the Spirit both enables the utterance of foreign tongues on the one hand even as the Spirit empowers the Christian witness to Jesus on the other. Hence Christian mission should include both authentic dialogue and sincere proclamation as two sides of one coin. Dialogue and proclamation together constitute authentic interreligious engagement (i.e., authentic engagement between individuals from different religious traditions). Further, dialogue and proclamation result in mutual transformation, at least of the minds of dialogue partners. At the very least, dialogue and proclamation are the means through which (a) inaccurate stereotypes and misunderstandings of religious others are corrected; (b) one's faith commitment is often deepened and strengthened; and (c) erroneous beliefs are exposed, criticized, and abandoned. In light of the Christian acknowledgment that our finite perspectives see through the glass dimly in anticipation of the eschatological revelation of God, a pneumatological theology of religions authorizes both dialogue and proclamation as essential aspects of the Christian encounter and engagement with other faiths.

The Spirit, the Religions, and Religious Conversion—But, given the interconnectedness between beliefs and practices, the interreligious dialogue can never remain merely conversational, and the mutual transformation can never remain merely cognitive. Authentic interreligious dialogue enables the kind of deepened understanding of religious otherness that produces various kinds of conversion. I suggest that a pneumatological approach to the religions provides theological (and not just pragmatic, missionary, or strategic) justification not only for interreligious encounter and engagement, but also for religious conversion.

At its most basic level, we convert to the religious other attitudinally when we take his or her testimony seriously. Just as the interreligious dialogue cannot be successful if either dialogue partner merely pretends to listen in order to gain a hearing, so also will the Christian mission be unsuccessful if Christians merely appear to listen, awaiting the opportunity to evangelize. We as Christians would be reluctant to listen to religious others who were thought to be interested only in proselytizing us rather than in the Christian message. Missionaries who "keep their distance" in order to avoid being implicated by other faiths will inevitably be handicapped in engaging those religious others with the gospel.

Of course, as we progress in this interreligious encounter, a deepened relationship develops. At any point when we even entertain the possibility of walking in the other's shoes, we are in effect contemplating the possibility of crossing over into the other's perspective, world view, and even way of life in some sense. I am using conversion at this point more in the phenomenological sense I introduced earlier (wherein it occurs variously in different domains of individual lives) rather than in the specifically Christian sense. At one level, doing so reflects simply the possibilities of empathy afforded by our common humanity. From a missiological perspective, however, we would be doing no less than following St. Paul in his confession: "I have become all things to all people, that I might by all means save some" (1 Cor 9:22). A pneumatological theology of conversion allows for the possibility of various levels of "conversion" to another religious perspective and for various degrees of participation in and inhabitation of another religious way of being in the world.

Of course, theoretically, going down this road there is always the possibility of religious conversion that results in the abandonment of Christian faith and the full adoption of another religious identity. My sense is that practically, however, such conversions rarely occur when dialogue partners come to the table committed to their own traditions. Still, two additional comments may be registered in response. First, I wonder about what it means to be "fully" converted. Even from a Christian perspective, I am powerless to fully convert myself to Jesus in the sense both that conversion is what happens to me as a gift of God, and that such full conversion is an eschatological rather than historical reality. Paul's noting, "I die daily," implies that our faith is a journey rather than a possession. Hence, isn't it also impossible to talk about "full" conversion to another religious tradition?

But second, the good news is that a pneumatological theology of religious conversion is predicated upon the workings of the spirit of God and the spirit of Christ. Hence, I believe that "conversion" to other faiths enabled by the Spirit will not contradict or compromise our commitment to Christ. What may happen is that the Christian perspective of Christ will be deepened or transformed. While unpredictable, genuine encounter and engagement with religious otherness will bring about some degree of conversion in and across the various dimensions—e.g., intellectual, aesthetic, moral, sociopolitical—of our lives. What will surely happen is that the grace of God that may be present and active in other faiths will be a catalyst for our own transformation as we cross over (convert) into the other way of life. In any case, a pneumatological theology of religious conversion will emphasize the need to be led by and to discern the Spirit in and through the dynamic process of encounter with those in other faiths. Hence, may I suggest that Christian mission marked by the authentic conversion of missionaries to other ways of life is simply an extension of the principle of incarnation whereby Christians follow in the footsteps of Christ and "become" part of and dwell among linguistic, cultural, and religious others in all their particularity (sin and idolatry excepted)?[14]

The Spirit and the Cross-Fertilization of Religions—The importance of dialogue (and proclamation) and conversion to Christian mission in a religiously plural world combine to inform the third implication of a pneumatological missiology: that of religious cross-fertilization. Authentic dialogue and sustained engagement with religious otherness results in the emergence of a new reality informed or cross-fertilized by that otherness. Here, I suggest that a pneumatological approach to the religions provides theological (and not just pragmatic, missionary, or strategic) justification for crossing over into other faiths in order to present the gospel.

Classical missiology has employed different terminology for what I call cross-fertilization, viz., inculturation (a more Catholic notion), indigenization (when dealing with "native," "primitive," or autochthonous people groups), and contextualization (more prominent among Protestants), among other terms. In each case, the goal is the communication of the gospel in a foreign situation: that of another culture in "inculturation"; that of other local categories, practices, and beliefs in "indigenization"; and that of other social, historical, and geographic contexts in "contextualization." Together, they constitute what I believe a pneumatological theology of religions enables: the "conversion" of the gospel into terms provided by other linguistic-cultural-religious traditions. At one level, this may be saying no more than that other faiths anticipate and point to the gospel as the religion of the ancient Hebrews and of postexilic Judaism pointed to Christ.

14. [The preceding discussion about conversion may to be confusing because it deals with the many different ways we change our minds and even our behaviors when some readers may understand conversion only in religious and soteriological terms. Here and elsewhere in this book, I do not minimize the centrality of Christ for Christian salvation. Rather, in this context, I am simply exploring how a pneumatological approach to religious phenomena can help us understand the dynamic character of religious life.]

Even here, however, we have to be careful about supersessionism and anti-Semitism (in the case of Judaism) on the one hand, and about the violating the integrity of other faiths on the other. Is it too much to expect that the Spirit of Pentecost who somehow enabled both the diversity of tongues and the testimony to the wondrous works of God can yet enable both the integrity of other faiths and their being vehicles for the good news of the kingdom of God?

A pneumatological theology is hopeful about an affirmative answer to this question. Jesus, for example, is the Christ (the messiah or anointed one in Hebraic religion) precisely as the one anointed by the spirit of God. As a historical person, there is no Jesus Christ apart from his maleness, (first-century) Jewishness, carpenter-hood, etc. Hence the incarnation of the Word means that there is no "pure" gospel apart from or unmediated by language, culture, and religion (in this case, Judaism). Jesus the Christ thereby fulfills, and in that sense, preserves the integrity of the Jewish tradition through the Spirit. Of course, Christians and Jews continue to differ about many things, and in that sense anticipate an eschatological resolution of their disagreements. Yet it was also the case that first-century followers of Jesus included both self-identifying Jews and Gentiles who were made one body by the spirit of God.

Now insofar as "Christianity" did emerge, to that extent we can say that a new synthesis developed out of the gospel's taking root in Jewish and Hellenistic cultures. Here, it is important to acknowledge both the "fine line" and the tension between a new "synthesis" and a new "syncresis."[15] The cross-fertilization of religions risks the improper blending of contradictory religious beliefs and practices—this would be syncretism in its pejorative form. At the same time, any genuine inculturation, indigenization, or contextualization of the gospel results in its being "formed" by another language, culture, and even religious tradition. As a theologian, I am interested in asking about how Christian theological reflection will be transformed if we engage not just Plato, Aristotle, and their traditions, as we have done for almost two millennia, but also the Buddha, Master Kong, and Shankara, among other perspectives, in the world religious context of the twenty-first century.[16] In the synthesizing process, the gospel informs and enriches the other, and vice versa (hence mutual transformation or cross-fertilization). On the other hand, the integrity of *both* Christian faith *and* other traditions are somehow dynamically preserved (otherwise, what we would have would

15. See my discussion of "Syncretism" in Corrie, ed., *Dictionary of Mission Theology*, 373–76.

16. Hence the very important question raised in the essay (and essay title) by McDermott, "What If Paul Had Been from China?"

be syncretism). How is this possible except through the spirit of God? The miracle of Pentecost—which preserves the authenticity of both the gospel and that of the diversity of tongues—is replicated on each occasion when the authentic cross-fertilization of gospel and culture and religion takes place.

REMAINING CHALLENGES FOR A PNEUMATOLOGICAL THEOLOGY OF CHRISTIAN MISSION IN A RELIGIOUSLY PLURAL WORLD

So far, I have sketched the basic elements of the pneumatological theology of religions (part I) and elaborated on its implications for Christian mission in the religiously plural world of the twenty-first century (part II). My suggestions that a pneumatological approach to other faiths provides theological justification for interreligious dialogue and proclamation, interreligious "conversion" (understood in terms of the principle of incarnation), and cross-religious fertilization (understood in terms of inculturation, indigenization, and contextualization) are perhaps bold and risky. Some of the broader theological questions that have been raised about this pneumatological theology of religions include: (a) the relationship between Christ and the Spirit, between Christology and pneumatology (and with this, the question of the *filioque*); (b) the difference between the universal presence and activity of the Spirit and the specific "salvation history" work of the Spirit at and through Pentecost; (c) the implications for theologies of revelation, creation, providence, and history; and (d) whether or not a suitable criteriology of discerning the Holy Spirit from other spirits can be developed to engage the interreligious encounter at the empirical, spiritual, and theological levels.[17] In what follows, I will gather these queries and objections together under three interrelated headings: those related to Christology; those related to soteriology; and those related to Christian revelation and Christian uniqueness.[18]

17. These are questions raised in reviews of two of my books: e.g., Tennent, "Review of *Beyond the Impasse*"; Langdon, "Review of *Beyond the Impasse*"; Robinson, "Review of *Discerning the Spirit(s)*"; Lord, "Principles for a Charismatic Approach to Other Faiths"; and Irvin, "Review of *Beyond the Impasse*." See also Kärkkäinen, *Introduction to Theology of Religions*, ch. 31.

18. I will take advantage of this occasion to respond explicitly to some of the questions raised by the fine thesis of Klaver, "In Search of Pentecostal-Charismatic Theology of Religions," especially those on Christology and revelation. As I have already corresponded with Mrs. Klaver on points of detail, and because her thesis is unpublished and not widely accessible (so far as I know), my response to her will be thematic rather than specific.

The Spirit and Christ in the World of Religions: One of the major challenges to a pneumatological theology of religions concerns the relationship between the Spirit and the Word Jesus Christ. Given the tendency to think in terms of correlating Spirit with universality and Christ with historical particularity, the concern arises that the Spirit's association with culture and the religions leads to disconnection from Christ and, by extension, the church. If the Holy Spirit is not any spirit but is the spirit of Jesus and the spirit of Christ, then how can the Spirit be present and active in the world's religious traditions when they neither name nor acknowledge Jesus Christ or (in some cases) explicitly reject the Christ of Christian faith (e.g., as in contemporary Judaism and Islam)?

Any response to this set of questions must include theological, hermeneutical, and eschatological perspectives. At the theological level, an explicitly Trinitarian framework will identify the Spirit as related to but not identical with the Word. Trinitarianism would become modalism if Spirit were identical with Word, or tritheism if Spirit were detached from Word. The theological challenge is to discern how to understand this relation, which implies distinction and conjunction simultaneously. Traditionally, the distinction has been specified in terms of the Word's generation and the Spirit's procession, and the conjunction has been explicated in terms of perichoresis and other like notions. Do these classical Trinitarian constructs carry over from their original Hellenistic and Scholastic contexts to those of our contemporary religiously plural world? I propose that in our time and religiously plural context, any understanding of the identities of both the Spirit and Christ, as well as the relationship of each to the other, has to pass through the crucible of the Christian encounter with other faiths.[19]

This leads to the hermeneutical level of response. To say that the Spirit testifies to Christ requires also that we specify the context of that testimony. The Spirit's living testimony to Christ always translates the scriptural and received ecclesial witnesses into the terms and categories of the new context. This context today involves the plurality of religious traditions. Put christologically, then, is it possible that the seeds of the Word sown into the hearts and lives of all persons everywhere (cf. John 1:9) have germinated, at least in part, in the world's religious traditions?[20] Answering this question involves a process of discernment enabled by the Holy Spirit. In the first century, Jesus was not recognized as the anointed Messiah by (most of) his fellow Jews, as he was said to be embodied in the prisoner, the naked, the hungry,

19. See Yong, "Globalizing Christology."

20. The "seeds of the Word" idea is an ancient tradition going back to the post-apostolic fathers; see Dupuis, *Christian Theology of Religious Pluralism*, ch. 2.

the sick, and even the (then-demonized) Samaritan. Do not the prisoners, the naked, the hungry, and the sick of today include not only Samaritans but also those in other religious traditions? Might we come to a deepened and transformed understanding of Christ when viewing him through the prisms of other faiths?

This line of thinking points, finally, to the coming Christ whose eschatological revelation will transform us, including our knowledge of him: "What we will be has not yet been revealed. What we do know is this: when he is revealed, we will be like him, for we will see him as he is" (1 John 3:2). While the coming Christ will not be ontologically different from the historical Jesus, his gloriousness (among other eschatological attributes) will so far exceed what was historically revealed that he may well be unrecognizable. On this point, the Apocalypse not only gives us a glimpse of this difference (Rev 1), but also clearly foretells that the kings and peoples of the nations will contribute their glory to that of the city of God's and of the Lamb's (Rev 21:22–26). As we now know that the identities of peoples and nations cannot be arbitrarily disconnected from their religious beliefs and practices, can we also suggest that aspects of the religions will be redeemed and will contribute to the glorious identity of the city of God and of the Lamb? Might not a pneumatological theology of religions facilitate historical discernment of that reality on this side of the eschaton?

The Spirit, Salvation, and the Religions: Related to but also distinct from the christological question is the soteriological question. "Religion" is, after all, interested in the salvation of human beings from the many problems with which they are confronted and afflicted. Traditionally, eschatological salvation was connected variously with knowing or confessing Jesus Christ (more pietistic traditions), or being baptized into the name of Jesus or into the body of Christ (the more sacramental traditions). However, since the other faiths provided none of these "windows" into eternal life, how could they be salvific? Hence, a pneumatological theology of religions that suggests the Spirit is present and active in other faiths apart from the proclamation and sacraments mediated by the body of Christ (e.g., her missionaries, evangelists, and pastoral agents) is also problematic since the traditional modes of salvation are bypassed.

It has been in response specifically to this soteriological question that the categories of exclusivism, inclusivism, and pluralism were originally formulated. The pluralistic response—the idea that all religions are different responses by their adherents and devotees to the one revelation of God, being analogous to the image of many roads heading up different sides of the same mountain and converging at the top—is problematic both because it assumes a suprahistorical vantage point from which to assess the many historical religious traditions, and because it denies the specificity of the various soteriological claims of the religions and imposes on them a Christian vision of the consummation. Hence if we are to take the interreligious dialogue seriously—along with the particular claims made by those in other faiths about the problem(s) of the human condition and the salvific response of their religious traditions—then Christians must remain agnostic on this side of the eschaton about the relationship of other faiths to salvation conceived in relation to the triune God.[21] This is expressed in popular Christian piety through the following saying: "when you get to heaven, there will be two surprises: there will be those who you expected to be there but will not be there, and there will be those who you did not expect to be there but are there!" The traditional Orthodox stance about knowing where salvation is (in Orthodox Christianity) but not knowing where salvation is not (outside of Orthodoxy) is a more sophisticated articulation of this insight.[22]

But if that is all that can be said about salvation in a pluralistic world from the perspective of a pneumatological theology of religions, does not the latter turn out to be a rather anemic theological platform? Let me venture three additional pneumatological emphases in response. First, if salvation is truly *both* a gift of divine graciousness *and yet* mediated concretely and historically, then the presence and activity of the Spirit *both* cannot be owned or controlled by the historical/empirical church that is constituted by human agents *and yet* must somehow be "carried" through but not limited by creaturely realities such as specific human actions (including those of Christians and of Christian institutions) or particular doctrinal propositions (including those of the ecclesial tradition). Whether or not these religious mediators would include aspects or elements of other faiths may be questions that a pneumatology theology of religions is better equipped to inquire into than other theological constructs. Second, if conversion is multidimensional, then so is salvation. Insofar as the various religious traditions emphasize divergent afflictions from which human beings need to be saved and specific soteriological instruments to attain the correlative salvation, in that sense, perhaps other faiths may also further illuminate the fallen human condition as well as the means of grace at the Spirit's disposal. A pneumatological soteriology that emphasizes the complexity of the conversion process brought about by the Spirit may be more capable of engaging this question in theology of religions than other less dynamic models. Finally, the vast majority of religious traditions discuss the source

---

21. A speculatively daring attempt to probe the depths of this Trinitarian mystery in relationship to a soteriology of religious pluralism is Heim, *Depth of Riches*.

22. On this Orthodox stance, see Bulgakov, *Bride of the Lamb*, 313.

of creaturely misery, despair, and suffering often using the language of the demonic. Modern rationalism has resulted not only in the deconstruction of the rhetoric of the demonic, but also in the dismissal of this category of discourse altogether. Yet the idea of the demonic remains central to the world of the religions. Perhaps a pneumatological theology of religions is more capable of finding a *via media* between the pervasive demonologies of religious naïveté and the scientist cynicism of materialistic skepticism, so as to do justice to this difficult topic.[23]

The Revealing Spirit and Christian Uniqueness: At the end of the day, a pneumatological approach to other faiths may remain under suspicion for conceptually undermining the logic of Christian mission. While this is an objection derived from Christian praxis—i.e., "reject a pneumatological theology of religions because accepting it will lead to the abandonment of the Christian witness"—it nevertheless deserves to be addressed. However, rather than responding "defensively" from a practical and explicitly mis-siological perspective, I wish to speak to this matter from an "offensive-minded" revisitation of the doctrine of Christian revelation. Detractors of a pneumatological theology of religions would claim that allowing for the possibility of the Spirit's presence and activity in the world of the religions levels out the uniqueness, authoritativeness, and normativeness of the revelation given to Israel and the church. I suggest that a pneumatological theology of Christian revelation as unique and normative can be secured, and that it bolsters rather than undercuts Christian mission.

That Christian revelation is "unique" is not necessarily newsworthy. At an ontological level, every particular thing is unique in its own way. Hence, each religious tradition is also unique from all others. Put another way, all religious traditions, when compared to other traditions, have continuities and discontinuities in various configurations. So most forms of Christianity have more in common with most forms of Judaism than with most forms of Buddhism, while some forms of Christianity have more in common with some forms of Buddhism than with some forms of Judaism. These complex-ities aside, religious traditions also have in common the human condition. Hence, arguments about uniqueness are in this sense overblown.

However, there is another conceptual distinction that may be help-ful. Gabriel Moran contrasts that which is uniquely exclusive (empha-sis on particularity) with that which is uniquely inclusive (emphasis on universality).[24] Arguably each of the world religious traditions has both

---

23. I overview some of the issues involved in *Discerning the Spirit(s)*, ch. 8, and "Spirit Possession, Living, and Dead."

24. See Moran, *Uniqueness*.

uniquely exclusive and uniquely inclusive features. At the same time, it is also arguable that the christological and the pneumatological symbols are supreme representations of the uniquely exclusive and uniquely inclusive elements of Christian faith respectively. With pneumatology, however, we have a uniquely inclusive dynamic wherein there is the potential unfolding of "Christianity" as a universalizing faith. This universalizing dynamic was latent in the Jewish tradition, even going back to Yahweh's promise to Abraham's blessing as reaching to all the families of the earth (Gen 12:3). At Pentecost, this latency was made manifest in the Spirit poured out on all flesh—hence Christianity's unique inclusivism. I suggest that Pentecost provides not just an anthropological commonality but a theological norm for assessing the encounter between faiths.

But the dynamism of the Spirit provides an internal safeguard against any merely human interpretation presuming to be the authoritative norm of divine revelation. As finite creatures, human beings long for security and often erect ideological fortification around their own "safe spaces." Yet if there is one consistent feature of the scriptural narratives about the Spirit, it is that the Spirit cannot be controlled by human ideologies; rather, like the wind, the Spirit's comings and goings cannot be predicted. This unpredictability applies not only to human interpretation of divine revelation, but also to the norms and criteria with which we attempt to discern the presence and activity of the Spirit and of other spirits. At one level, to say this is simply to acknowledge that even the discernment of spirits is a gift of the Holy Spirit rather than a creaturely capacity. At another level, to say this is to acknowledge that the norms of divine revelation are not a priori constructs but a posteriori acknowledgments (this beginning with the recognition "after the fact" of the scriptural canon itself).

Hence, the normativeness of Christian revelation vis-à-vis other faiths is not static but rather dynamic when set in pneumatological perspective. To discern other faiths in light of Christian revelation requires some measure of crossing over into another set of beliefs and practices, and inhabiting its way of life. Over time, one slowly gains facility in the categories of the other tradition (learning what is important from that religious perspective),[25] and then determining if and how Christian categories are or are not commensurable. Just as we need to proceed cautiously in any attempt to develop adequate comparative categories for apples and oranges, so also should we proceed even more vigilantly to develop adequate comparative categories for

---

25. On the challenge of developing adequate categories for understanding the world of the religions, see Baird, *Category Formation*.

Christian faith and another religious tradition.[26] Of course, in the process of crossing over and returning, even one's norms have been transformed. Hence a pneumatological theology of religions does not reject Christian normativity, but rather provides theological (rather than ideological) warrant for recognizing and working with the dynamic character of normative engagement.

In short, a pneumatological theology of revelation does not decide in advance about Christian uniqueness, but is willing to follow the Holy Spirit into history. What does the revelation of Jesus Christ mean in another religious context? How is Christianity uniquely inclusive vis-à-vis another faith? How do Christian norms function in this new religious framework? What is the Spirit saying and doing in this place and time? A pneumatological approach to other faiths therefore underwrites theologically what may be called a "Lakatosian research program" that seeks to engage Christian faith with other faiths, and engage Christian theological ideas with the religious ideas of other traditions.[27]

I suggest that in the longer run, the Christian mission will be established on a more sure theological footing through such a project in comparative religious ideas. At the same time, such a research project is not only missiological but self-defining since crossing over into another faith also results in our own transformation. Is there a risk involved? Absolutely! But it is the same risk taken by missionaries like Bartolomé de las Casas, Robert de Nobili, Matteo Ricci, Hudson Taylor, and many others who have left the comfort zones of their Christian world to enter into the religious worlds of others; and it is the same risk taken by God who so loved the world and condescended into the human condition to dwell among us.[28]

26. Comparative religious categories should capture what is important to each tradition that is being compared on its own terms even while being sufficiently nonbiased to be specified by elements from two or more traditions. We are only now beginning to realize the formidable task involved in doing comparative religion and comparative theology; see Neville, *Comparative Religious Ideas Project*.

27. The notion of a "Lakatosian research program" derives from the philosopher of science, Imre Lakatos; see Murphy, *Anglo-American Postmodernity*, passim. My own "research program" in comparative theology has focused so far on the Christian dialogue with Buddhism. See my articles on soteriology, demonology, methodology, and anthropology respectively: "Technologies of Liberation"; "Demonic in Pentecostal-Charismatic Christianity"; "Holy Spirit and World Religions"; and "Christian and Buddhist Perspectives." [My book-length monograph on this project is *Pneumatology and Christian-Buddhist Dialogue*.]

28. My thanks to Terry Muck for the invitation to participate in Asbury Theological Seminary's fall semester 2004 Seminar in Missiology. The main ideas of this paper were presented to the seminar on October 20, 2004. I am grateful to probing questions raised by students in response to my talk, which led to revisions of parts of this essay.

PART II

Pentecostal Missiology

Pragmatic Mission Theology

CHAPTER 4

The Spirit of Hospitality

Pentecostal Perspectives toward a Performative Theology of Interreligious Encounter

IN SOME RESPECTS, THE encounter between the world's religions is no less heated in the twenty-first century than before. This is especially the case when adherents of religious traditions adopt an aggressive stance toward proselytism, as do members of missionary and evangelistic movements like modern pentecostalism. Pentecostal scholars and theologians, however, have begun to recognize the need to cultivate a wider range of postures and approaches to the interreligious encounter more appropriate to the demands of a post-9/11 era.

I suggest that there are resources within the pentecostal tradition of biblical interpretation that can be harnessed for the purpose of developing a performative theology of the interreligious encounter, and that such an approach can benefit not only pentecostal praxis but also the evangelical mission of the church catholic. I will unfold this hypothesis in four steps, corresponding to the four sections of this paper. First, I discuss how our contemporary religiously plural world poses distinctive challenges to Christian movements that take the Great Commission seriously and the early Christian church's experience normatively, as do most pentecostal churches. Second, I present developments in pentecostal scholarship that have begun to explore the possibility of a pneumatological approach to theology of religions grounded in the motif of the Spirit poured out on all flesh on the Day of Pentecost. In section three I attempt to advance the discussion about theology of religions by proposing a pneumatological theology of hospitality from the narrative of Luke-Acts. The final part very briefly fleshes out how what I call a pneumatological theology of interreligious hospitality enables the performance of Christian mission (within and without the pentecostal churches) in ways that are more sensitive to the complexities of the interreligious encounter in the twenty-first century.

THE CHALLENGE OF RELIGIOUS PLURALISM FOR MODERN PENTECOSTALISM

From their beginnings early in the twentieth century, modern pentecostals have understood themselves in terms of their missionary and evangelistic vocation to take the gospel to the ends of the earth. The connections were already made then between the gift of the Holy Spirit, the gift of tongues, and the last days missionary movement of the church. Pentecostals sought the gift of the Holy Spirit because of the scriptural promise that "you will receive power when the Holy Spirit has come upon you; and you will be my witnesses in Jerusalem, in all Judea and Samaria, and to the ends of the earth" (Acts 1:8).[1] The gift of tongues, they initially surmised, enabled them to bear witness to the gospel to those who lived outside the Anglo-American West without having to spend years acquiring foreign languages. The urgency of the missionary task was fueled by the conviction that these were the last days and that the end would come only after the gospel message had gone out to the unreached peoples who lived afar from the Christianized world (cf. Matt. 24:14 and Acts 2:39). Although pentecostals quickly realized that the baptism of the Holy Spirit did not allow them to bypass a training process that would include language acquisition, nevertheless the basic missionary identity of modern pentecostalism was already established: the gift of the Holy Spirit brought with it the power to bear witness to the gospel to the ends of the earth.[2]

The central role of the Acts narrative has continued to shape the missionary and evangelistic approaches of pentecostal churches. If the outpouring of the Spirit on the Day of Pentecost resulted in the evangelization of the Mediterranean world, then the modern-day outpouring of the Holy Spirit is intended for the evangelization of the whole world. If signs and wonders such as the healings of the man at the beautiful gate and of many others (e.g., Acts 5:12–16) followed the ministry of the apostles, then they should also follow the ministry of those full of the Holy Spirit today. If the spread of the gospel was accomplished in part through power encounters

1. See also Faupel, "Glossolalia as Foreign Language."
2. Goff Jr., *Fields White unto Harvest*, and Faupel, *The Everlasting Gospel*.

such as that between the apostles and Simon the sorcerer, between Paul and Bar-Jesus, or between Paul and the slave girl in Philippi, then so also should there be power encounters between contemporary missionaries and evangelists and those who are oppressed by the power of the devil. If the early church was persecuted for sharing its faith with unbelievers, so also will the present church experience persecution for bearing witness to the gospel. And perhaps most importantly, if it was true during the time of the apostles that healing came in the name of Jesus Christ of Nazareth (Acts 3:6 and 16), and that "There is salvation in no one else, for there is no other name under heaven given among mortals by which we must be saved" (Acts 4:12), then it remains true today that healing and salvation are available under no other name.[3]

While it cannot be denied that pentecostals are biblical literalists with regard to understanding the Acts narrative as historically accurate, it should not be overlooked that they differ from fundamentalists who almost always think that the charismatic gifts of the Spirit have ceased since the days of the apostles. Against this cessationist stance,[4] pentecostals are convinced that the Holy Spirit enables them to inhabit the biblical story in such a way that the experiences of the early church remain normative even today. If the story of the church continues, then the modern pentecostal movement is an extension of the Lukan narrative into the twenty-ninth chapter of the book of Acts, as it were.

Yet it is precisely this embodiment of the early Christian story which presents challenges for pentecostal missions in a post-9/11 world. In a time when exclusive claims to truth are problematic in many quarters, pentecostals continue to proclaim salvation in the name of Jesus. The early apostles were apologists with regard to the resurrection of Jesus from the dead (Acts 4:2); spoke and taught in and about the name of Jesus (Acts 4:18; 5:28, 40–42; 28:31); declared that Jesus was the Son of God, the Anointed Messiah (Acts 9:20–22); and insisted that all repent, have faith in Jesus, and be baptized into Jesus' name (Acts 2:38 and 20:21).[5] Pentecostal missionary

---

3. Acts 4:12 has featured as a central point of contention in Christian theology of religions, as seen in book titles by exclusivists like Braaten, *No Other Gospel!*; inclusivists like Sanders, *No Other Name*; and pluralists like Knitter, *No Other Name?*

4. Ruthven, *Cessation of the Charismata*.

5. Oneness pentecostals baptize only in Jesus' name according to the Acts narrative (Acts 2:38, 8:16, 10:48, and 19:5). While they believe Jesus is the revealed name of God and that in Jesus, "the whole fullness of deity dwells bodily" (Col 2:9), they have rejected the traditional Trinitarian notion of God existing in three persons as a post-biblical invention, preferring instead a christocentric interpretation of the earlier modalistic understanding of the relationship between Father, Son, and Holy Spirit. For more on Oneness pentecostal theology and practice, see French, *Our God is One.*

and evangelistic proclamation has therefore been unabashedly christocentric, believed to be inspired by the Holy Spirit who anointed Jesus himself (Luke 4:18).

But the same narrative of the early church that lifts up the name of Jesus in this way also presents those in other religions in a rather negative light when compared to today's politically correct standards. While there is no scholarly consensus about how the author of Luke-Acts viewed the Jews,[6] any cursory reading of the book of Acts reveals at least the following portrait: that the Jews had been perennially resistant to the Holy Spirit in spite of repeated presentations of the gospel; that the Jews had not only refused the offer of the gospel, but had also persecuted the messengers who have borne witness to Jesus Christ; and that because of the Jews' rejection of the gospel, the good news was thus being proclaimed to the Gentiles. Now to be sure, a closer reading of Acts will uncover different portrayals of Judaizers versus Pharisees versus Hellenist Jews versus Jewish Christians,[7] along with tensions between these groups, such as those between the Hebraic- and Greek-speaking Jewish Christians in the early Christian community (Acts 6:1). Yet it is also clear that one of the underlying themes in Luke-Acts concerns the restoration of Israel, and that the author clearly believed this promise was being fulfilled in the coming of Jesus the Messiah and in the gift of the Holy Spirit.[8] In part for these reasons, pentecostals have aligned themselves with Dispensationalist interpretations which affirm, on the one hand, that the covenant with the Jews has not been abrogated but will be confirmed in the future,[9] even while insisting, on the other hand, that the Christian mission to the Jews should not be abated in the present age and that the gospel should be preached to the Jews so that they also can experience the salvation that is available only in the name of Jesus.

But what about the Gentiles in Luke-Acts? Here, we would also need to distinguish between proselytes to Judaism, God-fearers, and "pagans." It is the God-fearers who are represented positively in Acts and who respond to the gospel.[10] Pagan Gentiles, on the other hand, are repeatedly portrayed as ignorant of and in enmity against God, spiritually incapacitated, idolatrous,

---

6. See Tyson, *Luke, Judaism, and the Scholars*, and Tyson, ed., *Luke-Acts and the Jewish People*.

7. So, for example, while portrayed negatively in Luke, the Pharisees are presented mostly positively in Acts (many convert to Christ), with some like Gamaliel even defending Christianity, and others like Paul being paradigmatic for how all people should respond to the gospel; see Gowler, *Host, Guest, Enemy and Friend*.

8. Turner, *Power from on High*.

9. Blaising and Bock, *Dispensationalism, Israel and the Church*.

10. Jervell, "The Church of Jews and Godfearers."

guilty of moral-ethical sins, under the power of Satan, and under divine condemnation. While some Gentiles with no prior association with Jews did become Christians, most either misunderstood the gospel that was proclaimed to them or did not respond positively to its presentation.[11] Hence Christoph Stenschke concludes his study of the Gentiles in Luke-Acts on this note:

> The pagan life, so natural and deeply entrenched, is not a *preparatio evangelica* but determined by notions and values that need to be eradicated. The fact that even Gentile Christians, following their salvation and endowment with the Spirit, need continuous correction, instruction, exhortation and encouragement and still will sin, has negative implications for the capacities of Gentiles prior to faith. The impact of paganism in spiritual, intellectual and moral issues and consequently Luke's strong emphasis on correction including all the measures to ensure its continuity and effectiveness, implies the need of God's saving intervention. The capacities of a pagan mind-set so deep and thoroughly in need of correction should not be overestimated in the appropriation of salvation.[12]

This portrayal of the Gentiles in the book of Acts has been intuitively absorbed into the pentecostal world view. Unsurprisingly, then, pentecostals have traditionally emphasized apologetics rather than dialogue, exorcisms rather than social witness, and repentance and conversion rather than mutual prayer. The Lukan witness that leads pentecostals to pray for the baptism of the Spirit is the same text that demonstrates the power to witness boldly to those who are blinded by the principalities and powers of this age. Insofar as pentecostals embody the Spirit of Pentecost narrated about in Luke-Acts, so also, it seems, will the pentecostal encounter with those in other faiths be characterized primarily by proselytism rather than by dialogue.

11. Even if Luke-Acts is considered more of an apologetic to the Jews than to the Gentiles (on this, see Alexander, "The Acts of the Apostles as an Apologetic Text"), it would be difficult to deny that part of Luke's motivation in the first-century Mediterranean world was to show that the God Christians worshipped "was worth worshipping because he was more powerful and could offer a 'salvation' that the traditional [pagan] gods could not" (Strelan, *Strange Acts*, 24).

12. Stenschke, *Luke's Portrait of Gentiles*, 375–76. See also Gill and Winter, "Acts and Roman Religion," which highlights the pagan Gentile background behind the early church's concern about idolatry persisting among Gentile converts. Given these assessments, it is difficult to fathom Hans-Josef Klauck's claim that with regard to other cultures and religious practices, in Luke "we do not find any heavily aggressive polemic. . . . Luke cannot have had a very negative view of the human race" (*Magic and Paganism in Early Christianity*, 119).

Kerygmatic proclamation focused on eliciting conversion to Christ should never be de-emphasized for those committed to carrying out the Great Commission. However, in our post-9/11 context, is proclamation to persons of other faiths opposed to dialogue with those in other faiths, and is the verbal preaching of the gospel the only mode of interreligious engagement? While most pentecostals would probably answer in the negative to both of these questions, not many have attempted to articulate a theology of religions commensurate with such a pragmatic response. Yet a few proposals have recently appeared on the horizon,[13] and some of these have emerged, as have many other pentecostal theological insights, from the Lukan narrative of the book of Acts.

THE SPIRIT POURED OUT ON ALL FLESH: PENTECOSTAL PERSPECTIVES TOWARD A PNEUMATOLOGICAL THEOLOGY OF RELIGIONS

I suggest that pentecostal thinking about the religions can be developed along two trajectories: the theological and the practical. In this section, I provide an overview of theological approaches that have recently been proposed, as well as suggest how pentecostal missionary praxis can contribute new perspectives that further the conversation.

Elsewhere,[14] I have formulated a pentecostal theology of religions by going back to the core pentecostal narrative of the Holy Spirit being poured out on all flesh (Acts 2:17). My argument has proceeded in three steps. First, at the exegetical level, I have suggested that Luke-Acts presents a universal vision of the church and the kingdom of God that extended far beyond the Jewish self-understanding of a religion centered in Jerusalem. The universality of the gospel is not only announced at the beginning of Luke (2:31–32) and Acts (1:8), but is also prefigured in the fact that the many tongues understood on the Day of Pentecost are derived from the ancient Jewish table of nations and therefore represent all the peoples of the world.[15] But, second, at the phenomenological and pentecostal levels, it is not just the translatability of the gospel that is miraculous, but the fact that strange

13. Besides my own work (about which more momentarily), two other pentecostal theologians have begun to turn their attention to theology of religions: Veli-Matti Kärkkäinen (*Toward a Pneumatological Theology*, ch. 14; *Introduction to Theology of Religions*; and *Trinity and Religious Pluralism*) and Tony Richie ("Neither Naïve nor Narrow"; "God's Fairness to People of All Faiths"; and "Azusa-Era Optimism").

14. Yong, *Discerning the Spirit(s), Beyond the Impasse,* and *Spirit Poured Out on All Flesh,* ch. 6.

15. Scott, "Acts 2:9–11," and Bechard, *Paul Outside the Walls,* chs. 3–4.

tongues can indeed be vehicles of the gospel and can declare the wonders of God. And given the interconnections between language and culture, the Pentecost narrative both celebrates the divine affirmation of many tongues, and announces the divine embrace of the many cultures of the world.[16] This leads, third, to the constructive theological argument, which proceeds from our contemporary understanding of the interrelatedness between language, culture, and religion. At this level, the Pentecost narrative can be understood to hold forth the possibility of the redemption of the diversity of religions, but this does not mean that entire religious traditions are to be uncritically accepted or that every aspect of any particular religion is divinely sanctioned. Rather, languages, cultures, and the religions need to be discerned, and their demonic elements need to be confronted and purified so that if there is any truth, goodness, or beauty in them, such may be redeemed.[17] The result, I suggest, is both a pentecostal and pneumatological approach to theology of religions.

As this overview is rather abstract, what does it mean practically? I suggest that the pneumatological theology of religions I am proposing provides theological justification for a dialogical approach to Christian mission that many pentecostals are already practicing anyway. Pentecostal missionaries have long been operating according to what has been called in missiological circles the "indigenous principle": the church is best established, overseen, and developed by local (i.e., "native") leadership with (Western) missionaries serving primarily in the role of consultant.[18] At one level, the indigenous principle can be discerned even in the Acts narrative insofar as the early church debated about who should retain control of the Christian mission as it expanded beyond Judea: the core group of apostles centered in Jerusalem or itinerant Hellenist evangelists like Stephen or Philip.[19] I propose that as developed by pentecostals, the indigenous principle is an intuitive extrapolation of the Acts narrative applied to the theology of mission.

16. For a multicultural reading of the Acts narrative from a pentecostal perspective, see Morales Jr., "Babel, Mount Sinai, Pentecost"; for the argument connecting the translatability of the gospel with the redemption of culture, see Sanneh, *Translating the Message*.

17. For similar arguments regarding the demonic dimensions of the religions, but also of their possible redemption, see McDermott, *God's Rivals*.

18. Hodges, *Indigenous Church*.

19. See Bruce, "Philip and the Ethiopian," and Borgen, *Early Christianity and Hellenistic Judaism*, esp. ch. 9. In fact, the case can be made that the arrival of the gospel to Samaria and the ends of the earth culminates in the ministry of Philip in Acts 8, inasmuch as there is the conversion of Samaritans and insofar as Ethiopia represented in the person of the eunuch the far horizons of the known world in the first century; see Barreto, "Reading in Black and White."

Pentecostal missionaries are simply recognizing that the redemption of the many tongues on the Day of Pentecost translates into a mission strategy that embraces the linguistic and cultural diversity of humankind, and that the leaders of the churches should simply be those who have been filled by the Holy Spirit even if they are heretofore marginalized persons like women, ethnic minorities, or even slaves!

With regard to the encounter of religions, the indigenous principle works itself out practically on at least two levels. First, the transmission of the gospel privileges the language and culture of the people group being missionized or evangelized. This requires that missionaries and local leaders pay careful attention to and even learn from indigenous cultures and religious traditions. The effective translation, inculturation, and contextualization of the gospel cannot proceed apart from this process of discerning engagement with the local situation.[20] Second, the lives of local leaders who have converted to Christianity become the site wherein the gospel confronts and interacts with local cultural and religious realities. Herein emerges the reality of what Raimon Panikkar calls the "intrareligious dialogue," which occurs when multiple cultures and religions come together within individual lives.[21] Hence the question is not whether or not pentecostals should engage in interreligious dialogue, but how such engagement will occur and what, if any, will be its theological rationale.

To be sure, pentecostals will always be suspicious, and rightfully so, about any missionary approach that subordinates proclamation to dialogue. I need to be clear: that is not my agenda. At the same time, not only does effective proclamation require the dialogical moment, but our post-9/11 context favors the dialogical approach. This can also be seen in the Acts narrative, particularly in the expansion of the early church beyond Jerusalem and Judea. Before elaborating on the Christian expansion into Samaria—which is where I want to focus the bulk of my discussion—note the importance of the dialogical relationship revealed in the Cornelius episode. In the background is the debate about the transformation of the early Jesus movement from a Jewish sect to a predominantly Gentile religion. Precisely because the established boundaries between Jew and Gentile were not easily crossed, Peter needed a vision from God before he agreed to set foot

20. I suggest that this is the pentecostal version of what is otherwise known as postcolonial hermeneutics, which assumes a decentered or multicentered global interpretive situation; see also Segovia, "And They Began to Speak in Other Tongues."

21. See Panikkar, *The Intrareligious Dialogue*. A Lukan example of the intrareligious dialogue that occurs not in the lives of converts but in the lives of those who have been raised in multiple religious worlds is Timothy, born of a Jewish mother and a Gentile father (Acts 16:1).

in Cornelius's home.[22] But after actually interacting with Cornelius, Peter came to acknowledge, "I truly understand that God shows no partiality, but in every nation anyone who fears him and does what is right is acceptable to him" (Acts 10:34–35). The lesson to be learned is that it is precisely in and through his encounter with Cornelius that Peter's self-understanding is transformed. The dialogical relationship between those "inside" and "outside" the faith resulted in the changed lives of both the missionized and the missionary. I suggest that this intersubjective process characterizes the relationships of those operating under the indigenous principle.

More important, it is precisely a pneumatological approach to theology of religions that is open to the many surprises that the Spirit brings in our encounter with others who are different, especially those we consider to be religious others. That the early Christian community would expand beyond Jerusalem and Judea to include both Samaritans and Gentiles was shocking to the Jewish followers of Jesus and hence contested.[23] Elsewhere,[24] I have suggested contemporary theology of religions has much to learn from how the author of Luke-Acts portrays the Samaritans, particularly in the parable of the good Samaritan (Luke 10:25–37). Insofar as Jewish attitudes toward Samaritans in the first century parallel in many ways conservative Christian and pentecostal attitudes toward those in other faiths, the parable challenges our assumptions about what is or is not possible in the encounter between religions. Not only can Jews learn from Samaritans, but it is the religious other who shows the Jew how to embody God's love for the neighbor. This implies, of course, both that Christians can learn from religious others and that God might choose to reveal Godself through the religious in ways that we might not expect. While in that discussion I left open the question about whether or not the Samaritan is saved through his fulfilling the conditions for salvation—of loving God and neighbor—in this context I want to ask whether or not the counter-condition applies: do Jews need to love their neighbors in order to inherit eternal life, even if such neighbors were despised as their enemies?[25] Put in our context, do Christians not need to love their neighbors of other faiths in order to be saved? If so, don't Christians need those in other faiths for our own salvation as much as if not more

22. Cf. Plunkett, "Ethnocentricity and Salvation History in the Cornelius Episode."

23. The thesis of Francis Pereira (*Ephesus*) regarding Paul's Ephesian ministry to Jews and Gentiles together in Acts 19:9–10 is importantly precisely because it is the author of the Letter to the Ephesians who talks about the breaching of the walls between Jews and Gentiles through their one baptism into one new body by the Spirit (Eph 2).

24. Yong, *Spirit Poured Out on All Flesh*, 241–44.

25. Owczarek, *Sons of the Most High*, 199–213, discusses loving one's enemies in terms of Jews loving Samaritans; cf. Robbins, "The Sensory-Aesthetic Texture," 263.

than those in other faiths need Christians to bear witness to the gospel for their salvation? My point is not to advocate for a works-based salvation, but to explore how the interreligious encounter itself might reveal the saving presence and activity of the spirit of God in unexpected ways.[26]

The book of Acts further reveals how challenging the case of the Samaritans was for the early Jewish followers of Jesus. Two points may be made in this regard. First, note that one of those who converted to Christ though Philip's preaching was a certain Simon who had previously dazzled the inhabitants of that region through his sorcery. Simon evidently believed and was baptized (Acts 8:13). Yet he was also clearly astonished by the signs and wonders accomplished through the ministry of Philip, and later by the gift of the Holy Spirit mediated through the laying on of hands by Peter and John. Simon offers to purchase the power to give the Spirit through the laying on of hands, but he is rebuked by Peter. Luke ends this pericope with Simon's repentance and expression of remorse. Whatever happens later on with Simon—and here, be reminded that the traditional associations between this Simon and the Gnostic heresy are absent in the biblical text[27]—this passage reveals the complexities of the intrareligious dialogue referred to earlier. Conversion to Christ does not automatically remove previous religious habits, practices, and ideas. In Simon's case, he even "stayed constantly with Philip" (Acts 8:13), learning from him over a period of time. Still, he misunderstood the gift of the Spirit, and needed further discipleship. As missionaries who operate under the indigenous principle often come to realize, conversion to Christ and even ascension to church leadership does not mean that previous religious beliefs and practices no longer need to be reckoned with. In other words, we need to understand not only what we are converting to but also what we are converting from. In the latter case, much closer attention needs to be paid to the dynamics of the religious life nurtured by our previous faith commitments. For this purpose, the interreligious dialogue serves not only to clarify the nature of religious conversion, but also to illuminate the nature of the intrareligious issues that remain at work in the hearts and lives of converts.

Second, it is revealing that the gospel comes to Samaria first not through any of the original twelve apostles but through Philip, one of the Hellenist converts who was appointed by the apostles to oversee the distribution of food to the widows (Acts 6:1–6). More precisely, while the

---

26. Ian McDonald ("Alien Grace") suggests that the good Samaritan reveals the "alien grace" of God that comes through unexpected sources, but then also warns that those who refuse or reject this alien grace may then be subjected to the judgment of God.

27. Fitzmyer, *Acts of the Apostles*, 403–4.

apostles had reserved for themselves the task of prayer and the ministry of the word, it was the multiculturally formed deacon Philip who turned out to be the first one to preach the gospel beyond Judea.[28] Might it be that the task of engaging the Samaritans required not a Judean "insider" but a Hellenist "outsider," even if it was Peter and John who later came to reap the harvest sown by Philip? Similarly, might the task of engaging those in other faiths today be more effectively undertaken by our deacons rather than our preachers (even if we are not denying that deacons like Philip may well be excellent preachers; cf. Acts 8:4–5)? I suggest that the more abstract lesson of the good Samaritan parable is tested concretely when during the persecution of the early Christians all except the apostles were scattered.[29] In that sequence of events, it was the Hellenist deacon Philip who was obedient to the Spirit's leading to proceed in the direction of rather than away from Samaria. If the question posed by the parable of the good Samaritan is "Who proves to be the neighbor?,"[30] then Philip's willingness to undertake the mission to Samaria shows how the parable can be enacted historically. On the other side, in contrast to the previous generation of Samaritans who denied entry to Jesus (who was bound for Jerusalem, it must be admitted; cf. Luke 9:51–53), this generation received the stranger into their midst. This opens up to the possibility that a pneumatological theology of religions derived from the Pentecost narrative might also be further developed in the direction of a theology of hospitality.

THE SPIRIT OF HOSPITALITY: TOWARD A PNEUMATOLOGICAL THEOLOGY OF HOSPITALITY

So far, I have suggested how the narrative of Acts that lies at the heart of pentecostal spirituality and practice both orients pentecostals toward those in other faiths in ways that are challenging in a post-9/11 world (§I) and also provides us with pneumatological and theological resources to develop a dialogical approach to other faiths that is latent in the indigenous principle (§II). In this section, I suggest that one of the reasons for the success of the early church's mission to Samaria and the ends of the earth was because of its practice of hospitality. More specifically, I want to sketch an outline of what I call a pentecostal and pneumatological theology of hospitality that

28. González, *Acts*, 105.

29. Scott Jr., "Stephen's Defense," 133–34, suggests that it is precisely the sermonizing of another Hellenist Jew, Stephen, against the temple and its place in Jewish religion that precipitated the persecution; cf. Kee, *Good News to the Ends of the Earth*, 45–47.

30. Brown, *Unexpected News*, 110.

will both complement and extend the pneumatological theology of religions proposed in the previous section and enable us to cultivate the appropriate postures toward those in other faiths imperative for our time (§IV).[31]

There are three theses that constitute the pneumatological theology of hospitality I am proposing. *Thesis one*: Christian hospitality is grounded in the hospitable God who through the incarnation has received creation to himself and through Pentecost has given himself to creation. Brendan Byrne has suggested that the book of Luke can be understood in terms of the hospitality of God insofar as it provides an account of God's visitation in Christ that brings salvation to the world.[32] For Byrne, the hospitality of God describes not only God's receiving the world to himself in the incarnation, but also Jesus' embracing the world in his life, passion, and resurrection. Hospitality is further exemplified in the lives of those who reciprocated divine hospitality, such as Mary (who accepted and carried the Son of God in her womb), Peter and Zacchaeus (who hosted Jesus in their homes), and Joseph the Arimathean (who afforded Jesus a proper burial).

While Byrne's focus is on the Gospel of Luke, I suggest that the Acts narrative complements his thesis since it reveals the hospitality of God through the gift of the Holy Spirit to all flesh (read: Gentiles).[33] On the Day of Pentecost, the presence and activity of the Spirit was manifest in and through the strange tongues that came forth from human lips. Contemporary pentecostal experience continues to insist that the Holy Spirit is evidenced in tongues speech, in the supernatural healing of human bodies, and in the signs and wonders that are beyond human concoction. At one level, God gives of himself by the Holy Spirit at Pentecost to all flesh, and by doing so welcomes and embraces all of humanity; at another level, human beings receive the gift of God, effectively hosting the spirit of God in their bodies, as it were.[34] Incarnation and Pentecost, then, are the ultimate expressions and manifestations of divine hospitality through which God both gives of himself to the world and invites the world to receive the salvation that comes through divine visitation.

31. In this section, I am developing ideas about the theology of hospitality derived from my participation during 2003–2004 in the Bossey Consultation organized by the World Council of Churches networks of Faith and Order, Conference on World Mission and Evangelism, and the Office on Interreligious Relations and Dialogue. For the Consultation document, see Bossey Consultation, "Religious Plurality and Christian Self-Understanding."

32. Byrne, *Hospitality of God*; cf. Richard, *Living the Hospitality of God*.

33. See Arterbury, "The Custom of Hospitality in Antiquity."

34. In the words of the fourth-century Alexandrian theologian Didymus the Blind, the Holy Spirit is God's greatest gift to humankind even as human beings are the temple of the Holy Spirit (see Heston, *Spiritual Life and the Role of the Holy Ghost*, 48–51).

Such a Trinitarian theological understanding serves as the ground for *thesis two*: Christian hospitality is enacted by the charismatic practices of the church as its members are empowered by the Holy Spirit. From a pentecostal perspective, the charismatic gifts of healing and miraculous powers manifest in the early church remain significant for Christian mission since it is through such encounters with God that people are often initially moved to repentance and experience conversion. Without discounting the importance of the manifestation of such gifts in the life and ministry of the church, I wish to draw attention to the specifically Lukan emphases of the Spirit's anointing of Jesus. Under the power of the Spirit, Jesus not only preached good news to the poor and opened the eyes of the blind but also released the oppressed and announced the liberating year of the Lord's favor (Luke 4:18–19). Hence, the charismatic practices of the church include signs and wonders, works of mercy and compassion, and acts of social liberation. The hospitality of God is thus embodied in a hospitable church whose members are empowered by the Holy Spirit to stand in solidarity and serve with the sick, the poor, and the oppressed.[35]

This emphasis on salvation manifest through healing and liberation has already been shown by the late David Bosch to be a central missiological motif in Luke-Acts.[36] For Bosch, the mission of the church as manifested throughout Luke-Acts is not only to announce and practice the forgiveness of sins, but also to restructure relationships between the rich and the poor, between Jew and Gentile, between male and female, and between the socially accepted and the socially marginalized. The new body of Christ is the hospitality of God extended to the world through the entire range of the church's charismatic and prophetic witness. Here we must affirm the history of pentecostal missions and evangelism that has not only preached to the poor but also founded rescue missions, not only laid hands on the oppressed but also established rehabilitation ministries like Teen Challenge. At the same time, since the hospitality of God is revealed also in acts of social liberation, pentecostalism needs to be called to further account along at least three lines.[37] First, while the earliest pentecostals affirmed the ministry of women—as anticipated in the promise of the Spirit for men- and maidservants (Acts 2:17)—women remain marginalized from positions of authority in pentecostal denominations. Second, while the earliest pentecostals were a fellowship of the Spirit that realized that "the color line was

---

35. Cf. Rhoads, *Challenge of Diversity*, ch. 5.

36. Bosch, *Transforming Mission*, ch. 3.

37. See also Yong, *Spirit Poured Out on All Flesh*, ch. 4.

washed away in the blood"[38]—realizing initially both the multiculturalism on the Day of Pentecost and the divine embrace of Black Africa as revealed in the narrative of the Ethiopian eunuch[39]—this promise of a multiethnic and multiracial movement has not been sustained in pentecostal history. Finally, what about the structural, economic, and political realities that undermine peace and justice in the world? If the works of the Spirit include righteousness, peace, and justice (Isa 32:14–20), then why is pentecostal mission practically absent—or at least unheralded—in these domains?[40]

I suggest that since the Holy Spirit is present and active in these public spaces, pentecostals should pray for a fresh outpouring of the Spirit to empower their engagement with the principalities and powers of these realms. The result, for our purposes, is that pentecostal presence in the public square will provide another palpable expression of the hospitality of God that liberates all who are touched by the Spirit poured out through the charismatic ministries of the church.[41] More importantly, pentecostal solidarity with and liberation of the oppressed will open them up to the interreligious encounter both because there will be those of other faiths who will also be working in these arenas and because poverty, sickness, and oppression is no respecter of religious commitments. Insofar as all persons of faith are touched by injustice, war, and famine, so also will Spirit-empowered advocacy and activism in these domains engage pentecostals on the interreligious front.

This leads to *thesis three*: Christian hospitality is realizable in a world of many faiths only when it is reciprocated by those in other faiths, and such reciprocity is made possible by the Spirit who is poured out on all flesh. We have already seen that the hospitality of God manifest in Jesus was reciprocated by those who responded in obedience. With the outpouring of the Spirit at Pentecost, is it possible that this reciprocity was extended even to those in other faiths? Pentecostal theologian Jean-Jacques Suurmond suggests that the outpouring of the Spirit made it possible for human beings to encounter one another as authentically other rather than as projections of and for the self.[42] On the one side, the gift of the Spirit has reconciled Israel

---

38. The quotation is from one of the participant witnesses of the Azusa Street revival, Frank Bartleman (*Azusa Street*, 54); cf. Irvin, "Drawing All Together in One Bond of Love."

39. See Bays, *From Every People and Nation*, ch. 8, and Carson, "Do You Understand What You are Reading?"

40. See, for example, a Palestinian-Christian reading of the Pentecost narrative by Naim Ateek, "Pentecost and the Intifada."

41. Cf. Hawkins, *Shearing the Search*, chs. 5–6.

42. Suurmond, *Word and Spirit at Play*, 198–203.

to the Gentiles and enabled Jewish hospitality to them.[43] On yet another side, the Samaritans who were previously closed to Jesus' visitation are now graced with the capacity to embrace his message delivered through Philip,[44] and Gentiles around the Mediterranean world—Dorcas, Cornelius, Lydia, the Philippian jailer, Titius Justus, Jason, unnamed families of the city of Ephesus (cf. Acts 20:20), Publius, etc.—have now opened up their hearts by opening up their homes to receive the apostolic messengers.

Three aspects of this reciprocity thesis are important for a pneumatological theology of hospitality in a religiously plural world. First, the reciprocity thesis calls attention to the fact that relationships ordered by the Holy Spirit are fluid and dynamic, formed and shaped according to shifting circumstances. Thus, on some occasions, the apostolic messengers found themselves as hosts, on others as guests.[45] Similarly, God-fearing Gentiles both before and after conversion not only received the apostolic messengers into their homes, but were also visited by the hospitable God in the form of his servants emboldened by the Holy Spirit. Christian mission, as we can see, is dependent both on the spiritual and material welcoming offered by the missionized and on the ability of missionaries to be recipients of the hospitality of others. This reciprocity and mutuality is especially vital for Christian mission in a post-9/11 world of many faiths.

Second, the rules of hospitality in the first century revolved especially around purity laws of table fellowship. This not only explains why Peter needed a vision to be convinced he was to respond positively to Cornelius's invitation, but also illuminates the central role of eating together in the missionary and evangelistic endeavors of the early Christians.[46] In fact, Jesus' first set of instructions to his itinerant evangelists was: "Whenever you enter a town and its people welcome you, eat what is set before you" (Luke 10:8).[47] The early church's conviction was that the new people of God birthed by the Holy Spirit were not separated by gender, ethnicity, race, or class, and that this allowed them to gather around a common table of fellowship.[48] Our

43. See Dumm, "Luke 24:44–49 and Hospitality."

44. Note Spencer, *Journeying through Acts*, 96.

45. Koenig, *New Testament Hospitality*, 91–103.

46. Harold Dollar reminds us, "The very nature of salvation for the Jews was bound up with their eating habits," and that since salvation also included one's relationship to the church, "then for Luke table-fellowship is a soteriological issue" (*Biblical-Missiological Exploration*, 367–68). For more on table-fellowship evangelism and meal hospitality respectively, see also Méndez-Moratalla, *Paradigm of Conversion in Luke*, 217–22, and Resseguie, *Spiritual Landscape*, ch. 4.

47. Cf. Burn, "Hospitality and Incarnational Vulnerability in Luke 10:1–12."

48. But here I would not go as far as Bartchy, "*Agnōstos Theos*," who argues the

fear of strangers is overcome precisely through our eating together.[49] Might the hospitality of table fellowship be a neglected motif in pneumatological theologies of mission in a religiously plural world?

Finally, the reciprocity thesis opens up the possibility of authentic dialogue in the Christian encounter with those of other faiths. In their harrowing experience on the Adriatic sea, Luke and Paul prayed, ate, and worked together with the sailors to survive the storm (27:27–38).[50] Then, after suffering shipwreck on Malta, they were shown hospitality by the islanders. For a few days, Paul prayed for their sick and many were healed, but there is no explicit mention of kerygmatic proclamation under these circumstances. While we cannot assume too much from the silence of the text,[51] I suggest that these were unique situations that brought forth distinctive responses that in turn opened up opportunities for an intersubjective encounter. The Christian mission in a postcolonial and post-9/11 world is unique in its own way, requiring a more dialogical disposition and approach today. I suggest that the Pentecost motif of the Spirit poured out on all flesh provides a theological—more explicitly, pneumatological—rationale for interreligious dialogue made possible when Christians find themselves as guests who are hosted by members of other faiths.

A PNEUMATOLOGICAL THEOLOGY OF INTERRELIGIOUS HOSPITALITY: PERFORMING CHRISTIAN MISSION IN A RELIGIOUSLY PLURAL WORLD

The objective in this essay has been twofold: to build on previous pentecostal readings of Luke-Acts toward a pneumatological theology of religions,

---

debatable thesis that for Luke, Gentile conversion was not from a polytheistic to monotheistic conception of God as much as it was from notions of hostile communities (representing factions led by warring gods) to inclusive communities shaped by a vision of one God over all the nations of the world. The second positive claim of Bartchy could surely be true even if he was mistaken about the former negative argument.

49. See Berryhill, "From Dreaded Guest to Welcome Host."

50. Tannehill ("Paul Outside the Christian Ghetto") focuses on peaceful coexistence and even cooperation between Jews and Gentiles not only during the sea voyage of Acts 27 but also in the public accusation scenes of Acts 16—19.

51. Wordelman ("Cultural Divides and Dual Realities," esp. 217–19) suggests that Paul performs miracles but does not preach at Malta in part because these were not only pagan Gentiles but also barbarians (note the mention of *barbaroi* in Acts 28:2 and 4). However, I find it inconceivable that such barbarians would have "bestowed many honors on us, and when we were about to sail, they put on board all the provisions we needed" (28:10).

and to further pneumatological theology of religions through a retrieval of a theology of hospitality also from the narrative of Luke-Acts. This convergence of theology of religions and theology of hospitality—what I am calling a pneumatological theology of interreligious hospitality—is especially crucial in world in which members of many faiths appear to be more hostile and antagonistic to one another than ever before. From a Christian point of view, we cannot be responsible for the actions of others, but we can and should be responsible for our own attitudes and behaviors. Hence, I suggest that the pneumatological theology of interreligious hospitality derived from the Pentecost narrative (as I have attempted in the preceding pages) provides a specifically theological rather than politically correct rationale for pentecostals and other Christians to relate to members of other faiths dialogically and relationally rather than only kerygmatically or apologetically.

Put another way, I propose that the pneumatological theology of interreligious hospitality developed in this essay expands the range of possible postures, strategies, and actions available for pentecostal engagement with the world of many faiths. Whereas conservative evangelical and fundamentalist theologies of exclusivism focus on proclamation, apologetics, and conversion, and whereas liberal theologies of pluralism emphasize sociopolitical activism, the pneumatological theology I am recommending requires that we discern the best approach amidst the many different situations we might encounter. In this sense, such a pentecostal and pneumatological orientation is much more ambiguous than exclusivistic and pluralistic theologies of mission because it requires constant attention to context along with spiritual vigilance in attending to what the Holy Spirit might be saying and doing.

But between exclusivism and pluralism in the usual typologies is inclusivism. How does the pentecostal-pneumatological approach commended here compare or contrast with inclusivist theologies of mission? On the one hand, the proposal I am recommending agrees with inclusivists that the Spirit may be present and active in surprising ways in the religions,[52] and that Christians can learn from and be positively transformed in authentic encounters with God mediated through relationships with those in other faiths. On the other hand, inclusivism cannot but affirm that whatever is good, true, and beautiful in other faiths is of divine origin, and in that sense, inclusivistic theologies of the religions may ultimately deny other religionists the right to define their own beliefs and practices on their own terms. At one level, it may be argued that this was Luke's own view. But applied to

---

52. E.g., Pinnock, *Flame of Love*, esp. ch. 6.

the religions in our time, such a position leads to theological claims that are problematic in a postcolonial situation.[53]

I wonder if the pneumatological theology of interreligious hospitality approach recommended here bypasses the need to label the beliefs and practices of religious others in our terms. Does not the Spirit of Pentecost respect the integrity of each voice to testify to his or her experience in his or her own language? Does not the Spirit of hospitality embolden those on the margins to bear witness against the powers that be at the center? Does not the Spirit poured out on all flesh create a public space wherein Christian and those in other faiths can engage mutually in acts of hospitality, in meaningful interreligious conversation, and in liberating social action? In the process, I submit, pentecostals and all Christians can and should bear witness to Jesus the Christ in word and in deed, while listening to, observing, and receiving from the hospitality shown them by those in other faiths. The result may be either mutual transformation of an unexpected kind, perhaps akin to the transformation experienced by Peter as a result of his encounter with Cornelius, or perhaps even our very salvation, such as described in the parable of one whose life was received as a gift through the hand of the good Samaritan.

In the end, the pneumatological theology of interreligious hospitality I am advocating is offered not as an exercise in speculative theology but as a means of revitalizing Christian witness in a religiously plural world. We often find ourselves acting as guests and hosts, even to and with those in other faiths, but we (at least those of us in pentecostal and evangelical circles) have not usually been given permission by our theological traditions to do so. What I am suggesting, then, is a theology of religions that is performative insofar as assenting to this view of the religions opens up sacred space for us to practice and receive hospitality with members of other religious traditions. Such a theological position not only permits but also obliges us to cultivate different dispositions toward those in other faiths than those traditionally promoted; not only allows but also requires that we look for dialogical situations and opportunities involving religious others; not only allows but also necessitates our establishing friendships and opening our homes for table fellowship with those in other faiths.[54] As performative,

---

53. So, for example, some might say that the rejection of the Jews in Acts is only temporary, since the redemption of Israel will be accomplished eschatologically when the Jews embrace Jesus as the Messiah. However, as Heikki Räisänen ("The Redemption of Israel") notes, this is to insist that Jewish salvation is possible only on Christian terms, and results in a Lukan anti-Jewishness in another voice.

54. Chapter 1 of Bruce Rowlison's *Creative Hospitality* is titled "Converting the Enemy into a Guest"—precisely the point of the pneumatological theology of interreligious

such a theology is not only descriptive but also prescriptive and normative for Christian attitudes and actions in a postmodern, postcolonial, and
religiously plural world.

Hence, a pneumatological theology of interreligious hospitality is not
divorced from but emergent from and directive regarding Christian praxis
and the spiritual life. Further, it is also theology in the service of a Christian
witness that is both kerygmatic (at the appropriate moments) and socially
liberative (as the Spirit leads). Finally, this is a theological posture characterized by a genuine epistemological humility, open to the surprising presence
and activity of the Spirit now wherever she may blow on the one hand and
yet also to the eschatological revelation of God on the other. In this vision,
the many tongues of Pentecost lead us to anticipate that the final revelation
of God will not arbitrarily exclude the witnesses to God given by those in
other faiths, but will redeem those testimonies and our own in a harmonious rendition that we all now glimpse as if only through a glass, dimly. Is
this not, at least in part, what the Spirit poured out on all flesh might finally
mean?[55]

---

hospitality I am advocating.

55. An earlier version of this paper was presented to one of the plenary sessions
of the annual meeting of the American Society of Missiology, June 16–18, 2006, at
Techny Towers, Chicago, Illinois. My thanks to Professor Steven Bevans for inviting my
participation in this event. Thanks also to Thomas E. Phillips for helping ensure that
this theologian was not misusing Luke-Acts scholarship, and to my research assistant,
Chris Emerick, for proofreading the penultimate draft. The faults that remain are my
own, of course.

CHAPTER 5

Missiology and the Interreligious Encounter

(with Tony Richie)

PENTECOSTALS HAVE ALWAYS BEEN heavily involved in missions, and hold missionaries in high esteem as extraordinary heroes of the faith.[1] But they have traditionally not given as much thought to the topic of theology of religions, or interreligious dialogue and encounter, as to other theological loci.[2] Part of why this is the case may be related to the fact that academic pentecostalism is but a recent arrival to the theological scene, with her first generation of professionally trained theologians—as opposed to historians or biblical scholars—emerging only since the early 1990s.[3] Yet pentecostal scholars can no longer avoid giving serious attention to these topics for various reasons, whether that be because the pentecostal commitment to carrying out the Great Commission leads many of her missionaries and ministers into environments and situations in which they are interacting with people of other faiths, because the question of how Christianity is to respond to other religions has become a more intensely debated social, political, and ideological question in an increasingly globalized world after September 11, 2001, or simply because they are led to engage in the wider academic conversation. There is now no denying the need to think through the theological question of the religions from a distinctively pentecostal perspective.

1. Possibly the closest that pentecostals have come to hagiography has been in their praise of extraordinary missionaries. E.g., Humphrey, *J. H. Ingram*.

2. Yong discusses this in "Inviting Spirit."

3. Developments in pentecostal scholarship are documented in Yong's "Pentecostalism and the Theological Academy."

96

Of course, missiology, theology of religions, and interreligious dialogue are characterized by closely interlocking concerns. A fundamental focal point shared by all three is that of intentional Christian encounter with religious others. This chapter will first survey pentecostal theologies of mission and theologies of religions respectively before finally attempting to articulate a pentecostal theology of the interreligious encounter. Whereas the first two sections will present the state of the discussion in these areas, the final part will suggest one possible way forward for further pentecostal reflection on these matters.

PENTECOSTAL THEOLOGIES OF MISSION

While pentecostals are well and widely known for missionary practice, in many ways our reflection and articulation have been left behind. Recently, however, that has begun to change.[4] In this section we will discuss first earlier and then later theologies of mission among classical pentecostals, before turning to explore more recent developments in the wider domain of pentecostal-charismatic missiology. In a transitional section, we will note the growing importance of theology of religions and the interreligious encounter for pentecostal missiology.

Classical Pentecostal Missiology

Credited with developing the distinctive doctrine of tongues as initial evidence,[5] Charles Fox Parham has been recognized as the father or founder of the modern pentecostal movement. Yet the greatest legacy that he bequeathed to modern pentecostalism may well be his missionary vision. Goff Jr. notes that Parham "instilled within the movement a fervent missionary emphasis."[6] Though his belief in xenolalia (that is, tongues as known languages used in an unprecedented wave of end-time missionary activity and revival) failed on the mission field and was discarded by the embryonic movement, his emphasis on the gift of the Holy Spirit's power for evangelistic witness continues to be of central significance within pentecostalism. These motifs came together in one of the central scriptural texts for pentecostals: "But you will receive power when the Holy Spirit has come upon you; and

4. See Dempster et al., *Called and Empowered*, and Kärkkäinen, "Pentecostal Theology of Mission."

5. Goff Jr., "Initial Tongues in the Theology of Charles Fox Parham."

6. Goff Jr., "Parham, Charles Fox," 955. For Goff's definitive treatment of Parham see Goff Jr., *Fields White unto Harvest*.

you will be my witnesses in Jerusalem, in all Judea and Samaria, and to the ends of the earth" (Acts 1:8). When linked with Peter's explanation of the events of the Day of Pentecost (drawn from the prophet Joel), that this outpouring of the Spirit was God's special work in the last days (Acts 2:17), Parham's eschatological emphasis and sense of urgency has since provided pentecostalism immense missionary momentum.

Yet it needs noting that Parham's (one-time) disciple William J. Seymour and the Azusa Street Mission's actual and sacrificial missionary practices also deserve considerable credit for much of the effective missionary thrust of early pentecostalism.[7] If today's pentecostal denominations like to highlight their "evangelism distinctive," and talk about evangelism as part of "a unified experience of the Holy Spirit," it is largely due to the early influence of Parham and Seymour.[8] Parham guaranteed that Spirit Baptism and evangelism or missions would be permanently connected for most pentecostals, while Seymour's Azusa Street Mission was what actually launched a large number of the first pentecostal missionaries around the world.

But neither Parham nor Seymour, nor anyone else early in the movement for that matter, systematized pentecostal missiology. Melvin L. Hodges, an experienced missionary and prolific author, was the first to begin articulating a distinctive pentecostal missiology in the mid-twentieth century. While in some ways he basically followed previously trodden evangelical paths, his practical missionary expertise building indigenous churches and his overt pentecostal pneumatology greatly shaped his approach and contributed to its overall effectiveness.[9] Following the lead of Parham and other early pentecostal missionaries, Hodges took his missiological cues from the book of Acts. From this he discerned not only that the church is God's missionary agency to the ends of the earth, but also that the Spirit empowers the church for her ministry and mission in various contexts. At the level of the individual, all persons, including nominal Christians, are to be brought into an experiential knowledge of the gospel and "into the fellowship of the life in the Holy Spirit."[10] At the corporate level, the Christian mission is to establish self-propagating, self-governing, and self-supporting local congregations and ministries. These would be the dominant features of what Hodges calls "the indigenous church": established, overseen, organized, and developed by local (i.e., "native") leadership in their own lan-

---

7. See Robeck Jr., *Azusa Street Mission and Revival*, 235–80.

8. E.g., Hughes, *Church of God Distinctives*, 49–62, and Horton, *What Bible Says About the Holy Spirit*, 149.

9. See McGee, "Hodges, Melvin Lyle."

10. Hodges, *Theology of the Church and Its Mission*, 95.

guage and according to their own cultural customs, with missionaries (in Hodges's mind, from the West, although in our new context, perhaps not exclusively so) serving only in the role of consultant.[11]

Clearly the earliest pentecostal missionaries were motivated first and foremost by the practical exigencies of fulfilling the Great Commission. What was distinctive about pentecostal missiology during this early period, however, even if not as explicitly articulated as later generations might have hoped, was its being informed by the early Christian and apostolic paradigm. Hence the mission for the church, for classical pentecostals, was linked essentially to the outpouring of the Spirit on the Day of Pentecost. Even Hodges's indigenous principle is, in effect, a practical missionary vision shaped in part by the many tongues manifest and validated by the apostolic experience.[12]

Contemporary Pentecostal Missiologies

With Paul Pomerville, an Assemblies of God missionary, we have one of the first insider analyses of pentecostal missions from a more formal missiological perspective.[13] Pomerville follows the church growth movement but denies the evangelical argument that the primary motivation for missions is obedience to the Great Commission of Matthew 28:19–20. Rather, he insists that the Holy Spirit of Pentecost is a missionary Spirit and that makes the Spirit-filled church a missionary church. Furthermore, what is true collectively is also true individually. Every Spirit-filled believer is an evangelist or a witness of Christ. Pomerville hence emphasizes the centrality of Spirit Baptism and its accompanying impetus for pentecostal missions. Yet he resists defining and describing pentecostal missions one dimensionally. Accordingly, he lists five prescriptions for pentecostal missions: a thoroughgoing Trinitarian theology of mission based on the book of Acts; a reemphasis of Great Commission missions based on the power of the Spirit with accompanying charismatic confirmations; a holistic view of missions with a priority on evangelism; evangelism directed toward church planting, viewing the local church as the Holy Spirit's instrument and the pentecostal experience as its primary dynamic; and, especially in the non-Western world, respect for independent movements.[14] Pomerville's work can thus be

11. See Hodges, *Indigenous Church.*

12. Yong argues this point in his *Spirit Poured Out on All Flesh*, 123–24 and ch. 4.

13. See Pomerville, *Third Force in Missions.*

14. Pomerville, "Pentecostals and Growth."

seen as a contemporary retrieval but also reappropriation of classical pentecostal theologies of mission.

Similarly, Grant McClung, a Church of God (Cleveland) missionary
and educator, is convinced of the centrality of experiencing the power of the
Holy Spirit for pentecostal mission.[15] He observes that signs and wonders,
especially divine healing, can serve as powerful openings for evangelistic
opportunities.[16] Indeed, miracles often serve to draw unbelievers to Christ.
Such experiences can also function as great levelers, catapulting women,
the poor and illiterate, and other marginalized people into positions of
prominent ministry and thus multiplying the missionary task force. With
Hodges, then, McClung understands pentecostal missions in terms of indigenization. McClung also contends, in the tradition of Parham and the
early Azusa Street experience, that there is a need for a continuing sense of
eschatological urgency and for a strong commitment of vocational calling
for missionary effectiveness.[17] Overall he emphasizes pentecostal missions
as a process of explosion, motivation, and consolidation; gripped by an eschatological urgency, sense of destiny, and high regard for the supernatural
working of the Holy Spirit as the heart of pentecostal missions; combining
"a spontaneous strategy of the Spirit" with pragmatic calculation; having
parallels with the church growth movement; and possessing a visionary
commitment to the future, acknowledging concerns and preparing for challenges. McClung's contributions to a contemporary restatement of classical
pentecostal missiology cannot be overlooked.

Gary McGee [d. 2012] is historian and missiologist who teaches at
the Assemblies of God Theological Seminary. Drawing on historical perspectives for missiological application, he notes that opposition to signs
and wonders of the Spirit *and* expectation of their occurrence have been,
paradoxically, common throughout the church's existence in the extension
of its witness.[18] Pentecostalism's extensive utilization of this radical strategy
of divine power certainly has been significant for its success. Yet McGee is
also quick to contend that pentecostal missions needs to increase its un-

15. See McClung, *Azusa Street and Beyond*, esp. his "Introduction" for each
section; cf. McClung, *Globalbeliever.com.*

16. Along this line contemporary pentecostal New Testament scholar John Christopher Thomas argues for "an intricate and significant connection" between healing and
mission; see his *Spirit of the New Testament*, 47.

17. Other pentecostal scholars have also noted the connection between pneumatology, eschatology, and mission for pentecostalism; see, e.g., Klaus, "Holy Spirit and
Mission."

18. McGee, "Pentecostal Missiology." See further McGee, *This Gospel Shall be
Preached*, "Pentecostal and Charismatic Missions," and "Radical Strategy in Modern
Missions."

derstanding and practice of social ministry and activism if it is to meet the needs of oppressed and underprivileged peoples today. However, a biblical hermeneutic including powerful spiritual experience remains a key to missionary effectiveness in the non-Western world. Supernatural experiences or occurrences are a major element of missions, particularly of pentecostal missions. Clearly, missiologists like McGee, Pomerville, and McClung are working both to provide the discipline of missiology with distinctive pentecostal perspectives, and also to update classical pentecostal missiology in dialogue with the wider missiological conversation.

Recent Developments in Pentecostal-Charismatic Missiology

In many ways Walter J. Hollenweger is largely responsible for making the wider scholarly world more aware of pentecostalism.[19] A Swiss scholar of pentecostalism and an intercultural theologian, he has been the preeminent analyst of the world pentecostal movement from his post at the University of Birmingham.[20] Hollenweger insists pentecostals themselves need new appraisals of pentecostalism's relations with pre-Christian cultures and religions, especially in the so-called Third World. He suggests these have been "taken and transformed" by pentecostalism, but laments that pentecostals have not consistently acted on W. J. Seymour's ecumenism. As the real founder of the movement (according to Hollenweger), Seymour's roots in the black spirituality of his past provide important insights into the original and authentic nature of a pentecostal identity that is rich with ecumenical and interreligious possibilities.[21] Hollenweger suggests that pentecostals must come to grips with bewildering pluralism within the global movement, and that this can be done by attending to the pluralism at the origins of modern pentecostalism itself. Further, he argues that first-century Christians weren't "theologically homogeneous" either, and that idea could be helpful for pentecostals today. This is especially relevant since all Christianity and churches—including pentecostal churches—are syncretistic, taking "on board many customs and ideas from our pagan past."[22] Thus rather than the traditional "aggressive evangelism," Hollenweger proposes "dialogical evangelism" as a biblical model for mission in which pentecostals and charismatics can learn from those they are evangelizing as Peter learned from

19. See his now classic text, *Pentecostals*; cf. Hollenweger, *Pentecostalism*.
20. Cf. Bundy, "Hollenweger, Walter Jacob," 729.
21. Hollenweger, "Black Roots of Pentecostalism."
22. Hollenweger, "Critical Issues for Pentecostals," 185–86.

his encounter with Cornelius (in Acts 10).[23] In the end, his goal is to help pentecostals and charismatics guard against losing their original ecumenical vision, and perhaps even encourage its restoration.[24]

Alan Anderson, the successor to Hollenweger at Birmingham, agrees with Hollenweger that pentecostals "must rediscover their roots" lest they "betray the origins of the movement."[25] He particularly stresses the need for pentecostal social involvement, and suggests the essence of the pentecostal gospel is a pragmatic gospel that meets practical needs. Yet pentecostal spirituality includes both strong liberationist overtones and a high priority on evangelism. Anderson also says some pentecostals and charismatics have so adapted to their cultural and religious context that many Western pentecostals would probably doubt the Christian identity of such communities. He himself, however, tends to view authentic pentecostalism as much more diverse than may be common for classical pentecostals. For example, he observes that pentecostal interaction with (not capitulation to) Korean shamanism can be a positive development. There is an "inherent flexibility" in pentecostalism that "makes it more easily able to adjust to any context" and this is its missiological advantage.[26] Hence Anderson sees the major features of pentecostal missiological theology to include the interrelatedness of the missionary Spirit and church growth; the importance and prevalence of signs and wonders; connections between Spirit Baptism and global mission, including social activism; the significant experiential impact of pentecostal liturgy and indigenous churches; and the adaptability of pentecostal forms of evangelism.[27] Like Hollenweger before him, Anderson also is particularly insistent on the worldwide scope and variety of pentecostalism and pentecostal missions.[28]

Andrew Lord, an Anglican charismatic missiologist influenced by this "Birmingham school," grounds pentecostal missions more directly in pneumatology. For example, in comparing the pneumatology of pentecostal scholars and Jürgen Moltmann, he examines two key differences

---

23. See Richie, "Revamping Pentecostal Evangelism"; cf. Richie, "Pentecostal in Sheep's Clothing."

24. See Lynne Price's excellent study, *Theology Out of Place*, which shows that Hollenweger is deeply committed to the ecumenical and interreligious nature of pentecostalism and that his missiology is significantly shaped by it.

25. Anderson, "Global Pentecostalism in New Millennium," 210.

26. Anderson, "Introduction: World Pentecostalism at a Crossroads."

27. See Anderson, "Towards a Pentecostal Missiology."

28. This is a main point of Anderson's recent books, *Introduction to Pentecostalism* and *Spreading Fires*.

in understanding and their implications for missions.[29] First, pentecostals tend to focus on the "particular" and the "transcendent" whereas Moltmann emphasizes the "universal" and the "immanent." Related to this, second, pentecostals have adopted a more evangelical posture on mission in contrast to Moltmann's more ecumenical approach. Together, these differences are significant for the theology and practice of mission. Although both Moltmann and pentecostals share a desire for mission to be holistic and experiential, they differ over the means of mission and characteristics of mission. Pentecostal missions and evangelism have focused on salvation of the individual soul in contrast to ecumenical missions being focused on social presence and transformation. Lord suggests a way beyond these differences by presenting a pneumatological framework for grounding mission in movement of the Holy Spirit. The Spirit is universally present and active, as well as involved in the particularities of human embodiment and the personal transformation of human hearts in anticipation of eschatological salvation. Hence a pneumatological theology of mission is holistic, experiential, contextual, community-forming, and spirituality sensitive. In this way, pentecostals and charismatics are encouraged to develop a holistic missiological theology more cognizant of cultures and globalization.[30]

From Pentecostal Missiology to Theology of Religions and Interreligious Dialogue

We have seen in this brief survey of the field of pentecostal missiology a growing recognition of the importance of theology of religions and of the interreligious dialogue. These connections have also been observed by the Finnish pentecostal systematician Veli-Matti Kärkkäinen.[31] He suggests that the next steps for pentecostal missiology involve a threefold challenge: (1) to continue to highlight and articulate the theological basis of distinctive pentecostal mission; (2) to clarify the relationship between proclamation and social concern or service; and (3) to explore further how pentecostals should understand and interact with followers of other religions. With regard to the first two points, Kärkkäinen has proposed that the church needs to be seen as the Trinitarian movement sent by the Spirit into the world even as the Spirit participates in the sending of the Father on behalf of the Son (in this way opening up to a distinctively Trinitarian and pneumatological theology of mission), and that pentecostals need to realize that kingdom works

29. Lord, "Pentecostal-Moltmann Dialogue."
30. Lord, *Spirit-Shaped Mission*.
31. Kärkkäinen, "'Truth on Fire.'"

remain to be done today, and that social activism can have eschatological significance (in this way, further strengthening the connections made by Anderson and Lord, for example, between mission and social witness).

Our focus, however, lies in Kärkkäinen's point three: concerning pentecostal relations with other (world) religions and their adherents.[32] Pentecostals typically duck the issue. Often they default to standard (evangelical) exclusivism. That is no longer satisfactory—if it ever was. Dialogue with other Christians, such as Roman Catholics, increasingly challenges pentecostals to face up to the diversity within the Christian movement as well as to the plurality of Christian views regarding the religions. Furthermore, developing pneumatology within pentecostalism's own ranks suggests room is being made for the Spirit in the world and, perhaps, in the world's religions. Significantly, a pneumatological theology of religions does not and must not downplay the importance of evangelization.

A few summary remarks can be made at this point with regard to pentecostal missiology. First, that pneumatology is the area (or experience!) that makes pentecostal missions most distinctive seems generally assumed, but how that may specifically apply is not agreed upon. For example, do we view mission through pneumatology or pneumatology through mission or both through yet another lens such as eschatology? Interestingly, almost everyone agrees about the recipe itself but many remain unclear about how to assess the resulting shifts in missionary practice. Second, there are tensions between the historic versus contemporary aspects of pentecostalism. The former seems to some more exclusive, anti-ecumenical, and anti-interreligious, while the latter seems to others too open-ended and ideologically pluralistic. Again, one senses a growing movement in the latter direction, even while there is reluctance to abandon completely the legacy of the historic tradition. Finally, there is the question of emphasizing the evangelical identity of pentecostalism that may incline us to embrace a North American version with all of its cultural and geographical baggage, or of opting instead for an ecumenical vision of pentecostal identity that opens us up to a global charismatic movement based in the majority non-Western world with implications for relating to other religions. Again, one is tempted to argue that it doesn't have to be either/or, that it can be both/and. The trajectories of pentecostal missiology explored above certainly seem to suggest developments in ecumenical, global, and interreligious directions. Hence it appears that pentecostal missiology is intertwined with and cannot avoid thinking about theology of religions.

---

32. See also Yong, "Not Knowing Where the Spirit Blows."

PENTECOSTAL THEOLOGIES OF THE RELIGIONS

One of the oft-repeated errors regarding pentecostalism (frequently even by pentecostals!) is an assumption that the movement is monolithic. It is not, and this diversity is reflected in its theology of religions as well.[33] In the following discussion, we present the classical pentecostal exclusivist view regarding the religions, discuss the inclusivism that has reappeared more recently among pentecostals and charismatics, and then look at efforts to think theologically about the religions from a distinctively pentecostal perspective. In a transitional section, we will note that there is a general correlation between developments in pentecostal theologies of mission (as presented above) and pentecostal theologies of religions.

Classical Pentecostal "Exclusivism"

As used in the context of the discipline of the theology of religions, "exclusivism" reflects a closed attitude, positing that a conscious personal response to the preached gospel is not only normative but necessary for salvation. It basically argues there is no salvation outside the church or apart from the church's proclamation of the gospel. On the other end of the spectrum, "pluralism" essentially equates all religions while denying superiority to any. It focuses at the more general level of God or "ultimate reality" rather than on the particularity of Christ (or Buddha or Mohammed, etc.). The moderating position, "inclusivism," is a christocentric and pneumatic openness regarding the present state and eternal fate of the unevangelized or adherents of other religions. It affirms salvation ultimately of and by Christ, even if it allows for the possibility that the unevangelized or adherents of other faiths may experience salvation according to the mysterious grace and mercy of God. But a great deal of ambiguity and overlap admittedly exists among these broad categories.[34]

Usually pentecostals are assumed to be exclusivists, and indeed there is a track record to that effect. At one level, pentecostal exclusivism is connected to its understanding of the Great Commission. The call to go into the world and proclaim the gospel to everyone has led them to view religious others narrowly, primarily as objects of evangelism. Hence pentecostals have asserted that the Spirit's saving work is limited to the church, and it is precisely as members of the church allow themselves to be used by the Spirit

33. Cf. Kärkkäinen, *Introduction to Theology of Religions*, 139–40.

34. For the classic presentation of the categories of exclusivism, inclusivism, and pluralism in theology of religions, see Race, *Christians and Religious Pluralism*.

to witness to their non-Christian neighbors, even those of other religions, that salvation is also made available to the world.[35] Insofar as pentecostals think the evangelism mandate and the inclusivist openness to the possibility of the salvation of the unevangelized (not to mention pluralism) are incompatible, their ardent evangelistic orientation requires, they assume, that they must be exclusivists.

Another way to understand pentecostal exclusivism is to note their historical connections with fundamentalism and conservative evangelicalism. The historic pentecostal closed-mindedness may be a remnant of their landing on the fundamentalist side of the fundamentalist-liberal (or modernist) divide during the first quarter of the twentieth century, with an excessively literalist approach to biblical hermeneutics, and an overall suspicion toward ecumenism in general.[36] Since the early pentecostals were shunned on both the left and the right—by liberals because of pentecostalism's uncultured and unsophisticated spirituality, and by fundamentalists because of their charismatic enthusiasm and experientialism—pentecostals have imbibed a sectarian mentality, almost as if for reasons of self-preservation. This rejection has produced a long history of ecumenical isolationism vis-à-vis the other churches as well as a theological exclusivism vis-à-vis other religions. And since pentecostals have not given serious thought to developing a formal theology of religions of their own until very recently, they have historically not felt the need to go beyond the exclusivism they shared with evangelicals (and fundamentalists) regarding the religions.

Of course, there is also the gloomy possibility that pentecostals are just exclusivists by nature, and without further evidence deciding is difficult. Fortunately, there is further evidence for investigation.[37]

Pentecostal-Charismatic "Inclusivism"

Clark Pinnock, himself a charismatic Baptist, has worked closely with pentecostal scholars and thus built a relationship of mutual respect. He is clearly inclusivist in his theology of religions.[38] While continuing to affirm unequivocally the incarnation and revelation of God in the person of Jesus Christ, he refuses to restrict the Spirit's reach to those who have specifically heard the gospel. In fact, it has been precisely his commitment to biblical authority and a high Christology that has led Pinnock to develop his pneu-

---

35. Cf. Kärkkäinen, *Introduction to the Theology of Religions*, 140–42.

36. Yong, *Discerning the Spirit(s)*, 185–87.

37. See, e.g., Richie, "Precedents and Possibilities."

38. Pinnock, *Wideness in God's Mercy.*

matology. The result has been an openly and optimistically inclusivist stance wherein he seeks to avoid the twin errors of overemphasizing either universality or particularity to the exclusion of the other. For Pinnock, the Spirit (though not entirely or only) represents universality and the Son (though not entirely or only) represents particularity.[39] This is not an either/or but a both/and proposition. Building upon John Wesley's concept of "prevenient grace" (the grace that goes before), Pinnock posits the Spirit's presence in the religions bringing God's revelation into contact with some who will receive it and then perhaps be saved. He does not see non-Christian religions as vehicles of salvation, yet he resists restricting God the Spirit to the church. One may discern this prevenient process in action through the presence of the Spirit's fruit. Pinnock, therefore, refers in hope to the unevangelized or adherents of other religions as "pre-Christian" rather than "non-Christian."[40]

No doubt some pentecostals have been influenced by Pinnock. But is inclusivism simply a choice between historic pentecostal and contemporary charismatic stances? No, because even in historic, classical pentecostalism "strands of openness" to religious others crop up sporadically in the midst of a history and environment of exclusivity.[41] Tony Richie has recently drawn attention to the fact that early and original elements of pentecostalism had significant inclusivist strains.[42] Such a stance may be gleaned from the theology of none other than Charles Fox Parham. Parham advocated an eschatological inclusivism of uncompromising loyalty to Christ coupled with compassionate openness to devout adherents of other religions.[43] For Parham commitment to the absolute uniqueness and necessity of Jesus Christ as Lord and Savior complemented openness to a possibility of divine reality and redemption in extra-Christian religions that are consummated in the eschaton by Christ.

Contemporary pentecostals can also respond to the challenges of religious pluralism through an appropriation of the optimistic and hopeful theology of Bishop J. H. King, an important and early pentecostal pioneer, leader, and thinker.[44] Central and crucial for King was the universal significance of Christ, a refined doctrine of universal atonement, the reality and

---

39. Pinnock, *Flame of Love*, 185–214.

40. For further discussion of Pinnock's charismatic and inclusivist theology of religions, see Yong, "Whither Theological Inclusivism?"

41. See Yong, *Discerning the Spirit(s)*, 187–97.

42. Richie, "Unity of the Spirit."

43. Richie, "Eschatological Inclusivism."

44. Richie, "Azusa-Era Optimism."

efficacy of general revelation, a qualified acceptance of religious experience over rigid doctrinal propositionalism, and, though somewhat less directly, a dynamic and progressive view of the process of salvation. King also accepted that "the religion of Christ"—the religion centered in the person of Christ himself rather than in institutional Christianity—predates and exists apart from ecclesial Christianity, even among other world religions, though Christianity may in a special sense be called "the only true religion." When put together to address the questions of religious pluralism, Bishop King's theology invites a more inclusive stance toward the religions than the rhetoric of classical pentecostalism suggests.

In fact, we suggest, a generally and genuinely inclusive theology of religions flows quite naturally out of the Wesleyan-Arminian heritage of the Holiness-pentecostal revival.[45] The time is ripe for pentecostals to explore a "balanced Pentecostal approach to Christian theology of religions."[46] Hollenweger's suggestion of "dialogical evangelism" provides an interactive mode of engaging religious others that is not contradictory to but compatible with pentecostal history, identity, missiology, spirituality, and theology. Neither dialogical evangelism nor traditional pentecostal evangelism usurps the other but both are appraised as attractive options in their appropriate places. Such an inclusive pentecostal theology of religions, especially of the kind articulated by Richie in dialogue with major streams of the early pentecostal tradition, is a "back to the future" approach that simultaneously looks backward and forward, and stresses both continuity and creativity.

Toward a Pentecostal Theology of Religions

One recognized pentecostal theologian who has led the way on the issue of theology of religions is Veli-Matti Kärkkäinen.[47] If theology of religions "attempts to account theologically for the meaning and value of other religions,"[48] then a distinctively Christian theology of religions, Kärkkäinen suggests, must be Trinitarian. Very briefly, Kärkkäinen's Trinitarian theology of religions suggests that Trinitarian theology serves as a critique of

45. See Richie, "John Wesley and Mohammed," and Yong, *Spirit Poured Out on All Flesh*, ch. 6.

46. Richie, "Neither Naïve nor Narrow."

47. For an explication of how Kärkkäinen's pentecostal identity informs his work as a theologian in general and as a theologian of religions in particular, see Yong, "Whither Evangelical Theology?" [This article has been reprinted as chapter 5 in Yong's *The Dialogical Spirit*.]

48. See especially Kärkkäinen, *Trinity and Religious Pluralism*, 2; cf. also his *Toward a Pneumatological Theology*, ch. 14.

a so-called "normative" pluralism (which usually collapses the differences between religions); that the triune God of the Bible is unique; that a high Christology plays a critical role in the doctrine of the Trinity; that the church in the power of the Holy Spirit anticipates the kingdom of God, always pointing beyond itself to the eschaton, or the coming of the kingdom and unity of all people under one God; that the doctrine of the Trinity indicates the communal nature of God capable of relating in unity and difference; and that Trinitarian communion can include critical relationship with religious others in tolerance. Essentially, Kärkkäinen is suggesting that a full-orbed Trinitarian theology emphasizes the role of the Spirit not only in the Trinitarian life of God but also in the presence of the relationship between God and the church and in the relationship between the church and the world.

Obviously pneumatologically robust, Kärkkäinen is nonetheless faithfully christocentric and ecclesiological.[49] The Spirit who reaches out beyond the church into the kingdom and into the world is always the spirit of Christ who abides in unique relation with his church. No wedge is driven between the Spirit and Christ, or between the Spirit and the church. Thus other religions are not salvific but discerning appreciation for the presence of the triune God in their midst is possible. This opens the way wide for relational engagement, and includes a responsibility for genuinely appreciative and cautiously critical interreligious dialogue and encounter. For Kärkkäinen, a truly Trinitarian theology of religions enables interreligious dialogue as a mutually respectful process of learning and sharing.

If Kärkkäinen has reflected theologically on the religions as a pentecostal, it has been Amos Yong who has attempted to develop a distinctively pentecostal theology of religions.[50] He advises fellow pentecostals to develop a theology of religions because of their international roots and global presence, because of their need to attend to urgent missiological issues such as syncretism, the relations between gospel and culture, and the balance between proclamation and social justice, and because of the importance of this topic for further delineating pentecostal identity. Yet the pentecostal experience produces its own "pneumatological imagination"—a way of thinking and theologizing informed by the pentecostal-charismatic experience of and orientation toward the Holy Spirit—that suggests the possibility of the Spirit's presence and influence in the world in general and in the world's religions more particularly. Further, such a pentecostal theology is also sensitive to the fact that there are many "spirits" in the world, much

49. E.g., Kärkkäinen, "Toward a Pneumatological Theology of Religions" and "How to Speak of the Spirit among Religions."

50. See Yong, *Discerning the Spirit(s)* and *Beyond the Impasse.*

less in the world of the religions, which require Christian discernment. The criteria for discerning the Holy Spirit from other spirits, then, includes the fruits of the Spirit, ethical conduct, and the signs of the coming kingdom. In such a pentecostal theological framework, then, Yong also emphasizes that "the pneumatological imagination derived from the outpouring of the Spirit" enables a relatively impartial, sympathetic, yet critical engagement with the religions.[51]

For Kärkkäinen and Yong, then, it is important that a pentecostal theology of religions should help pentecostal Christians engage the religions through discernment rather than through any a priori views about the religions. This means that people of other faiths need to be heard first on their own terms, even while (pentecostal) Christians would also be invited or even required to testify in their own tongues. The key here is to be able to comprehend other religions according to their own self-understanding, without prejudging or defining them according to our own Christian (or pentecostal) theological categories (for example, in exclusivist, inclusivist, or pluralist terms). Such a pentecostal approach thus sustains and motivates the interreligious encounter, and does so as part of the Christian mission.

Assessing Pentecostal Theologies of Religions

We will momentarily expand on these insights toward a pentecostal and pneumatological theology of religions. Before doing so, however, some assessment is in order. To begin, we should clearly state, as Kärkkäinen has already pointed out, that pluralism is not an option for pentecostals.[52] At the same time, a narrow exclusivism, that is, a view that Christ and the Spirit are restricted entirely to the church or its members, sits uncomfortably with the theology of religions proposed by Pinnock, Richie, Kärkkäinen, and Yong. However, as a more open inclusivism could fit with any of them, it is noteworthy that those working most directly and pointedly in the area of pentecostal theology of religions seem to be developing in generally inclusivist directions. As of yet, no major theological voice from within the movement itself is sounding an alarm (even while recognized pentecostal theologians like Frank Macchia are turning in what might be called inclusivist directions).[53] Though that may happen at some point, likely the burden of proof rests with those seeking to limit or restrict the Spirit.

51. Yong, *Spirit Poured Out on All Flesh*, 254.

52. See Kärkkäinen, "Response to Tony 'Richie's Azusa-Era Optimism.'"

53. While Macchia rejects the philosophy of religious pluralism, he skillfully argues that Christ's role as Spirit Baptizer indicates the church is the locus of the Spirit's

But it is interesting to ask why pentecostal scholars and theologians who are publishing on the religions have not resorted to the established categories of exclusivism, inclusivism, etc. Perhaps there are more exclusivists present than we are aware of, but if they are not explicitly using (or defending) the exclusivist model in their writings, they would be identifiable as exclusivistic only with difficulty.[54] Hence, concluding that inclusivism has won or will win the day is premature.

Of course, inclusivism itself is not without its challenges. One of the major hurdles that inclusivists need to confront is that their theological paradigm remains wedded to the soteriological question about the salvation of the unevangelized or of those in other religions. Inclusivism, in other words, was developed more for Christian self-understanding than for answering the questions related to theology of religions. Hence, inclusivism is inappropriate when applied in a dialogue with people of other faiths, since that would entail Christians either granting salvation to people of other faiths who are not seeking such salvation (of union with God in Christ), or Christians labeling people of other faiths according to categories foreign to those religious traditions. In our contemporary pluralistic world, the challenge is to understand religious others on their own terms even while remaining committed to our own religious vision, including that of bearing witness to Christ in the power of the Spirit.

In a real sense, the theologies of religions of Kärkkäinen and Yong are in search of ways to resolve this inclusivist dilemma. Both emphasize a robust Trinitarian pneumatology (even if Kärkkäinen stresses the Trinitarian a bit more and Yong the pneumatology) precisely in order to open up theological space to appreciate the particularities of the religions and their differences from Christian faith. While Kärkkäinen's emphasis is on how the real Trinitarian distinctions may correlate with real differences between the religions, Yong's "pneumatological imagination" is designed to both recognize and yet bridge the vast chasm separating Christian faith from other religions. In this sense, both recognize the shortcomings of the dominant categories of exclusivism, inclusivism, and pluralism and have explored the

---

work, and that the Spirit still works in the wider religious world because the kingdom extends in gracious ways beyond ecclesial borders. Pluralist equalizations of all religions are thereby refuted without falling into the equal and opposite error of exclusivist incriminations. Accordingly, Macchia adds his voice to others assisting pentecostals in advancing toward a mature, moderate theology of religions. See Macchia, *Baptized in the Spirit*, 178–90.

54. For example, it appears that the exclusivist position is defended in Gallagher, "The Holy Spirit in the World," although the author does not put it in those terms.

questions of if and how we might advance beyond this paradigm.[55] Yet their efforts, along with those of Pinnock and Richie, are also indications that a pentecostal theology of religions is an exciting but complex undertaking. They suggest pentecostals are ready to take their place in the global community amidst the interreligious encounter. Might pentecostal approaches to mission and the theology of religions point the way forward for such a task?

PENTECOSTALISM, MISSIONS, AND THE CONTEMPORARY INTERRELIGIOUS ENCOUNTER

In this final part of our essay, we will focus both on pneumatological-theological issues and on performative-practical proposals for pentecostal pneumatological theology of religions. First, we will argue that the many tongues of Pentecost could represent the religious traditions of the world, and second, that this same multiplicity of tongues invites and empowers various kinds of practices for the interfaith encounter. Our goal in the following is to make explicit the connections between a distinctive pentecostal missiology (which we discussed in part I above) and a distinctive pentecostal theology of religions (which we just introduced), with an eye to explicitly fleshing out how such a pentecostal and pneumatological approach to the religions works itself out in the practice of missions.

Toward a Pentecostal and Pneumatological Theology of Religions

As we have seen, one of the main problems that plagues traditional theologies of religions is how to honor and respect the particularities of other faiths even while remaining committed to one's own (in our case, pentecostal Christianity). This is parallel to the perennial philosophical challenge of the relationship between the one and the many. Historically, responses have either privileged the one, which risks rejecting the many, or emphasized the many, which lapses into anarchy or relativism.[56] Does a pentecostal and pneumatological perspective shed light on this ancient debate?

---

55. As suggested in Yong, "Can We Get 'Beyond the Paradigm'?" Note that Kärkkäinen himself organized his introductory textbook, *Introduction to Theology of Religions,* using a different set of categories than exclusivism, inclusivism, and pluralism. For further discussion of the unresolved difficulties for each of these approaches, see Yong, "Spirit, Christian Practices, and Religions," esp. 6–13.

56. See Copleston, *Religion and the One.*

The Day of Pentecost narrative in Acts 2 provides some perspective on this issue. Two observations can be made.[57] First, it should be noted that the one outpouring of the Spirit did not cancel out but rather enabled an eruption of a diversity of tongues. On the one hand, there is a cacophony of tongues, yet on the other there is a harmony of testimonies, each witnessing in their own way to God's deeds of power. Correlatively, there is both mass confusion but yet also an astonishment born of understanding.[58] In these ways, Pentecost signifies, perhaps, a unique resolution of the one and the many: the many (tongues) retain their particularities even as they participate in the one (the Spirit's outpouring).[59] Whereas before there were just the many tongues, now the many tongues are brought together, not so that they might cancel or drown one another out, but so that precisely out of the plurality of utterances strangers might be brought together and the goodness of God might be declared.

This leads, second, to the observation that the many tongues of Pentecost did indeed signify the many cultures of the ancient Mediterranean world. Whereas the cultural and religious domains of human life are neither identical nor synonymous, we argue that they are also not completely distinct. Rather, languages are related to cultures and both are related to religious traditions, even if each is a distinguishable aspect of human life. Given this interrelationship, however, might we suggest the many tongues of Pentecost not only represent many cultures but also, at least potentially, many religious traditions? If so, then the outpouring of the Spirit points not only to the redemption of the many languages, but also to the redemption of many cultures and perhaps of many religious traditions.

What we mean by redemption, however, should be qualified. First, the claim about the redemption of other faiths is an eschatological one: "In the last days it will be, God declares, that I will pour out my Spirit upon all flesh" (Acts 2:17a). If the eschatological gift of the Spirit means, in part, that the outpouring of the Spirit has occurred, is occurring, and will continue to occur, then the redemption of anything, the religions included, may have past, present, and, most importantly, future aspects to it. In that sense, then, every person, including those in other faiths, is a candidate for the future reception of the Spirit (if not already having been touched by the Spirit whose winds blow where they may), and such reception may depend in part on

57. What follows is a condensed version of what Yong has argued at greater length elsewhere: "As the Spirit Gives Utterance . . . " ; "The Spirit Bears Witness"; and *Spirit Poured Out on All Flesh*, ch. 4.

58. On these points, we follow the brilliant reading of the Acts 2 narrative provided by Welker, *God the Spirit*, ch. 5.

59. Cf. Suurmond, *Word and Spirit at Play*, 201.

their interactions with us (as Christians). How we approach or respond to people of other faiths may determine if and when the gift of the Spirit will be given to them. And, given the fact that there are varying degrees of ignorance and knowledge about Christ, we would underscore God's redemptive work in the lives of individuals as a dynamic process depending not on our certification of their salvation, but on the gracious gift of God in Christ and the Holy Spirit. So then in anticipating the possibility of the redemption of the religions, we are saying neither that Luke means every person since the Day of Pentecost has received the Spirit nor that all people of other faiths are already saved.

Second, in speaking about the redemption of cultures and of religious traditions, we are by no means suggesting that all cultures or religious traditions as wholes are now conduits of the saving grace of God. Cultures and religions, like languages, are not monolithic, and aspects of each of them are antithetical to the purposes of God (hence their fallenness). At the same time, neither are languages, cultures, and religions static, so that whatever in them might be hostile to the purposes of God today will not necessarily be so tomorrow. The Day of Pentecost attests to God's gracious and incomprehensible freedom to redeem—take up and use—the diversity of languages for his purposes. Similarly, we suggest, God has the freedom to do this redemptive work with the various cultures and religions of the world.

But, further, we must also avoid any unqualified optimism, as critics of inclusivism have warned. Hence discussion of the redemption of the religions, even if understood in eschatological perspective, must provide guidelines for discerning engagement with them on this side of the eschaton. If our position is to avoid both a universalistic soteriology in which all people are finally saved (which we repudiate), and a blanket endorsement of the religions as already redeemed of God (which we reject), then what is the proper posture with which we should approach people of other faiths? For this task, we must be discerning not only of the many tongues (beliefs or doctrines) of other religious traditions, but also of their many practices. Let us outline a pentecostal and pneumatological approach to discerning the religions, then, that avoids the pitfalls identified above in the traditional approaches.

To begin, a pentecostal and pneumatological theology of religions underwrites an a posteriori approach to interreligious engagement. Just as in a congregational context, "Let two or three prophets speak, and let the others weigh what is said" (1 Cor 14:29), so also in the interfaith encounter: we must look and listen carefully before rendering judgment. The goal is to allow the tongues (testimonies) of other religious people to be heard first on their own "insider's" terms (just as we clamor to be heard on our terms). Any theology *of religions*, even a pneumatological one, must be deeply informed by the empirical reality of the religions, rather than be an a priori projection of the Christian imagination.

Second, a pentecostal and pneumatological theology of religions engages in critical analysis (discernment) of the religious phenomenon or teaching under scrutiny. Here we might bring to bear a multitude of disciplinary perspectives, being cautious about not imposing a reductionist interpretation on what we are attempting to discern. Also here, we attempt to compare and contrast what we are looking at or listening to with our Christian convictions (beliefs and practices).[60] Such analysis is not always straightforward. At one level, we might be attempting to compare very disparate realities, and if so, any conclusions will have missed the point.[61] Part of the task involves application of what might be called a "hermeneutics of charity" that attempts to empathize with the other faith perspective as much as possible from their point of view. Always at work, however, will be the Christian (and pentecostal) "hermeneutics of suspicion" (regarding the other faith) that is vigilant about the urgency of the gospel.

At some point in the discerning process, we might have to "come to a decision." So long as we remember that any such judgments are always provisional, subject to later confirmation (or not), we recognize that as historically situated beings, life requires that we discern the Holy Spirit's presence and activity to the best of our ability. Decision is followed by action. The hermeneutical circle requires, however, if we are to be honest, that we then reassess the process of discernment to see if we've missed the mark.

Many Tongues, Many Practices: Hospitality, Missions, and Interfaith Practices

We have suggested that a pentecostal-pneumatological perspective sheds new light on the perennial question of the one and the many in ways that allow us to affirm the diversity of tongues, cultures, and religions without being uncritical in our affirmation. We proposed that holding together our conviction about Christian faith amidst the many religions invites a posture of engagement and discernment. Now we expand on this by arguing that a pneumatological approach that begins with the many tongues of Pentecost opens up to the many practices of the empowering Spirit. More precisely, we

60. Yong describes the task of comparative theology in a religiously plural world in *Beyond the Impasse*, ch. 7.

61. The difficulties associated with obtaining adequate comparative categories across religious lines are discussed extensively throughout Neville, *Comparative Religious Ideas Project*.

argue that the Spirit of encounter is also the Spirit of hospitality, and that a pneumatological theology of hospitality nourishes many practices through which Christians can and need to bear witness to the gospel in a pluralistic world. We present this line of thought first by looking at the life of Jesus, and then that of the early church. As pentecostal theologians, we turn to the two volumes of Luke and Acts.[62]

Jesus himself can be understood both as the paradigmatic host of God's hospitality, and as the exemplary recipient of hospitality. From his conception in Mary's womb (by the Holy Spirit) to his birth in a manger through to his burial (in a tomb of Joseph of Arimathea), Jesus was dependent on the welcome and hospitality of others. As "the Son of Man has nowhere to lay his head" (Luke 9:58), he relied on the goodwill of many, staying in their homes and receiving whatever they served. But it is in his role as guest that Jesus also announces and enacts the hospitality of God. Empowered by the Spirit, he heals the sick, casts out demons, and declares the arrival of the reign of God in the midst of the downtrodden, the oppressed, and the marginalized. While he is the "journeying prophet" who eats at the tables of others, he also proclaims and brings to pass the eschatological banquet of God for all who are willing to receive it. So sometimes Jesus breaks the rules of hospitality, upsets the social conventions of meal fellowship (e.g., Jesus does not wash before dinner), and even goes so far as to rebuke his hosts. Luke thus shows that it is Jesus who is the broker of God's authority, and it is on this basis that Jesus establishes the inclusive hospitality of the kingdom to the marginalized of his day (women, children, and the "disabled").

This more inclusive vision of divine hospitality is most clearly seen in the parable of the good Samaritan (10:25–37). It is the Samaritan, the religious "other" of the first-century Jewish world, who fulfills the law, loves his neighbor, and embodies divine hospitality. What are the implications of this parable for contemporary interreligious relationships? Might those who are "others" to us Christians not only be instruments through whom God's revelation comes afresh, but also perhaps be able to fulfill the requirements for inheriting eternal life (10:25) precisely through the hospitality that they show to us, their neighbors?[63]

In Acts, the hospitality of God manifested in Jesus the anointed one (the Christ) is now extended through the early church by the power of the same Holy Spirit. As with Jesus, his followers are anointed by the Spirit to be guests and hosts, in either case representing the hospitality of God. St.

62. What follows condenses lengthier arguments in Yong's "Guests, Hosts, and the Holy Ghost," part I, and Yong, *Hospitality and the Other*, esp. chs. 2 and 4.

63. Yong probes these questions at greater length in *Spirit Poured Out on All Flesh*, 241–44.

Paul, for example, was both a recipient and conduit of God's hospitality. He was the beneficiary of divine hospitality through those who led him by the hand, Judas (on Straight Street), Ananias, other believers who helped him escape from conspiring enemies, and Barnabas. Then during his missionary journeys, he is a guest of Lydia, a new convert, and has his wounds treated by the Philippian jailer. Paul the traveling missionary is also a guest of Jason of Thessalonica, Prisca and Aquilla and Titius Justus at Corinth, Philip the evangelist (and his daughters) at Caesarea, Mnason in Jerusalem, and unnamed disciples at Troas, Tyre, Ptolemais, and Sidon, etc. Along the way, Paul is escorted by Bereans, protected by Roman centurions, and entertained by Felix the governor. During the storm threatening the voyage to Rome, Paul hosts the breaking of bread. After the shipwreck, Paul is a guest of the Maltese islanders (*barbaroi*, according to the original Greek of Acts 28:2) in general and of Publius the chief official in particular, and then later of some brothers on Puteoli. Acts closes with Paul as host, welcoming all who were open to receiving the hospitality of God. Throughout, Paul is the paradigmatic guest and host representing the practices of the earliest Christians who took the gospel to the ends of the earth by the power of the Holy Spirit.

The Spirit's empowerment to bear witness to the gospel takes the form of many different practices in the lives of Jesus and the early Christians, each related to being guests and hosts in various times and places. We suggest that these many practices of the Spirit are related to the diversity of tongues spoken on the Day of Pentecost. Even as the many tongues of the Spirit announce the redemptive hospitality of God, so also do the many works of the Spirit enact God's salvation through many hospitable practices. As believers interact with and receive the hospitality, kindness, and gifts of strangers of all sorts, even Samaritans, public or governmental officials, and "barbarians," a diversity of practices ensue. In short, many tongues require many hospitable practices because of the church's mission in a pluralistic world.

How do these many practices redeem the traditional theologies of exclusivism, inclusivism, and pluralism? We suggest that a Lukan, pentecostal, and pneumatological theology of hospitality allows us to retrieve and reappropriate the wide range of practices implicit in these models without having to endorse the full scope of their theological assertions. From the pluralist perspective, for example, an emphasis on social justice is prevalent in Jesus' concerns for the poor and the marginalized, and in the Spirit's producing a new community, the church, in which the traditional barriers of class, gender, and ethnicity no longer hold; but pluralism's "all roads lead to God" idea can be rejected. The inclusivist insistence on recognizing the possibility of divine revelation and activity among the unevangelized is likewise preserved, especially given the pentecostal conviction regarding the miraculous gift of the Spirit that enables understanding amidst the cacophony of many tongues; at the same time, inclusivism's crypto-imperialistic stance can be recognized and guarded against. And finally, the exclusivist commitment to the proclamation of the gospel is upheld since authentic hospitality is redemptive, and this includes declaration of the gospel in the proper time and place; but exclusivism's triumphalism and arrogance can be rejected. In short, the practices of the models are redeemed without their theological and attitudinal liabilities.

Hence, a pneumatological theology of hospitality empowers a much wider range of interreligious practices more conducive to meeting the demands of our time. This is in part because Christians often find themselves as guest or as hosts, sometimes (as in the lives of Jesus and Paul) simultaneously. In these various circumstances, there are many sociocultural protocols that will inform Christian practices. Sometimes, Christians will defer to their hosts, embodying epistemic humility, and in the process be enriched by their interactions with people of other faiths. In other cases, Christians are hosts, with the responsibility to care for their guests of other faiths, and to do so at the many levels at which such care can be given (the physical, the material, the intellectual, the spiritual, etc.). In all cases, however, the conventions of hospitality will resist imperialistic approaches or better-than-thou attitudes, even as such conventions mediate honest dialogue and mutual interaction.

Perhaps most importantly, a pentecostal-pneumatological approach to theology of religions opens up to the kinds of Christian practices through which Christians themselves are transformed and even saved. A parallel parable to the good Samaritan is that of the sheep and the goats (Matt 25:31–46), and in this case, the salvation of the sheep was mediated by their ministering to Jesus through their encounter with the poor, the naked, the hungry, and those in prison. Of course, many people of faith, both Christian and non-Christian, are poor, hungry, and marginalized. Will we who have experienced the redemptive hospitality of God in turn show hospitality to such people? And if so, the Spirit has surely empowered us to bear witness to the gospel in these encounters. But at the same time, such hospitable interactions become the means of the Spirit to lavish on us the ongoing salvific hospitality of God. In these cases, rather than "looking down" on those in other faiths because we have something they don't, we are ourselves in a position similar to that of the Jewish man by the wayside in the parable of the good Samaritan: thankful to the God of Jesus Christ for revealing himself to us and saving us by the power of the Holy Spirit in and through the lives of our many neighbors in a pluralistic world.

We have suggested that pentecostal missiology, theology of religions, and interreligious encounter and dialogue are or ought to be interrelated and interdependent. These important disciplines should not be developed or practiced in isolation. Further, we have suggested that fresh and vigorous pentecostal-pneumatological insights, while building upon long-standing classical commitments, yield exciting possibilities for their theological development and practical implementation. Continuity and creativity here may be integrated and applied profitably. While existing conceptual categories—such as exclusivism, pluralism, and inclusivism—are relatively helpful, the conversation needs to be able to move past those boundaries to explore potentially fertile regions beyond. The challenge for today is for pentecostal scholars, missionaries, theologians, dialogue participants, and others to move forward into the future under the powerful anointing of the Holy Spirit.

CHAPTER 6

From Demonization to Kin-domization

The Witness of the Spirit and the Renewal of Missions in a Pluralistic World

THIS CONCLUDING CHAPTER BUILDS upon the theologies of mission suggested in the preceding chapters, but goes beyond them to attempt to adjudicate the urgent missiological questions.[1] We will attempt to chart the way forward to viable theological views regarding interreligious interactions in the twenty-first century, especially as these might enable the renewal and reinvigoration of mission in the present pluralistic age. To do so, we begin by confronting squarely the discourses of demonization so prevalent in renewal circles.[2] The central and longest part of these concluding pages will suggest, in dialogue with the authors of the preceding chapters, a series of antidemonization strategies for renewal missiology from the book of Acts. The emergent result, I proffer, is a "kin-domization" model that counters the discursive rhetoric of demonization and does so by anticipating the formation of the new people of God beyond the historical divisions that have separated humankind. Such is the eschatological community that is reflected in the miracle of human communication manifested in the Day

1. [As this is the concluding chapter to Yong and Clarke, eds., *Global Renewal, Religious Pluralism, Great Commission*, I will insert notes with the titles of the other chapters when reference is made to them in what follows.]

2. My use of "renewal" and its cognates in what follows is inclusive of classical pentecostalism, neo-pentecostalism, the charismatic movement, and those from other related revival and revitalization movements in the Euro-American West and across the global South that feature charismatic spirituality and phenomenology.

of Pentecost narrative in the book of Acts, and that is unfolded in the relationality and mutuality of the apostolic encounter with those in other faiths.

DEMONIZATION AND THE RELIGIOUS OTHER: THE CHALLENGE FOR RENEWAL MISSIOLOGY

Renewalists have always presumed a demonology from their plain reading of the Bible. While this is neither the time nor the place to undertake a critical analysis of such ideas,[3] it is important to note that renewal demonology resonates with and maps onto much of the cosmological intuitions of populations in the global South. Hence practices like exorcism, deliverance, and spiritual warfare are prominent in certain renewal circles. When enacted vis-à-vis the interreligious encounter, however, such demonological discursive practices are problematic and, in some cases, lethal.

For example, one potentially explosive form of renewalist engagement with the pluralistic public square of late modernity involves the political demonization of the opposition party or opposing candidate that is from the "other" religious tradition. Given the dualistic framework of much of renewal cosmology, Jesus' words, "Whoever is not with me is against me" (Luke 11:23) lend themselves to the conclusion that the non-Christian option receives its mandate, empowerment, and agenda from the prince of darkness himself.[4] Yet this can be taken even further, as when the rhetoric and cosmology of demonization is extended to provide theological legitimation for egregious political and military activity. The most prominent example concerns the Sandinista government of Ríos Montt in Guatemala in the early 1980s.[5] Montt, at that time, had testified of a pentecostal conversion, and submitted himself to the spiritual advisement of a neo-pentecostal church. In response to the accusations of human rights atrocities committed against the indigenous people of Guatemala by Montt's army, Verbo Church pastors said: "The Army doesn't massacre the Indians. It massacres demons, the Indians are demon possessed; they are communists. We hold Brother Efraín Ríos Montt like King David of the Old Testament. He is the king of

---

3. I provide such a critical account partly in ch. 4 of my *In the Days of Caesar*. [See also Yong, *Spirit of Creation*, ch. 5, and Kärkkäinen et al., *Interdisciplinary and Religio-Cultural Discourses*.]

4. Meyer, "Power of Money," esp. 32–33.

5. I present an overview of the issues in my *Spirit Poured Out on All Flesh*, 35–37. Regrettably, I did not then come out forcefully against the crimes that Montt's government perpetrated against the indigenous people of Guatemala.

the New Testament."[6] At a broader level, as this quotation suggests, such reasoning also serves as theological justification for international military operations, whether in the past against the Muslim infidels (during the Crusades) or against the advance of communism and socialism (during the Cold War era) or in the present at the vanguard of American-led forays into the Muslim-dominated Middle Eastern arena.[7] At this point the lines between the American renewal movement and the wider evangelical and conservative Christian "right" become blurred. Unfortunately, renewalists have, in general, supported such political agendas with their own distinctive theological rationales rather than prophetically protested against these developments.

Cephas Omenyo's chapter on renewal in West Africa also is suggestive for understanding how renewal demonology engages with a pluralistic world with violent consequences, even when not specifically sanctioned by the political powers that be.[8] The Nigerian case especially invites further comment.[9] The emergence of renewal churches and Christians in Nigeria during the last thirty years has complicated an already hotly contested interreligious arena. Besides revitalizing Christianity in general in terms of competing for the allegiance of the Christian faithful with historic Protestant and Roman Catholic churches in Nigeria, renewalists have also aggressively engaged the interreligious arena. On the one hand, they have picked up on earlier missionary polemics against African traditional religions, to the point of being very concerned that even the retrieval of African culture— e.g., such as occurred at FESTAC 1977 (the 2nd Black and African Festival of Arts and Culture)—was and would be "an open door to the demonic" in terms of reinstilling the covenants with the indigenous religious traditions and their spiritual entities.[10] On the other hand, renewalists are not only

6. Diamond, *Spiritual Warfare*, 166, quoting from *Sectas y religiosidad en America Latina* (October 1984), 23.

7. At the popular level, few pentecostals would question this statement: "The US military machine was God's way of defending the peace so that his message of salvation could be made known. Washington's adversaries around the world therefore continue to be God's adversaries, and evangelizing the world continues to hinge on US power"; see Stoll, *Is Latin America Turning Protestant?*, 67. For an account of the gradual transformation of the Assemblies of God in the USA from a pacifist denomination into one supporting an idolatrous form of nationalism and its accompanying militarism, see Alexander, *Peace to War*.

8. [See Omenyo, "Renewal, Christian Mission, and Encounter with the Other."]

9. This and the next paragraph are adapted from my *Hospitality and the Other*, 25–27.

10. Thompson, "Rising from Mediocre to Miraculous," esp. 26–28. For more coverage of this issue, see Hackett, "Discourses of Demonization in Africa and Beyond," and

countering the Islamization of Nigeria, but have sought to do so by evangelizing both the nation and, as we have seen in renowned evangelist Reinhard Bonnke's "Africa for Christ" crusades, the entire continent.[11]

For our purposes, it is important to note not just the fact of the renewalist commitment to mission and evangelism, but the tactics and, especially, rhetoric that is often employed. The inflammatory nature of renewalist modes of evangelization can be identified at multiple levels. First, renewal "political theology" is based not on political action but on fasting, prayer, spiritual warfare, and even exorcism and deliverance ministries against the principalities, powers, and covenants of the heavenly realms.[12] Following from this, second, there is the consistent demonization not only of African religions but also of Islam in renewalist literature. For renewalists, Ishmael is outside the covenant, born out of the Abraham's lack of faith to Hagar "the bondwoman" (cf. Gal 4:22–31), Mohammad is not a prophet but an epileptic and womanizer, and Allah is not the supreme God but one of 360 in the Ka'abah of pre-Islamic Arabia; hence, Islam is idolatry, Muslims are caught up "in Satan's bondage," and renewalists reject as demonic core Islamic symbols such as the moon, the star, and Islamic rituals.[13] Third, and perhaps most provocative in terms of its practical effects, renewalists have employed the full range of media and technology in their evangelism campaigns—loud speaker public address systems, cassettes, videos, CDs, DVDs, radio, TV, the Internet—all of which not only clearly publicize the renewalist understanding of other religions but also generate new forms of interreligious animosity and hostility.[14] Of course, such defamatory literature and media communications are also now being produced by Muslims, but the result is an intensification of interreligious "hate" rhetoric that fur-

---

the work of Ogbu U. Kalu—e.g., "Estranged Bedfellows?"

11. Thus the back cover of Olonade, *Battle Cry for the Nations,* announces that the book is designed to mobilize the church to evangelize the "unreached millions" caught up in "idolatry and Islam."

12. Kalu, *Power, Poverty and Prayer,* ch. 5.

13. See Brouwer et al., *Exporting American Gospel,* 173–75; Hackett, "Radical Christian Revivalism in Nigeria and Ghana," esp. 252; Hackett, "Managing or Manipulating Religious Conflict in Nigerian Media," esp. 58; Marshall-Fratani, "Mediating Global and Local in Nigerian Pentecostalism," esp. 102–3; Kalu, "Sharia and Islam in Nigerian Pentecostal Rhetoric, 1970–2003," esp. 256–58; and Ojo, "American Pentecostalism and Growth of Pentecostal-Charismatic Movements in Nigeria," esp. 167. The reference to "Satan's bondage" is in Gifford, *New Crusaders,* 111, while the renewalist assertion that Allah is not the supreme God builds on the highly polemical book by a Muslim convert, Moshay, *Who is This Allah?*

14. See Hackett, "Devil Bustin' Satellites." Thanks to Professor Hackett for sending me a draft copy of this paper before publication.

ther destabilizes the region rather than provides a platform for building a harmonious multifaith Nigeria.[15] Partly as a result of such developments, set within the sociopolitical and economic backdrop of an otherwise extremely contested Christian-Muslim public space, there have followed a series of serious and tragic violent conflicts particularly in the Muslim-dominated regions of northern Nigeria.[16]

In her chapter, Kirsteen Kim also calls attention to the violence attending some of the interreligious interactions in the South Asian context.[17] The enactment of martyrdom in the name of religion and in the call for liberation and emancipation highlight the potential that the rhetoric of demonization can play in such extreme political environments. On the one hand, the martyrs are resisting the oppressiveness under which they and their peoples are burdened, and such situations of injustice certainly must be called demonic. On the other hand, the radical acts of martyrdom also surely should be interpreted as a manifestation of the demonic character of reality that must be otherwise opposed with the full range of nonviolent means of resistance (instead of passive resignation at the hands of violent perpetrators). Renewalists find themselves across this spectrum of responses, and not infrequently engage in their own theological analyses of the demonic character of their political experiences.

As people of the book, like most other Protestant Christians, renewalists believe their notions about the demonic are scripturally grounded. The biblical categories that divide the light from the darkness, good from evil, and the children of God from the children of the devil are certainly present across the pages of especially the New Testament.[18] Missiologically, this leads practically to an understanding that only believers in Christ (i.e., converts) are children of light, while all others (i.e., nonconverts) remain children of darkness.[19] With regard to the interfaith encounter, then, a similar theme emerges: only followers of Christ are the children of God, while people of

15. Toyin Falola points out that in light of the emerging Muslim literary and media propaganda, some renewalists have sought to rationalize hate crimes in religious terms: "the holy books provide psychological support for all sorts of crimes, including murder" (*Violence in Nigeria*, 264).

16. I detail and discuss these in my *Hospitality and the Other*, 16–19.

17. [See Kim, "Theologies of Religious Pluralism."]

18. I have taken up this issue at some length in my article focused on the Gospel of John: "'Light Shines in the Darkness.'"

19. This is the gist of Birgit Meyer's analysis that focuses on the Christian mission to convert the heathen by insisting that they do what is indicated in the main title of her by now almost-classic essay: "'Make a Complete Break with the Past.'"

other false religions should only be evangelized, if not engaged with other more forceful strategies of missionization and even Christianization.

To be sure, few if any contemporary texts in renewal missiology either utilize this rhetoric of demonization or advocate its corollary missional practices. However the problem persists at least at the following two levels: (1) in the popular arena, lay renewalists continue to imbibe a remnant mentality that situates themselves over and against those not within their own group amidst an apocalyptic understanding of the impending eschatological conflagration between the forces of light and of darkness, and (2) even among the ecclesiastical hierarchy, many of whom are involved in organizing, mobilizing, and securing funding for mission projects and ventures, the dualistic world view of the New Testament narratives implicitly informs the renewal self-understanding of having to engage in spiritual warfare "against the rulers, against the authorities, against the cosmic powers of this present darkness, against the spiritual forces of evil in the heavenly places" (Eph 6:12). These renewal demonologies need to be critically interrogated, especially for the purposes of constructing a more relevant theology of mission in a religiously plural world.

THE MISSIOLOGY OF RENEWAL AND THE RENEWAL OF MISSIOLOGY: APOSTOLIC INSIGHTS IN A PLURALISTIC WORLD

In this section I sketch a renewal missiology that simultaneously serves to renew the Christian mission in a pluralistic twenty-first century. Such a renewal, I proffer, proceeds less from a polemical demonization of religious others than it does from a respectful, even deferential posture toward them, albeit one informed deeply by theological convictions rather than merely driven by pragmatic or politically correct concerns. In order to accomplish this objective, I want to bring the perspectives registered by the authors in this book into dialogue with Luke, especially his narrative of the earliest or apostolic Christian encounter with religious diversity in the book of Acts.[20] On the one hand, I recognize that there is a dualistic strain even in Acts, which accents evangelistic urgency precisely to turn people "from darkness to light and from the power of Satan to God" (Acts 26:18), even as I also

20. My work has repeatedly focused on the Acts narrative not only because this second Lukan volume has been, historically, the canon within the canon for renewal spirituality and theology, but also because of the renewal restorationist hermeneutic that has consistently sought to enter into the apostolic experience of the earliest Christians. For more on the use of Acts for the purposes of renewal theology, see my *In the Days of Caesar*, chs. 3.1–3.2.

realize that Paul confronts Elymas, the shaman on the island of Cyprus, as a "son of the devil, [an] enemy of all righteousness, full of all deceit and villainy" (Acts 13:10), and that he later exorcises evil spirits from the Jewish sons of Sceva (Acts 19:13–16). On the other hand, I believe that this strategy of demonization is neither dominant in the Acts narrative nor that it best describes the early Christian encounter with those in other religions. In the following, I focus on five occasions of apostolic interaction with people of other faiths,[21] highlighting especially the practical dimensions of such encounters.[22] This will set the stage for the discussion in the final section, when we draw some overarching theological and missiological conclusions. We proceed in reverse, arguing from the end of Acts to the beginning of the book.

Acts 28

The first part of this chapter describes the encounter between Paul and his travel companions with the Maltese islanders, which Luke identifies (in the original Greek) as βαρβαροι, transliterated as "barbarians" (Acts 28:2, 4). Three observations are especially noteworthy vis-à-vis a renewal missiology in a pluralistic world. First, there is no explicit reference to the proclamation of the *kerygma* in this passage. This means neither that such did not occur nor that there were no conversions to Christ (although the text is equally silent about that as well). Second, Paul and his comrades are repeatedly described in this passage as having received the hospitality of the barbarian islanders (Acts 28:2, 7, 10). Third, whereas elsewhere in Acts the apostles had resisted obeisance from those who thought them deserving of gestures usually reserved for deity or had strongly corrected misapprehensions by pagans about their divinity (i.e., Acts 10:25–26, 14:11–18), in this case, there is no noted response to the islanders thinking that Paul, because he had escaped death expected from a snakebite, was divine (Acts 28:3–6). This indicates that while often Christians find themselves as hosts of people in other faiths—an important set of interreligious practices—equally important but often neglected is a theological self-understanding that involves consideration of how to be guests in the presence of religious others. The

21. The following discussions of Acts 28, 19, 17, 7–8, and 6 condenses but also expands my discussions, in reverse order, in *Who is the Holy Spirit?*, chs. 14, 16, 18, 33, 35, and 39.

22. My focus on practices derives from my convictions regarding their centrality—over and against more abstract theological or theoretical emphases—for renewal missiology; see my essays, "Spirit, Christian Practices, and Religions," "The Spirit of Hospitality," and "Inviting Spirit."

combined missiological effect of this passage should not be underestimated. While there are certainly occasions for overt proclamation of the gospel, Christians need to be sensitive to their missional contexts and, especially when being guests of those in other faiths, need to interact with their hosts in ways that are respectful of their traditions. This does not undermine the variegated expressions of the Christian mission, in the Maltese case involving the ministry of healing the sick (Acts 28:8–9).

What I find remarkable is that whereas much of the history of Christian missions has demonized pagans and barbarians of the world, in this text, Paul and his fellow missionaries receive the generosity of their Maltese hosts instead. There is no indication of any suspicion regarding the islanders and their gifts. There is an authentic mutuality: the hosts opened up their homes and gave of their possessions to the visitors and the latter ministered healing to the former in turn. Although it may have been that Paul and his friends simply found themselves as guests of these barbarians because of the shipwreck and hence cannot be said to ever have intended to engage in the formal evangelization of the island, these developments highlight the importance of being ready, as Christians, to be hosted by those in other faiths. In fact, in a globally shrinking world of massive immigration, exile, and refugee experiences, more often than not we find ourselves cast in the presence of religious others without ever having asked to be put in those situations. So even in stable societies, Christians need to pause and ask themselves: how often do we put ourselves in the position of being invited over as guests of folk in other religions? There is a form of relationality and neighborliness that Paul manifests in his encounter with the Maltese pagans that should model for us the character of the missionary posture that anticipates the coming of the Day of the Lord in which the hostilities between human beings will be no more.

Further, the value of Luke's discussion of Paul's shipwreck on Malta is especially lifted up in light of Clifton Clarke's urging that we take non-Western and non-Enlightenment epistemologies, traditions, and perspectives into account.[23] Clarke's focus is on the African continent, in particular on the import of African world views, use of symbolisms, and cultural orality. The Lukan missiology of guests would invite further consideration of how to defer to local norms and ways of knowing in articulating and living out the Christian faith. Such a call for contextualization, however, is not limited to what occurs only in the global South, as in Clarke's example. Rather, I would suggest that the contextualization of the gospel of Christ is a universal phenomenon and obligation, one that begins and is reflected in

23. [Clarke, "Dialogue or Diatribe," esp. 32–37.]

the apostolic experience itself. In this case, then, other religious traditions are not just "objects" to be overcome, but realities to be respected, carefully engaged, and even received as guests in certain contexts. To be sure, on some occasions, the proper Christian response is a discerning rejection of that local reality; on other occasions, however, what Walter Hollenweger calls a theologically responsible syncretism is the appropriate result, when the gospel is enriched by the local cultural forms, even as the latter are transformed in light of the power of the Spirit.[24]

Acts 19

The riot in Ephesus described in the last half of this chapter is the occasion that provides us with another glimpse of how the early Christians encountered other religions. In this case, the economy of Ephesus was being shaken by the growth and expansion of the messianic community. Not only had conversions to Christ resulted in the rejection of the magical practices that had been prominent in that community, but the local economy had also suffered in the process since sales of the silver shrines of Artemis had plummeted. Part of the accusation by the craftsmen, intended to rile up the crowd in defense of Artemis and against Paul and his missionary friends, was that "Paul has persuaded and drawn away a considerable number of people by saying that gods made with hands are not gods" (Acts 19:26). Yet the response of the city clerk, intended to quiet the mob, was equally straightforward: "You have brought these men here who are neither temple-robbers nor blasphemers of our goddess" (Acts 19:37). On the one hand, the accusations of the craftsmen may have been true in some respect—after all, Paul had said elsewhere that, "no idol in the world really exists" (1 Cor 8:4); on the other hand, it is also clear that the clerk's insistence that more formal charges be brought to try the missionaries never materialized, and in that sense, the apostles were vindicated as having been deferential, or at least nonblasphemous, in their approaches to the cult of Artemis. Rather than demonizing Artemis or her cult, the Christian mission to Ephesus appears to have been conducted with respect vis-à-vis the pagan deities.

Renewalists have a good deal to learn about being respectful of the beliefs and even practices of those in other faiths from this account. On the one hand, public expressions of faith in Christ are by no means out of order, as the burning of books devoted to magical practices attests (Acts

---

24. See Hollenweger, *Pentecostalism*, ch. 11. I address some aspects of the complex issues of culture and syncretism for missiology in my articles "Culture" and "Syncretism" in Corrie, *Dictionary of Mission Theology*.

19:18–19). On the other hand, such practices can and did, in this case, occur quite apart from irreverent polemics against other religious traditions and their practices, doctrines, and even deities. For purposes of thinking theologically and missionally about the religions, the task of negative apologetics—being against or tearing down the religious others' beliefs and practices—is less important than is a positive witness to the transformative power of the gospel. Our goal is not to exacerbate interreligious enmities but to be sufficiently deferential in order to establish dialogical relationships with those in other faiths.

Further, Steven Studebaker's claim that the religions are culturally situated is also pertinent vis-à-vis this account of what transpired at Ephesus.[25] Studebaker's argument is that insofar as the religions are constituted at least in part by wider cultural realities, to that same extent the universal presence and activity of the Spirit in such wider cultural domains suggests the presence and activity of the Spirit in the religions as well. The Acts narrative acknowledges the complex and interrelated nature of religion and economics at Ephesus. Not only does religion, especially its conversion dynamics, have an economic dimension, but economics also has religious implications and consequences. In short, any theology of religions, such as that proposed by Studebaker, must be consistent with theological reflection on the various domains that comprise human life, including not only the economic but also the social and the political, among others.[26]

Acts 17

Luke's discussion of Paul at the Areopagus has, of course, been consistently mined for missiological insights. Here, let me make only the following observations before bringing the discussion into dialogue with the proposals of Richie and Kärkkäinen.[27] First, Luke repeatedly highlights Paul's dialogical approach. Thus the word διελεγετο, often translated into English as "argued" (Acts 17:17), can also be translated as "dialogued," as it includes both the disputative and conversational character of Paul's exchanges with the Athenians. Second, as perennially noted, Paul enters into the discussion with the Epicurean and Stoic thinkers on their own philosophical terrain, quoting from their own poets and authorities (Acts 17: 28). Most

25. [Studebaker, "Christian Mission and Religions."]

26. For further elaboration on the interconnectedness of these theological domains, see my *Spirit-Word-Community*, parts II and III. [See also Studebaker, *From Pentecost to the Triune God*, esp. ch. 7, for further development of these theology of religions ideas.]

27. [See Richie, "Wide Reach of the Spirit," and Kärkkäinen, "*Dukkha* and *Passio*."]

importantly for our purposes, however, is that Paul articulates an inclusive theology, cosmology, and anthropology, one that does not divide the world between "us" and "them" but which suggests that the unknown god of the Athenians was the God of Jesus Christ, and that emphasizes the one world (Acts 17:24, 26) and the common humanity between himself and his heathen interlocutors (Acts 17:25, 27). From this Paul approvingly quotes from pagan sources, "*we* are God's offspring" (Acts 17:29, my italics), in a way which binds him and his interlocutors together. Paul thus begins with the theological and anthropological common ground: humankind is one family, children of the one God.

All of this is consistent with our preceding deliberations from Acts 19 and 28, including Clarke's advocacy of contextualization of local traditions,[28] even if in this case St. Paul engages with what later emerged as being part of the dominant philosophical tradition of the Western world. As important, rather than mocking the Athenians, deprecating their idolatry, or demonizing their theological ideas, Paul's approach to the religious traditions of the Athenians is to treat their beliefs and practices with respect, albeit firmly also suggesting alternate ways of understanding these realities as well. Hence witness is borne through the Spirit regarding the possibility of overcoming the estrangement that divides family members from each other.

What, then, are the implications of this Lukan passage for the contemporary interreligious encounter? I see at least two lines of convergences with the proposals made in this book. First, Richie's advocacy of an inclusivist approach to the religions deserves comment in light of these developments at the Areopagus.[29] For Richie, theological inclusivism is pneumatologically expansive but christologically tethered, ecclesiologically connected, and missionally driven. Such an inclusivist vision is, arguably, Lukan and Pauline, at least as refracted in this text. The inclusive theology, cosmology, and anthropology recorded as proclaimed to the Athenian philosophers nevertheless neither presumed a chasm between synagogue (where the believers gathered) and marketplace (Acts 17:17), nor neglected the judgment of God appointed through the man who was raised from the dead (Acts 17:31). It is precisely such an inclusivist dynamic that allows for open and honest but also respectful encounter between the religions. Without common ground, there would be no possibility of encounter; but without differences, there would be nothing to discuss.[30]

28. [Clarke, "Dialogue or Diatribe."]

29. [Richie, "Wide Reach of the Spirit."]

30. Richie has developed his theology of interreligious dialogue further in his *Speaking by the Spirit.*

Kärkkäinen's chapter presents a clear example of how the interreligious dialogue can proceed, which can be profitably compared and contrasted with Paul's dialogical strategy.[31] First, Kärkkäinen proceeds carefully and contextually, focused on the Southeast Asian Theravadan Buddhist contexts, and thus is mindful about Theravadan Buddhists, texts, concerns, and issues. His chapter is a model of respectful and deferential engagement with the religious other at least initially on its own terms, rather than by imposing a Christian interpretive framework.[32] Second, such serious interaction with local voices and perspectives is not then left to its own, but taken up within the response of the gospel. What I mean here is that Theravadan Buddhist concerns call forth a renewal response, but one that heeds the insights of the former. What emerges is a renewal theology of suffering, a theme not otherwise given much attention by renewalists because of a triumphalism that usually overlooks (at best) or suppresses (at worst) such realities. But, finally, the result nevertheless allows the gospel to speak forth, albeit this time within the resonances of the Southeast Asian Theravadan Buddhist self-understanding. Thus Buddhist *apatheia* encounters, informs, and is transformed by renewal *orthopathos* in the process. Hence here we have a genuine dialogue, one that unfolds as a theologically responsible syncretism, on the one hand taking up the indigenous religious concerns but on the other hand enabling the good news of divine, redemptive, and integrative healing to be registered in local idiom. In the process, Christians and Buddhists learn how to meet each other potentially as equals, at least in their common humanity, and even perhaps in anticipation of the eschatological community that will be full of surprises for both sides.[33]

31. [Kärkkäinen, "*Dukkha* and *Passio*."]

32. This importance of this approach is discussed and debated in my coauthored essay with Frank D. Macchia, Ralph Del Colle, and Dale T. Irvin, "Christ and Spirit."

33. My own attempts to engage with Buddhist traditions include the following essays: "Technologies of Liberation"; "The Holy Spirit and World Religions"; "Christian and Buddhist Perspectives"; "Buddhist-Christian Encounter in the USA"; "Mind and Life, Religion and Science"; and "From Azusa Street to Bo Tree and Back." Two book-length proposals are in the making. [These have now been published as Yong, *Pneumatology and Christian-Buddhist Dialogue*, and *Cosmic Breath*; "Buddhist-Christian Encounter in the USA" is reprinted as ch. 8 of this book, and "Mind and Life, Religion and Science" has been reprinted as ch. 8 of my *Dialogical Spirit*.]

Acts 8–7

The expansion of the gospel into Samaria as recounted in Acts 8 is not often viewed as an interreligious encounter.[34] While the narrative is dominated by the apostolic interaction with Simon Magus, we need first to emphasize that the antagonism between Jews and Samaritans was so palpable—i.e., John mentions that "Jews do not share things in common with Samaritans" (John 4:9)—that they can be considered to have inhabited, by the time of the first century, two distinct religious traditions. In fact, things had so degenerated between Jews and Samaritans that the former had already begun to engage in the rhetorical demonization of the latter; thus does John record the Jewish leadership's polemic against Jesus: "you are a Samaritan and have a demon" (John 8:48)! Yet Philip, when driven out of Jerusalem by persecution, did not (perhaps unlike the other deacons and leaders) avoid Samaria. More pointedly, Philip did not evade Simon, well known as a powerful religious leader (Acts 8:10–11), but fairly engaged his world.

I suggest, however, that there is more involved in the mission to Samaria than simply the miraculous signs and wonders among the Samaritans and their conversion, as important as these are. Rather, when it is understood that Jews and Samaritans had different theological self-understandings, and that within these theological schemes the place of worship of the one true God was centrally important and served as a dividing theological line—with Jews worshiping at Jerusalem and Samaritans at Mount Gerizim (John 4:20–22)—then Stephen's speech before the Sanhedrin illuminates how the mission to Samaria can be understood as transforming the early Jewish messianic theology as well. This is because Stephen, as a Hellenist Jew, had come to see that the Jewish insistence on localizing the presence and activity of God in the temple at Jerusalem reflected a parochial theological viewpoint. Instead, God did not dwell in local temples, nor was God's domain geographically or regionally limited (Acts 7:48–49). It was this radical theological revisioning that made it possible, I suggest, for Philip, another Hellenist, to venture out into Samaria, in contrast with the other Judean apostolic leaders who stayed put in Jerusalem (Acts 8:1), perhaps because they had more conservative or classical Jewish views that restricted the divine presence and activity. It was also this thorough theological reconstruction that enabled Philip to preach Christ, not just a place, and to insist that the apostles come up to Samaria rather than that the converted Samaritans go down to Jerusalem.

---

34. I treat it as such in my *Spirit Poured Out on All Flesh*, 241–44.

Put more strongly, might it be more appropriately suggested that it was precisely the possibility if not the actuality of the gospel in Samaritan dress, shorn of its Jerusalemite centeredness and presuppositions, that inspired Stephen's own theological transformation and, eventually and unfortunately, brought about his martyrdom? Is it possible to see that whereas the Jews had rejected as demonic the Samaritan idea of worship at Mount Gerizim, it was precisely the Samaritan intuition about true worship not being bound to Jerusalem that was central to the Hellenistic Jewish-Christian insight into the universal scope of the work of the God of Jesus Christ, and that motivated the expansion of the Christian mission beyond the confines of Judea toward Samaria initially and then later to the ends of the earth?

Again, these insights highlight the importance of the proposals of Clifton Clarke and Veli-Matti Kärkkäinen to allow the perspectives and voices of religious others to be heard on their terms.[35] What are the possibilities for the effective and powerful witness of the gospel when spoken according to the terms, categories, idioms, and commitments of the world's religious traditions? My suggestion is that just as Samaritan theology, deemed demonic by traditional Jews, can be understood to have provided a critical perspective on the received Jewish theological understanding, so also can the religious traditions of the world, similarly demonized as were the Samaritans from the Jewish point of view, provide critical but no less helpful perspectives for understanding the gospel amidst the pluralistic realities of the twenty-first century. If this is the case, the religions are less demonic realities to be overcome—without denying that there are demonic elements in all religious traditions, including within institutional Christianity itself—than they are invitations to understand the potentiality of the gospel to transform the world. People in other faiths, then, are also less opponents or enemies to be overcome (or destroyed!), than there are potential friends, even family members, if our hearts might first be converted to them.[36]

Acts 6

Going back before Philip's mission to Samaria and Stephen's speech and martyrdom, we come upon the series of events that drew them both

---

35. [Clarke, "Dialogue or Diatribe," and Kärkkäinen, "*Dukkha* and *Passio*."]

36. Thus, for example, Peter experienced conversion on two fronts in his encounter with Cornelius in Acts 9–10: first a conversion that allowed him to enter into the home of an unclean Gentile, and then second, a conversion that allowed him to embrace the Gentile as an equal, despite the fact that this Gentile remained a Gentile rather than becoming a Jew. See Maimela, "Practice of Mission and Evangelism."

together initially. We meet both Philip and Stephen first as Hellenists, probably from Asia Minor (Acts 6:5). They had somehow been drawn into Judea, with their families and many others, it appears, and gotten caught up in the new messianic movement. What emerged given the explosion of this new movement was, literally, an intercultural phenomenon. If we follow Studebaker's assertion regarding the overlapping of religion and culture,[37] then this sequence of developments demands closer scrutiny vis-à-vis the interreligious encounter.

What we see is that all intercultural encounters are fraught with pitfalls. The Hebraic Jewish widows and the Hellenist Jewish widows at first could not work things out. The emergent conflicts were no doubt felt and interpreted by some as of demonic provenance. The details are sketchy about where the disagreements lay,[38] but I suggest that there were not only linguistic barriers, cultural differences, and economic disparities but also theological dissonances, and these are no doubt sometimes understood spiritually and, hence, demonically. The last aspect, the religious and theological dimension, unfolded in the opposition to the Hellenist deaconship of Stephen by other Hellenists with very traditional Jewish commitments (Acts 6:9–10). This was a particularly contentious issue, even demonic, especially when viewed in light of the end of the story that saw the martyrdom of Stephen. But even such highly polemical encounters have a redemptive dimension, and since I have already commented on the potential such intercultural encounters have for the cross-fertilization and transformation of theological understandings, I will say no more about the matter here.

What I want to highlight in this passage, however, is that which is lifted up when read in the context of Kirsteen Kim's discussion of Dalit Christianity in India.[39] As Kim notes in her chapter, renewal Christianity has taken root among the Dalits, even if the results have been mixed. While in many cases Dalits have experienced uplift as a result of conversion to Christianity, in just as many other cases the older oppressions and prejudices have resurfaced within renewal churches.[40] So, on the one hand, renewal Christianity has contributed in some respects to the liberation of the untouchables in India, but on the other hand, renewal churches have also not been immune to being co-opted by the forces of oppression operating at the cultural, political, social, and economic levels. What Luke's report in Acts 6 challenges

37. [Studebaker, "Christian Missions and the Religions."]

38. A full discussion of all the complex social, historical, cultural, and other issues is Finger, *Of Widows and Meals*.

39. [Kim, "Theologies of Religious Pluralism."]

40. I discuss Dalit renewal in my *Spirit Poured Out on All Flesh*, 54–58.

renewalists to do is to follow through with the egalitarian commitments at the heart of the Pentecost narrative—which levels out the hierarchicalism between men and women, old and young, and slave and free (Acts 2:17–18)—and put the minorities in charge! Who the minorities are will vary from context to context, whether considered numerically or demographically, culturally, economically, socially, or theologically.

In the Judean context, the minorities were the Hellenists from the surrounding Mediterranean world. Some might argue in hindsight that this may have been a mistake, that to put Hellenists in charge of food distribution to both Hellenist and Hebraic widows was to just ask for further divisiveness, resulting in the failed experiment of what some have considered as an early Christian form of communism. I will debate neither the merits nor demerits of such possibilities. More important for our purposes, however, are the intercultural and interreligious implications for the formation of ecclesial communities and for Christian witness, mission, and evangelization. This early messianic community had the potential to model the relationality and mutuality of the coming Day of Lord in ways that invited deference to the leadership and even authority of those initially outside the community of faith. In short, putting minorities in charge not only invites a letting go of power, an elevation of the other, a respectful interface, and a meaningful interdependence, but also a expresses a willingness to allow the identity of the community to be transformed by the influx of outside differences. This had the potential to transform the inequalities of the first-century Palestinian world, even as it still holds forth possibilities today for experiencing the transformation of injustices that plague not only Dalit communities in the South Asian continent but various people everywhere.

MISSION AND KIN-DOMIZATION: PENTECOST AND MISSION IN A PLURALISTIC WORLD

Our overarching goal in this concluding chapter in particular and in this volume as a whole has been to suggest how renewal Christianity can continue to engage in the missionary task in a religiously plural world but do so in a manner that neither compromises its core theological convictions on the one hand nor undermines the gospel's capacity to bear witness on the other. More particularly, such an objective is even more urgent given the tendency in renewal missionary and evangelistic practice to demonize the religious other. I have attempted in the preceding to craft a renewal missiology by identifying nondemonization beliefs and practices among the Spirit-empowered experiences of the early messianic believers. With these final remarks, then, I want to make three broad theological claims for a renewal missiology in a pluralistic world, all informed by the apostolic practices that highlight and allow for interreligious engagement rather than demonization.

First, our considerations of the book of Acts suggest a renewal missiology as an extension of the Day of Pentecost narrative in which many different tongues and languages were involved in "speaking about God's deeds of power" (Acts 2:11). Analogically, whereas the many tongues denoted the many languages and cultures around the Mediterranean world gathered in Jerusalem for the celebration of the Feast Day of Pentecost, in today's pluralistic world the many cultures of the religions of the world are also potentially conduits for the Spirit's presence and activity in revealing the mystery of Christ and manifesting the wondrous works of God. By extrapolating from what I have suggested in the preceding, renewal approaches to the other religious traditions and to the interreligious encounter should be contextually discerned, taking into consideration the particularities and distinctives of each cultural-religious situation, and being informed and transformed by them in turn.[41] This does not lead to any bland universalism since the cross-cultural comprehension and cross-linguistic communication on the Day of Pentecost enabled only a declaration of the wondrous works of God (Acts 2:11), not necessarily resulting in the salvation of all speakers and hearers. Similarly, my minimal claim is that the outpouring of the Spirit makes possible the kinship of those who have otherwise been estranged linguistically, culturally, and even religiously, although this in turn certainly has implications for mission and for the eschatological renewal of all creation.

Second, such a dynamic renewal missiology continuously stretches the boundaries of the church and its self-understanding precisely by its poly-contextual set of interactions with its surroundings. Historically, such a project was understood in terms of Christianization, and involved the conversion of the world to the lordship of Christ. The complex interdependence of church, culture, and the political, however, resulted just as often, if not more often, in the transformation of the world according to the image of the missionary and his/her sending culture rather than the image of Christ. In short, Christianization became Westernization, and the dynamics of the church became the accommodation of the church to the world. It is thusly that in our post-Western world, we must either get behind Christianization or go beyond it.[42] This involves a rejection of the colonial model of missions

41. I sketch the outlines of such a contextual soteriology in Yong, "Salvation, Society, and the Spirit."

42. The following summarizes the arguments in my essays "Many Tongues, Many Practices," and "Church and Mission Theology in a Post-Constantinian Era" [the latter

and a retrieval and renewal of the apostolic practices instead.[43] From the perspective of the interreligious encounter, what is required is deferentiality toward the religious other that does not devolve into an uncritical acquiescence to the other. Urgently needed is the cultivation of a spiritual discernment that is capable of building bridges with people of other faiths but yet is wary of the demonic realities that threaten all faiths. This involves the turn to the religious other that enables us to hear and understand them first on their own terms, rather than an a priori demonization of the other before we have had a chance to get to know them.

Third, the call to mission and witness involves, as we have seen with Stephen in the apostolic era and in countless other examples delineated by Kim and Omenyo,[44] the call to martyrdom (Acts 1:8). What Kärkkäinen calls a theology of suffering is simultaneously an *orthopathos* that manifests the suffering love of God for a dying world,[45] a world that includes people of all faiths and no faith. Christian witness may involve, in our pluralistic context, less the capacity to talk louder and do more to Christianize the world than the capacity to defer to others and receive from them, even to the point of death. The renewal of the Spirit may be liberative for the marginalized, but at the expense of our own lives; but even in these cases, our martyrdom is for the glory of God and on behalf of our fellow human beings, motivated by the hope that death sows the seeds of later reconciliation between humanity and with God. While such an approach may render us vulnerable to the demonic realities of the world, it also has the capacity to undermine the demonic expressions in our own faith and equips us with the weapons of the gospel of peace instead.

This common humanity, testified to by St. Paul on the Areopagus, means that rather than a demonization of the (religious) other, we must work for the kin-domization of the gospel of Christ, with others, even across religious lines, to the level that is possible.[46] Remember that the author of the book of Acts himself records Jesus addressing the impossibility of salvation: "What is impossible for mortals is possible for God[!]" (Luke 18:27). The miracle of Pentecost was precisely the impossible relationality

---

being ch. 9 of this book].

43. See also my "Missiology of Jamestown." [Reproduced as ch. 7 of this volume.]

44. [Kim, "Theologies of Religious Pluralism," and Omenyo, "Renewal, Christian Mission, and Encounter with the Other."]

45. [Kärkkäinen, "*Dukkha* and *Passio*."]

46. My use of "kin-domization" affirms the feminist attempt to avoid perpetuating the sexist, elitist, and hierarchical connotations that have accrued in the classical theological notion of "kingdom"; see Isasi-Diaz, *Mujerista Theology*, ch. 5, and also Pittman, "Dialogical Discernment and the 'Kin-dom' of God."

and mutuality of human diversity caught up in the Spirit's redemptive work: the redemption of the pluralism of human tongues inaugurated on that day initiated a kin-dom movement that stretched from Jerusalem to Judea to Samaria and still yet aspires to reach the ends of the earth. It is that same Spirit's work that enables—in the book of Acts and stretching in human history through the present unto the eschaton—human interaction, dialogue, and comprehension across the many differences that otherwise separate us. If Jews and Gentiles who were before aliens and strangers to one another are now in effect kin, joined together in Christ and by his Spirit (Eph 2:12–13), is it possible that there may be a form of relationality and mutuality between Christians and those of other faiths, one that also anticipates the kin-dom?

Thus it is that the goal of such Spirit-enabled encounters cannot be merely the expansion of the church as an institution—that is in part what it means to say that we live in a post-Christian world—but must be the dawning of the kin-dom of God proclaimed by Jesus the Messiah. It is also in this sense that I urge viewing the interreligious encounter as an occasion for the manifestation of the kin-dom, an opportunity to do the works of the kin-dom, and as an opening for the coming of the kin-dom. This is the Spirit's invitation to inhabit the kin-dom beyond the superficial boundaries of race, class, gender, culture, ethnicity, and perhaps even religion. It is the work of the Spirit to bring about the redemption of all people and even to enable peoples from many tribes, tongues, and languages and their kings and leaders to bring their riches, purified of all things unholy by the glory of Christ, into the new heavens and new earth (Rev 21:24, 26), the kin-dom that is now here somehow, but that is also yet to come.[47]

47. Thanks to my graduate assistant, Tim Lim, and to my coeditor Clifton Clarke, for their comments on a previous draft of this essay.

PART III

North American Missiology

Theology of Mission Post-Christendom

CHAPTER 7

The Missiology of Jamestown 1607–2007 and Beyond

Toward a Postcolonial Theology of Mission in North America

WE NEED TO CONTINUE to seriously consider the "hard questions" that have been raised in the preceding pages.[1] In this concluding reflection, I want to engage these questions at two levels—the theological and the missiological—and then sketch in response what a postcolonial theology of mission might look like in North America in the twenty-first century.

THEOLOGICAL QUESTIONS AFTER JAMESTOWN

There are many difficult issues that are discussed in the chapters in this volume. I will begin by noting one of the overarching concerns: that concerning the Christian story considered as a metanarrative. By using this term, I am intentionally engaging debates occasioned by the postmodern "incredulity toward metanarratives."[2] While I am sympathetic to the counterargument that insofar as the Christian story is based on a faithful reception of the ancient Israelite and apostolic witness it is unlike the metanarratives based

---

1. [This was originally the concluding chapter to Yong and Zikmund, eds., *Remembering Jamestown*. I will insert notes with the titles of the other chapters when reference is made to them in what follows.]

2. Most prominently propounded by Lyotard, *Postmodern Condition*, esp. xxiv.

on universal reason that have been rejected by postmodern thinkers,[3] from another perspective, no hard-and-fast lines can be drawn between the two since the perpetuation of even faith-based narratives must be amenable to reason and, further, the big picture of the Christian story has always had missionary impulses that have inevitably engaged aliens and strangers to the Hebraic and Hellenistic Greek ways of life. Yet it is precisely this missionary character of the Christian story that is problematized in light of the history of mission before, during, and after Jamestown.

Most problematic is that intertwining of the Christian story and both the Doctrine of Discovery and the Manifest Destiny agenda of the colonial American experience and the nation's westward expansion. As rendered with stark clarity by both Robert Miller and Edward Bond,[4] both sets of ideas were shot through with Christian motifs and rationalizations. In fact, both were predicated fundamentally on the Christian missionary enterprise itself, and were understood in part as the unfolding of the Great Commission to take the gospel to the ends of the earth. I am certainly not denying that there were also other ideological factors involved in their articulation and implementation. But we cannot minimize or ignore how the Discovery and Manifest Destiny Doctrines were intertwined with the Christian self-understanding of how their story would continue to unfold in the New World. In other words, it is difficult now to simply say these were aberrations in the history of Christianity; rather, they were self-consciously promulgated as legitimate and even necessary theological expansions of the Christian narrative that was destined to conquer the world.[5]

Of course, the problem is that Christian Europeans ran into a recalcitrant indigenous population. Setting aside the issues of land ownership, the quest to secure resources, and other deeply troubling aspects of the European encounter with Native America,[6] there was also the challenge of introducing Christian monotheism to the native inhabitants. Here, Barbara Mann points to the clash of world views underneath the confrontation.[7] In her analysis, Christianity's One-Thinking was fundamentally incommen-

---

3. For an articulate defense of this view, see Smith, *Who's Afraid of Postmodernism?*, ch. 3.

4. [Miller, "Christianity, American Indians" and Bond, "Colonial Virginia Mission Attitudes."]

5. That this discover-and-conquer destiny is tied in with the main strands of the biblical narrative is aptly delineated in Warrior, "A Native American Perspective."

6. As one popular textbook puts it, the colonial mission to Native America was motivated by the pursuit of "gold, glory, and God," in that order. Baker, *Religion in America*, I:6.

7. [Mann, "A Failure to Communicate."]

surate with native Two-Thinking. While some may contest either Mann's association of monotheism with One-Thinking or her incommensurability thesis, or others may counter that Mann's Two-Thinking world view actually has reconstructed the "other" (the European Christian) within the framework of in its own binary terms, there is no disputing that the Christian missionaries were faced with serious theological challenges in their mission to Native Americans. Even if Mann's claim that Christian and native ways of thinking are "incompatible paradigms" is too strong, it is important to acknowledge that not many Christian missionaries seriously undertook the effort to enter into the native way of life on its own terms; that few if any valued native culture and spirituality in comparison to what the missionaries had to offer; and that it was well nigh impossible for the missionaries to critically reexamine their modern, Western, and European assumptions from the various indigenous perspectives. The result, to put it bluntly, following Tinker, was the "cultural genocide" of Native America, legitimated theologically by doctrines like those of Discovery and Manifest Destiny.[8]

Might there be a way forward theologically after Jamestown and its horrendous history? Is it possible to retrieve and redeem the Christian story in light of the "failed encounter" (Mann) between Christianity and Native America? Richard Twiss's chapter undertakes some first steps in this direction, albeit with great trepidation.[9] As a member of the Lakota/Sioux Tribe, Twiss wrestles deeply with what it means to be a Native American and a Christian. The latter dimension of his identity affirms his relationship with Jesus the Christ. But how is Twiss able to embrace this confession, given the long history of genocide conducted against his people in the name of Jesus?[10] Twiss's proposal is to connect with Jesus as "an aboriginal boy" in the midst of empire, one who therefore can empathize with the plight of Native Americans at the hands of their colonial conquerors.

At one level, one can respond to Twiss's aboriginal Christology by simply understanding it as an attempt at theological contextualization or indigenization. Thus Native American perspectives on the Jesus story naturally highlight the parallels between the life of Christ and the contemporary horizon, perhaps an allowable correlation given the biblical insistence that Jesus "had to become like his brothers and sisters in every respect" (Heb 2:17a). Yet at a deeper level, note that Twiss must necessarily reach over the historical mediations of Christ through the church, and that in effect, he

8. Tinker, *Missionary Conquest*.

9. [Twiss, "Living in Transition, Embracing Community."]

10. Chapter 4 of Tinker's *American Indian Liberation* explicates the challenges confronting the articulation of a Native American Christology.

arrives back at a more primordial Jesus, a cosmic and universal Jesus who is capable of meeting the people of Native America not on the terms of those who originally introduced him, but on indigenous terms. To be sure, as an evangelical follower of Jesus, Twiss is committed to the portrait presented by the gospel evangelists; however, his reportrayal of the tribal Jesus is rather far afield from how Jesus is understood in white American evangelicalism.

At a third level, however, I suggest that Twiss's approach is more the theological norm than the exception in that it emphasizes the agency of recipients of the gospel message.[11] Each people, as well as each generation, will need to meet Jesus on their terms, rather than on the terms of the missionaries or of their parents.[12] I would go further to claim that this is a legitimate expansion of the incarnational principle: that the Christian conviction that the Word became flesh means not only that Jesus came as a first-century Mediterranean Jew, but also that the Word continues to meet all peoples and individuals where they are. Later on, I will suggest that when combined with a pentecostal and pneumatological principle, this view does not succumb to philosophical relativism but instead underwrites the universal relevance of the gospel.

MISSIOLOGICAL PROSPECTS AFTER JAMESTOWN

For the moment, however, I want to turn from theological (and christological) issues to specifically missiological ones. To cut to the chase, the major question before us in light of this history of mission to Native American before, during, and after Jamestown is this: Whither the Christian mission? In his chapter, Tinker puts it forcefully thus: "Given the disastrous history of euro-western mission practices—to the cultures and the peoplehood of those missionized—it would seem that there are no missiological projects that we might conceive that would have legitimacy of any kind."[13] Recall that Tinker's concerns are informed by the history of Christian aggressions against Native America that have been recounted by him and many others.

---

11. This is in contrast to the view that Native Americans were coerced into or were passive digesters of the missionary message. For accounts of Native agency in fashioning the Christian religion for their own (important) purposes, see Griffiths and Cervantes, *Spiritual Encounters*; a specific case study is provided by Salisbury, "'I Love the Place of My Dwelling.'"

12. That people inevitably receive the gospel on their own terms in some respects is clearly seen in anthropological research that specifically asks about indigenous or Native viewpoints regarding their conversion experiences; see, e.g., Vilaça and Wright, *Native Christians*.

13. [Tinker, "Romance and Tragedy of Christian Mission," quotation from 26–27.]

If some might think that things are better now in the late-modern world, Tinker would retort that an even more insidious form of colonialism is currently afoot, one that engages in the ongoing "colonialism of the mind" by continuously communicating the inferiority of the Native American way of life in contrast to the modern, Western Christian one.[14] So from this perspective, it is not *how* the mission to Native America should proceed, but *whether* such should proceed at all. The response is: No! Ongoing calls for the conversion of Native Americans perpetuate the Christian quest to eradicate indigenous cultures, and there is no time to be idle in the face of such threats.

On the one hand, of course, Tinker is aware that such a stark response is simplistic in view of the complexities of the interface between Native Americans and the Christian America. On the other hand, however, it would also be a mistake to undertake the Christian mission as usual, as if reparations have now been made, as if healing and reconciliation either has already begun or is in the wings. Sure, there have been tremendous strides made in Native American-Christian relations, but there remains much difficult work to be done.

Missiologists Rick Waldrop and Corky Alexander both realize the enormity of the task in light of the specifically pentecostal mission to Native America.[15] The ignominious history of mission after Jamestown has been exacerbated by the zealousness of pentecostal missions in the twentieth century precisely because of the sectarian pentecostal attitude toward culture. The outworking of this in the pentecostal missionary enterprise has been a devaluation of things native, a rhetoric that has intensified the colonial attack on indigenous culture, and a set of conversion practices that have demanded a rejection of many, if not most, traditional forms of life.[16]

Waldrop and Alexander thus struggle to reformulate pentecostal missiology in light of this "failed encounter."[17] Their approach is to emphasize the Trinitarian character of God's mission, especially as marked by the incarnation and Pentecost. Their intuitions are headed in the right direction, even if both aspects of their proposal can be made more explicit with regard to the challenge of mission to Native America today. First, the incarnation marks God's entry into human history in all of its specificities, including the

14. Confirmation for Tinker's claim comes from those quite unconnected to his project. See, for example, Blossom, "Evangelists of Destruction," whose analysis of four contemporary films on the Christian mission to Native America uncovers the ongoing agenda to undermine the indigenous world view and way of life.

15. [Waldrop and Alexander Jr., "Salvation History and Mission of God."]

16. As documented by Dombrowski, *Against Culture*.

17. [See the title of Mann's chapter, "Failure to Communicate."]

diversity that constitutes this history of Native America. Second, the Spirit of Pentecost is also the Spirit who hovered over the primordial creation, and hence has already been present to the peoples of Native America, and may even be preserved in its myths and stories. But Waldrop and Alexander could have gone further to retrieve the indigenous principle at the heart of historic pentecostal missiology and to call for its more rigorous and intentional application in the Native American case.[18] The performance of such a pentecostally and pneumatologically informed indigenous principle would have invited Native Americans to receive the gospel on their own terms, or, to put it in more specifically pentecostal language, in their own tongues.

Yet as Waldrop and Alexander acknowledge, the proof in the pentecostal missionary pudding is in the kinds of practices, structures, and relations that come out of the Christian encounter with Native America. This now touches on Tinker's suggestion that what will really count in the future of Christian mission is not so much the proclamation of the gospel but the embodiment of the message of Jesus as peace, justice, and love. Shanta Premawardhana and William Burrows thus both emphasize a more praxis-oriented missiology of reconciliation designed to live rather than just preach Christ.[19] Premawardhana's emphasis, following the Asian Indian Christian theologian M. M. Thomas, is on the *missio humanitatis*, highlighting the central role of humanization as the goal of mission. This is certainly in keeping with the major themes that have unfolded in the last century of mainline Protestant missiologies. Deeply aware of the problematic 400-year history of Jamestown, the ecumenical churches have tended to thoroughly reconsider the nature of the Christian mission. Premawardhana's description of joint mission captures the partnership aspect of the ecumenical approach involving collaboration on goals related to human flourishing and well-being. There is much to be said about such a missiological proposal. And even if the ecumenical reluctance to be offensive to non-Christians tends to produce a bland all-inclusive gospel, it is nevertheless important for us not to quickly forget the offenses that were part and parcel of the missiology of Jamestown.

So, if Mann (explicitly) and Tinker (at least on the surface) call for the withering of mission in light of the history of Jamestown, reading more deeply, I think we can say that Tinker, along with Waldrop, Alexander, and Premawardhana each ask instead, whither the Christian mission? It is safe to say that none of the Christians in this volume deny the essentially

18. I discuss this in my *Spirit Poured Out on All Flesh*, 123–24.

19. [Premawardhana, "Jamestown and Future of Mission," and Burrows, "Moving beyond Christian Imperialism."]

missionary character of their faith; yet the question after Jamestown concerns the *how* of this mission going forward. Each is concerned about the integrity of the Native American side of the encounter. Is there a way to craft a "missiology after Jamestown" that preserves the Native American voice and perspective on theological rather politically correct grounds?

TOWARD A POSTCOLONIAL THEOLOGY OF MISSION IN NORTH AMERICA

In effect, what we are searching for can be understood as a postcolonial theology of mission for the specifically North American context.[20] I would like to propose for consideration what is hinted at but undeveloped in Waldrop and Alexander's and Twiss's chapters: a robustly Trinitarian theology of mission resulting particularly from a thoroughly pentecostal and pneumatological emphasis.[21] Such an approach is consistent with the incarnational and Trinitarian model they present, but the pneumatological dimension is not just subsumed within the broader theological framework. Rather, the pneumatological trajectory opens up substantive theological space for rethinking Christian missionary praxis in ways that are consistent with a postcolonial emphasis on Native American agency and perspective. Let me flesh out five aspects of such a postcolonial and pneumatological theology of mission for twenty-first-century North America.

First, a postcolonial and pneumatological theology of mission draws fundamentally from the many tongues of the Pentecost narrative. As many languages were empowered by the Spirit to speak about God's deeds of power on that day (Acts 2:11), so also are many languages required to bear witness to the glory of God today. Such a pentecostal theology of mission thus requires attentiveness to the diversity of testimonies that characterize the life of humankind. Testimonies are, after all, the most powerful forms of religious proclamation. Richard Twiss's confessions of Christ are effective precisely because they emerge out of his own journey in search of a tribal or aboriginal Jesus.[22] But the wildness and weirdness of the many tongues

20. My use of the notion of "postcolonial" is shorthand for "after Jamestown." For initial articulations of a postcolonial missiology in an Asian context, see Dharmaraj, *Colonialism and Christian Mission*.

21. I have written extensively about pneumatological theology. For my most recent and sustained attempt to elaborate a pneumatological theology of mission in a pluralistic world, see Yong, *Hospitality and the Other*.

22. For a book-length argument regarding the centrality of testimonial biography and autobiography to religious proclamation and even theological formulation, see McClendon Jr., *Biography as Theology*.

of Pentecost also suggest that when we encounter testimonies that fit only with difficulty or even not at all with those we feel called to perpetuate—like those of Barbara Mann's—we may need to be especially attentive rather than refuse to listen. We cannot simply reject, silence, or neglect such uncomfortable voices, since they bear witness to truths that we ignore to our own detriment.

Of course, discerning exactly what those truths are is complicated (as complicated as is discerning the truths of Twiss's testimony), but we cannot proceed to discernment apart from first listening. This leads to my second point: that the many tongues of Pentecost presume the importance of listening to the many voices. Here I wish to expand William Burrows's proposal for a *missiologia crucis* in a pneumatological direction.[23] If Burrows highlights the centrality of a humble missiology based on the cross of Christ (rather than a triumphalist missiology based only on the resurrection), I would further emphasize that such humility attempts to follow the winds of the Spirit who has been poured out upon all flesh (Acts 2:17) and thus potentially is capable of speaking through the many strange tongues of others. In practice, this means that in the initial encounter, we efface ourselves in humility before (religious) others. Missiologists Terry Muck and Frances Adeney talk about this in terms of bracketing our convictions (and especially prejudices) sufficiently in order to be able to sympathetically listen to, interact with, and maybe even experience another language, culture, and religious tradition.[24] Such bracketing is absolutely imperative for a postcolonial theology of mission in light of Jamestown.[25]

Of course, such bracketing is only an initial moment in the encounter, and it is questionable whether it can really be achieved. But, and this is my third point, such bracketing is grounded incarnationally and pentecostally (pneumatologically) in the work of God who has really entered human history. Thus God achieves the conversion of humanity but not before emptying himself in Christ and pouring out himself in the Spirit. Hence any evaluation and assessment of the religious other—always necessary and unavoidable moments of the interreligious encounter—in the postcolonial theology of mission I am proposing always already presumes some kind conversion toward the other in and through the encounter. This mutual conversion is most aptly illuminated by Twiss's aboriginal Christology, which involves both a transformation of Christian and native identities simultaneously.

23. [Burrows, "Moving beyond Christian Imperialism," 152–53.]

24. See Muck and Adeney, *Christianity Encountering World Religions*, esp. part III.

25. I have also previously called for a bracketing of theological convictions for purposes of forestalling imperialistic approaches and of allowing religious others to be present to us first on their own terms; see Yong, *Beyond the Impasse*, esp. ch. 7.

Of course, such a mutual transformation will be rejected either by those (conservative Christians) who deem such as syncretism or by others (Native Americans who remain suspicious of Christianity) who see such as a disguised form of imperialism. While there is no way to completely quell the fears of either side (since syncretism and imperialism always remain real possibilities), I am optimistic such a postcolonial and pneumatological theology of mission allows for a healthy tension that takes seriously the task of reinterpreting Christian faith while respecting the Native American context.[26]

But, fourth, the many tongues of Pentecost also open up to many missionary practices. I base this on the cultural-linguistic model that correlates human languages with whole forms of life. This means that different tongues emerge out of and shape a diverse set of cultural and even religious practices. From this pentecostal and pneumatological insight, then, a postcolonial theology of mission embraces, enables, and empowers a plurality of missionary modes of engagement. Shanta Premawardhana's insights regarding the *missio humanitatis* highlight the need for a diversity of approaches in light of the many different ills that plague humankind, and the divergent conditions from out of which we all need salvation. Whatever eschatological salvation consists of is at least in part continuous with our experience of salvation, healing, wholeness, reconciliation, and forgiveness in the present life. We need to creatively participate in the work of the Spirit to develop many more liturgical forms and other social practices that can facilitate the healing and salvation needed to respond to the reprehensible mission history of Jamestown. On these matters, Native American input is not optional, but essential.[27]

Finally, then, a postcolonial theology of mission after Jamestown cannot but emphasize a genuinely dialogical (Burrows) mutuality between Christianity and Native America. I have called for such under the rubric of a pneumatological theology of hospitality that follows the ways of the Spirit wherever the Spirit goes. In such a journeying missiology, Christians are no longer in control; rather than only being hosts to Native Americans, Christians are just as often, if not more so, guests in what is still a New World.[28]

---

26. For a parallel hermeneutical project, see Richard, "Indigenous Biblical Hermeneutics."

27. See, e.g., Brewer, "Touching the Past, Teaching Ways Forward."

28. Here, and below, I draw from John Howard Yoder's post-Christendom theology of exile in which he calls for Christians to cease striving to "be in charge"; see Yoder's "On Not Being in Charge," ch. 9 of his *The Jewish-Christian Schism Revisited*. Cf. also further discussion and application of Yoder's diasporic theology in my *In the Days of Caesar*, §5.2.1.

To be sure, the Christian impact on the Americas cannot be discounted and we cannot return to the days before Columbus. However, the time has come for the Native American voice and perspective to be registered on the form of life we call Christianity in North America. A truly indigenous and contextual theology is not only a Native American Christian theology; rather it is a theology that emerges out of a genuinely mutual encounter of Christianity and Native American culture, tradition, and spirituality. We have barely begun such a conversation simply because Christians have not perceived themselves as guests in a strange land being hosted by others. But following the biblical metanarrative, Christians can never be completely at home. Instead, we can always only be exiles in diaspora, always only be "strangers and foreigners on the earth" (Heb 11:13) who are looking for a homeland in another city. From this perspective, Christians are guests to others in their following in the footsteps of Christ,[29] who went forth into a strange and far country, and in their being carried by the Spirit, who has been poured out indeed upon all flesh, even to the ends of the earth.

Neither this concluding essay nor this book pretends to present the "final answer" to the question, Whither missiology after Jamestown? Rather, both my reflections as well as those of the contributors above merely seek to confront the hard questions of Christian mission in our pluralistic historical context. Perhaps some of the proposals in these pages will survive the test of time; they are at least presented in this spirit of humble anticipation.[30]

29. See here Udho, *Guest Christology*.

30. For further discussion of the constructive proposal in these final paragraphs, see Collins Winn and Yong, "Apocalypse of Colonialism." Thanks to my graduate assistant Timothy Lim Teck Ngern for proofreading this essay; needless to say, I take full responsibility for any infelicities that remain.

CHAPTER 8

The Buddhist-Christian Encounter in the USA

Reflections on Christian Practices[1]

THE CHRISTIAN ENCOUNTER WITH Buddhism stretches back perhaps fifteen millennia to when Nestorian missionaries first traveled the Silk Road and arrived in East Asia.[2] Along the way, Christians have engaged in a wide range of practices in their interactions with Buddhists. Some missionaries and apologists have debated with Buddhists while others have adopted what we today might call more a dialogical approach that resulted in "Buddhistic" forms of Chinese Christianity.[3] Both strategies, as well as others, can be seen in the Christian encounter with Buddhism in America.

1. I am delighted to have been invited to participate in this festschrift for Professor Irving Hexham. I met Irving in the fall of 2000 at a conference at Regent College in Vancouver, BC, where we were both invited to present papers that were then published in Stackhouse Jr., *No Other Gods before Me?*. Irving later wrote a very nice commendation for my book, *Beyond the Impasse*. I have always appreciated his scholarship on new religious movements, and used his texts when I taught on that subject while on the faculty at Bethel University (St. Paul, Minnesota). It is with gratefulness that I present this essay as a token of my appreciation and respect for his scholarly contributions.

2. On the Nestorian mission to China, see Saeki, *Nestorian Monument in China*, esp. 118–61; Foster, *Church of the T'ang Dynasty*; Bundy, "Missiological Reflections on Nestorian Christianity in China"; and Tang, *Study of the History of Nestorian Christianity in China*.

3. On medieval Christian apologetics, see Scott, "Medieval Christian Responses to Buddhism"; Young, "*Deus Unus* or *Dei Plures Sunt*?"; Klimkeit, "Christian-Buddhist Encounter in Medieval Central Asia"; and Irvin and Sunquist, *History of the World Christian Movement*, vol. 1, chs. 25 and 35. For Chinese Christian sutras that summarize the gospel in Buddhist terminology, see Coakley and Sterk, *Readings in World*

My goals in this essay are twofold, corresponding to the two parts of that follow: first, to provide a broad historical overview of the various ways in which Christians and Buddhists have interacted in America, and second, to reflect theologically and missiologically on Christian practices vis-à-vis American Buddhism in particular and the Christian encounter with other faiths in general. My thesis is that Christian interreligious practices have perennially been multifaceted, in various ways shaped by the many situations and contexts Christians find themselves in relationship to people of other faiths. In this paper, I will seek to illustrate this thesis by looking specifically at the history of the relationship between Buddhism and Christianity in America.

THE BUDDHIST-CHRISTIAN ENCOUNTER IN AMERICA: A BRIEF OVERVIEW

The first Buddhists to arrive in America were Chinese and Japanese workers and immigrants in the mid-nineteenth century.[4] Yet for most of these families and individuals, Buddhism did not function as a religion in their lives as Christianity might have for Christians. Rather, as with many East Asians throughout history, Buddhism has been interwoven with strands of Daoism, Confucianism, and local religious practices so that it is unidentifiable as a distinctive religious identity. Further, the fact of the matter is that without access to temples or prior to the establishment of a sangha, Buddhist practices were more-or-less individualized, if maintained at all. It would not be until 1899 that the first Jodo Shinshu missionaries from Japan (representing the Pure Land Buddhist tradition) would arrive in San Francisco in order to specifically establish that branch of Buddhism in North America.[5]

Yet during the nineteenth century, Caucasian Americans also began to discover Buddhism. This American fascination with Buddhism can be traced back to intellectuals like Emerson, Thoreau, Whitman, Bronson Alcott, Edwin Arnold, and many others. Thomas Tweed has described this as the encounter between Victorian culture and Buddhism on American soil.[6] In his account, while overall initial American images of Buddhism were fairly negative—in terms of its passivity, its atheism, and its impersonalism, at least in some readings—the Buddha and his Dharma did find a hearing among a small group of intellectuals. Those in pursuit of esoteric religious

---

Christian History, 1:247–51.

4. This story is told by Fields, *How Swans Came to Lake*, esp. ch. 5.

5. See Tanaka, *Ocean*, ch. 4.

6. Tweed, *American Encounter with Buddhism 1844–1912*.

and philosophical ideas found in Buddhism lofty and yet intriguing ideals on the one hand, as well as a new way of understanding the traditional Christian idea of the immortality of the soul (in terms of karmic reincarnation) on the other. Others who were drawn to the romantic movement saw in Buddhism a naturalistic world view that was a congenial alternative to traditional theism. Still others found in Buddhism a rational philosophy that did not necessarily require the rejection of Christianity but helped to stabilize theism on a more secure foundation in the face of higher criticism, Darwinism and modern science, and the emerging discourse of comparative religion. For many, Buddhism was compatible with Victorian cultural themes, especially with regard to how the Buddhist articulation of a noble personal ethic fit with the Victorian emphasis on self-reliance. Ironically, as Tweed's portrayal shows, it was Buddhist ideas that in a sense rescued the theistic faith of some of these interreligious explorers, albeit while providing further religious and philosophical rationale for late–nineteenth-century American values like individualism, activism, and cultural optimism.

These nineteenth-century developments culminated at the World's Parliament of Religions (WPR) held alongside the World's Columbian Exposition Fair in Chicago in 1893.[7] Representatives of all the major religious traditions of the world had a platform to present their ideas. Speaking on behalf of Buddhism were Anagarika Dharmapala (1864–1933) from Theravada Ceylon and the Japanese Zen master Shaku Soen (1859–1919). The former focused on the commandments of (Theravada) Buddhism while the latter spoke on the laws of cause and effect, arguing for the compatibility of Buddhism with the world of modern science.[8] As their ideas were accessibly presented, the WPR communicated the impression that Buddhism had by now secured its place on the stage of world religions. These speakers were careful, however, as well-behaved guests, to neither overemphasize the major differences between Buddhism and Christianity, nor insist too blatantly on Buddhism's superiority to Christian faith.

In the wake of the WPR, Dharmapala, Soen, and other Buddhists traveled throughout the United States introducing Buddhism to interested audiences. Soen's personal secretary at the WPR, D. T. Suzuki (1870–1966), would carry on his teacher's work into the next century.[9] Widely published

7. A centenary assessment of the WPR's significance is provided by Seager, *World's Parliament of Religions*.

8. Their speeches have been published in numerous venues—e.g., Barrows, *World's Parliament of Religions*, 2:829–31 and 862–80, and Seager, ed., *Dawn of Religious Pluralism*, chs. 52–53.

9. For the significance of Suzuki's contributions to spreading the Buddhist Dharma across North America, see Haar and Abe, *A Zen Life*.

both at the scholarly and lay levels,[10] perhaps it is Suzuki who has done more than anyone else to demystify Buddhism in general and Zen Buddhism in particular for Americans. By the mid-twentieth century, his students had emerged as leaders of the movement to Westernize Zen Buddhism in the American context. Chief among these were Dwight Goddard (1861–1939), whose *The Buddhist Bible* (1938) was to leave a lasting impression among Christian inquirers into Buddhism;[11] Alan Watts (1915–1973), a one-time Episcopal priest whose initial exposure to Buddhism was through the lectures and writings of Suzuki;[12] and, later, Beat generation poets like Allen Ginsberg (1926–1997), Jack Kerouac (1922–1969), and Gary Snyder (b. 1930).

Given these developments, it would be unsurprising to find that those in the Zen Buddhist tradition have been the most eager to engage in the more formal scholarly dialogues between Buddhists and Christians in the United States. Yet at the same time, the broad spectrum of Buddhist and Christian traditions was represented in the emerging American dialogue scene. With the abolition in 1965 of the national-origins quotas limiting immigration from Eastern hemisphere countries and the development of religious studies programs and departments in American colleges and universities shortly thereafter, the academic study of Buddhism took on the task of interpreting Buddhism not just as an Eastern religious tradition but also as a dynamic and flourishing form of American religiosity.

In this context, the first International Buddhist-Christian Conference was called and held at the University of Hawaii in 1980, organized by scholar-practitioners David W. Chappell and George Tanabe Jr. Out of this and subsequent meetings, the Society of Buddhist-Christian Studies was formed (with its annual journal *Buddhist-Christian Studies*) and other dialogical conferences were envisioned and then held. Out of these conferences one especially vibrant set of interchanges that occurred on various occasions over the course of two decades (1984–2004) was the International Buddhist-Christian Theological Encounter Group, cochaired by Zen Buddhist philosopher Masao Abe and Christian theologian John B. Cobb Jr.[13] By the time of the first meeting, the latter had already published a major book on Buddhist-Christian dialogue, engaging specifically with the Japanese tradition of Pure Land or Amida Buddhism, while Abe was on the verge of

10. Suzuki's historical and textual scholarship is primarily in Japanese, although some of these works have been translated into English. A selection from his books and many essays is in Barrett, ed., *Zen Buddhism*.

11. See Goddard, ed., *A Buddhist Bible*.

12. See Keightley, *Into Every Life a Little Zen Must Fall*.

13. See Gross, "International Buddhist-Christian Theological Encounter."

becoming a household name in Buddhist-Christian dialogue circles, with many of his books and essays translated into English during and since that time.[14]

While it is beyond the scope of this paper to go into the details of these dialogues,[15] allow me to briefly summarize some of their key features. First, given the breadth of Christian and Buddhist traditions represented at the dialogues, participants deployed a wide range of philosophical, hermeneutical, and theological perspectives and methods in their approaches; this range was even further expanded when Jewish thinkers were invited into the conversation.[16] Second, proselytism and apologetics were a secondary concern at best, especially since individuals were found on both sides of the dialogue table that had begun in one tradition but by now either had converted or were in the process of negotiating dual religious identities. In either of these cases, the other side knew just as much if not more about the two religious traditions as their conversation partners. Often, participants came out of the dialogues even more deeply committed to their own tradition, although certainly also having been transformed variously in the process of engaging the discussion. Finally, the dialogues involved theologians, philosophers, and scholars who were also practitioners of their respective religious traditions. Hence the dialogues were engaged at a high academic level, but were at the same time deeply informed by confessional commitments and practices.

This confluence between dialogue and practices has been the central feature in discussions between Christian and Buddhist monastics. In these encounters, there are often scheduled periods of personal and group meditation, with the latter sometimes involving members of both traditions meditating together in silence, rotating between formal and informal dialogue sessions.[17] Of course, since Protestant churches lack a developed contemplative tradition, most of the Christians involved in these monastic dialogues with Buddhist practitioners come from the Roman Catholic tradition. In any case, while similar to the academic conversations in which

14. See Cobb Jr., *Beyond Dialogue*, and—representative of Abe's work—Abe, *Zen and Western Thought*.

15. Those interested can consult Lai and von Brück, *Christianity and Buddhism*.

16. The multireligious character of the dialogue is seen most clearly in one of the main publications out of the Cobb-Abe group: Ives, ed., *Divine Emptiness and Historical Fullness*.

17. Representative volumes from these dialogues include Mitchell and Wiseman, eds., *The Gethsemani Encounter*, and Barnhart and Wong, eds., *Purity of Heart and Contemplation*. See also *Monastic Studies* 19 (1991), the entire issue of which is devoted to "Buddhist and Christian Monasticism," as well as the *Bulletin of the Monastic Interreligious Dialogue* at http://monasticdialog.com/bulletins.php.

mutual understanding and exploration are prioritized over proselytism or apologetics, the monastic interreligious encounters are different in that the goals of personal transformation are much more central and pronounced because of the commitment to meditative practice. But in the midst of the alternating silence and conversation, there is a deep sense of communion testified to by participants from both traditions. There is something that happens when sitting together that nurtures this kind of affinity, which does not happen when engaged in the more formal academic exchanges of paper presentations and responses.

Yet these developments on the monastic front mirror developments "on the ground" in American. Most non-Asian and nonimmigrant lay-people who may or may not be formal converts to Buddhism come from across the sociopolitical and economic spectrum of American society and are inevitably drawn especially to the Buddhist practice of meditation. Ever since the 1960s, meditation centers from across the Buddhist spectrum can now be found all over the country. Yet as adaptations of the various Tibetan, Nepalese, Tantric, Theravadan (also known as Vipassana or insight meditation), and Ch'an/Zen traditions arise, what may be unique in the American context is the hybridity that continually shapes Buddhist meditative practices. Practitioners and their instructors and teachers are less likely to insist that there is the unique or pure form of Buddhist practice; rather, a blending of Buddhist traditions with psychotherapeutic strategies, medicinal and health care prescriptions and recommendations, and, to a growing extent, socially aware and engaged practices are increasingly the norm.

Mention of socially Engaged Buddhism in the West requires further comment.[18] Buddhist mindfulness and compassion, its practitioners insist, produces an engaged rather than detached Buddhist disposition. Whether it be the Buddhist Peace Fellowship, prison Zen practice, the International Network of Engaged Buddhists, the Benevolent Organisation for Development, Health and Insight, the Free Tibet movement, the Friends of the Western Buddhist Order, or others, Engaged Buddhists recognize the interdependence that characterizes life on this planet and therefore are committed to addressing important issues related to the flourishing of all people as part of their practice. As with other forms of American Buddhism, Engaged Buddhists hail from the wide range of Buddhist traditions, often combin-

---

18. There is a growing literature on Engaged Buddhism in general, especially focusing on Asian Engaged Buddhist movements. For Engaged Buddhism in the Western hemisphere, see Eppsteiner, ed., *Path of Compassion*; Hanh, *Interbeing*; Queen, ed., *Engaged Buddhism in the West*; and Queen et al., eds., *Action Dharma*, esp. the essays in parts II and III. King's *Being Benevolence* focuses on Asian Engaged Buddhists; we await her analysis of Western Engaged Buddhism.

ing insights and practices from various streams of Buddhism in their lives. And as is increasingly the case with socially mindful movements, Engaged Buddhists are generally nonsectarian, seeking alliances with any and all, including those in other faiths, who are willing to work with them on issues of common concern.

I now wish to turn our attention back to 1965 when, as mentioned previously, immigration and naturalization laws were liberalized to reopen America's doors to Asia. With the influx of Asian immigrants came not only the Hare Krishnas and Hindu gurus of all stripes, but also the masses of East Asians (Chinese, Korean, and Japanese) whose identities have been shaped over time by various traditions of Buddhism. Further, refugees from Tibet, Sri Lanka, and Southeast Asia (including Vietnam, Laos, and Cambodia) have brought with them varying forms of Buddhist belief and practices as well. The result is that over the course of the last generation, immigrants from across the Asian continent have erected temples, built educational institutions of different types and sizes, and established transnational Buddhist networks.[19] The concerns of these immigrant Buddhists, of course, are much different from nonimmigrant and non-Asian American practitioners and converts to Buddhism. The former are worried about assimilation and adaptation, as well as about linguistic, social, and economic factors that do not impinge in the same way on the latter. Yet the Buddhist commitments of Asian immigrants are perhaps for these reasons all the more intense, to the point that Buddhist missionaries are now arriving on Western shores in greater numbers than ever before. Their motivations have been not only the pastoral care of the growing Buddhist diaspora but also the commitment to seeking American converts.[20]

This explosion of Buddhism resulting from Asian immigration to America raises many interesting issues regarding the present and future of Buddhism in this country.[21] I note the following rather generalized comparisons and contrasts:

1. Whereas Asian immigrant Buddhists are almost always ethnically constituted, American Buddhists were at one point almost all white, but now are increasingly diversified.

---

19. For the dizzying shape of immigrant Buddhism in America, see Seager, *Buddhism in America*, part II; and Prebish and Tanaka, eds., *Faces of Buddhism in America*.

20. See Learman, "Introduction."

21. Here, I follow especially Das, "Emergent Trends in Western Dharma," and Prebish, *Luminous Passage*, esp. ch. 2.

2. Whereas Asian Buddhist traditions have generally viewed the monastic life as a higher vocational calling, Asian American and American Buddhists tend to emphasize lay expressions of the tradition.

3. Whereas Asian Buddhist traditions have tended to be hierarchical and authoritarian, American Buddhism has been much more democratic and egalitarian.

4. Whereas Asian Buddhism has generally been patriarchal, American Buddhist traditions have been much more open to the participation of and leadership by women.

5. Whereas some Asian Buddhists have focused on the centrality of the enlightenment experience and others on the ceremonial aspects of the tradition, Asian American and American Buddhists are much more focused on everyday life and experiences.

6. Whereas Asian Buddhism has emphasized the doctrinal elements of the Dharma, American Buddhism has been much more focused on the practical expressions of the Dharma.

7. Whereas traditional Buddhism has evolved a number of highly standardized and ritualized forms, American Buddhism has been more exploratory, innovative, and experimental in its approaches.

8. Whereas ethnic Buddhism in America has retained a palpable Asian sensibility, the Americanized version of Buddhism has a distinctively "Protestant" character (e.g., there are now Buddhist "Sunday schools," churches, and ministers).

9. Relatedly, whereas ethnic Buddhism is generally sectarian, American Buddhism is generally ecumenical, less concerned about maintaining proper boundaries, and more open to intra- and inter-Buddhist cooperation.

Now I should also be quick to emphasize that these are broad generalizations that mask continuities amidst the apparent discontinuities and vice versa. At the same time, these observations highlight the important issues confronting American Buddhists of all stripes. Perhaps most important of these may be two major questions: that which concerns the transition between the first and second generations of ethnic or immigrant Buddhism in America and that which concerns American Buddhist identity overall. With regard to the former, the issues are familiar. Demographic changes have produced more diffused patterns of immigration, meaning in any given place that there may be either more temples (and as a result, stiffer competition) or fewer temples (and as a result, lack of accessibility in order to sustain ties to the Buddhist community). Further, the costs of building, maintaining, and perhaps later expanding physical structures are usually greater than immigrant communities can bear.[22] Finally, and most importantly, the second generation usually does not have the same religious commitments as their parents. More often than not, Americanization involves a process of assimilation and accommodation that leaves the "religion of the parents" less attractive to those who were born and/or grew up in America.[23] Interestingly, however, this question of the second generation affects not only immigrant or ethnic Buddhist communities but also the white baby boomer generation that embraced Buddhist meditational practice and then got married and began raising children. Generations X and Y (also known as the "millennial" group) were usually not brought up in self-consciously Buddhist homes or environments and often left to find their own way.

All of these issues open up what may be an obvious question: what does it mean to be an American Buddhist, or what is the definition of American Buddhism? From the viewpoint of immigrant Buddhists, at least those from East and Southeast Asia (in contrast to South Asia), the Buddhist identity is never defined in any distinctive manner. Rather these Asian identities are complex wholes of interwoven strands drawn deeply from various religious, philosophical, and ritual traditions. It is perhaps among some white converts to Buddhism that the taking of the Three Refuges—in the Buddha, the Dharma, and the Sangha—provides the basis for a distinctive Buddhist identity. But just as many if not more white practitioners of the Buddhist path go so far as to say that to embrace a Buddhist "identity" requires no formal doctrinal commitments whatsoever.[24] And finally, there are also American Buddhists who do not consider Buddhist practice to be exclusive of other religious ways of life.[25] A common "testimony" among these "converts" is the ironic admission that for them, "Buddhism was also a gateway [back] to Christianity."[26] How should Christians respond in the face of this fluid and dynamic American Buddhist landscape?

22. These issues are brought out nicely in Cadge, *Heartwood*, 199–201.

23. An interesting case study is Tanabe Jr., "Grafting identity."

24. See, e.g., Batchelor, *Buddhism without Beliefs*.

25. See the essays in part I of Gross and Muck, eds., *Buddhists Talk about Jesus, Christians Talk about the Buddha*.

26. Tworkov, *Zen in America*, 181.

TOWARD A CHRISTIAN THEOLOGY OF INTERRELIGIOUS PRACTICES IN DIALOGUE WITH BUDDHISM

The preceding overview of Buddhism in America has been succinct in the extreme and does not do justice to the complexities of the American Buddhist experience. Nevertheless, my interests as a Christian theologian are to simply sketch what might be called the "lay of the land" with regard to American Buddhism, in order that we might chart some ways forward for the Buddhist-Christian encounter in the twenty-first century. In the remainder of this essay, I suggest that Christians should learn from the history of Buddhism in America that a wide range of postures, attitudes, and practices are essential for a vital interchange. This includes at least three overall approaches that I will call *social engagement, interreligious dialogue,* and *evangelical.*

There are at three aspects to the Buddhist-Christian encounter at the level of *social engagement*: the interpersonal, the communal, and the sociopolitical. With regard to the interpersonal dimension, I am thinking specifically about refugee Buddhist communities. Insofar as American Christians have been and remain hosts to a large number of Asian Buddhists who are forced refugees from their land of birth, to that same degree our primary obligation is to demonstrate what I have elsewhere called the hospitality of God.[27] Motivated here by the parables of the good Samaritan and of the sheep and the goats, I suggest that Christian hospitality to the stranger, the naked, the hungry, and the poor must include religious others who are also refugees, exiles, and immigrants of various types. Whether it is enabling their setting down new roots, learning new languages, adapting to new social customs, or simply obtaining needed employment or other forms of relief and assistance, the Christian task is to meet the needs of their (new) neighbors, when it is in Christians' means to do so.

This level of interpersonal engagement leads naturally to a discussion about community building. What I have in mind here is the kinds of local projects such as housing developments, institutional formation, and social networking that are essential for any new community to find its bearings in a strange land. The focus here, however, is on specific local communities so that the level of engagement is midway between that of merely interpersonal relationships and that of overly cumbersome bureaucratic structures. Projects at this level might include Christian contributions to the development

27. See my essays "Guests, Hosts, and the Holy Ghost" and "Spirit of Hospitality"; cf. also Yong, *Hospitality and the Other*, chs. 4–5.

of community centers and even religious sites. This is the praxis of what might be called communal hospitality.

A a third level of social engagement, however, might be that involving Christians and Buddhists forging alliances (that may not be exclusive of those in other faiths) to address common social, political, and economic concerns. We have already discussed the emergence of Engaged Buddhism. These are individuals committed to a compassionate engagement with social issues because they are drawn to the ideal of the Bodhisattva's vow to desist from entering into Nirvana so long as there remain any suffering sentient beings. At this level, then, social engagement focused on alleviating poverty, injustice, crime, and war, among other social ills, requires the goodwill of many people working patiently and persistently across religious boundaries.[28] Here Christians can, should, and must join forces with all whom God might raise up—and this would include their Engaged Buddhist coreligionists—to realize the peace, justice, and righteousness that anticipates the eschatological kingdom of God.[29]

A second level of Christian engagement with American Buddhism is what I call *interreligious dialogue*. Now of course, social engagement cannot proceed without dialogue of some kind. But socially engaging dialogue may or may not turn to explicitly religious—explicitly Christian or Buddhist—concerns. The interreligious dialogue I am now discussing, however, is focused precisely on religious matters. In the following, I will flesh this out in terms of academic dialogue, the dialogue of spiritual practices, and the dialogue of religious ideas. (Before doing so, however, I want to specifically identify, and reject, any notion that what I am calling interreligious dialogue in this discussion is understood merely instrumentally to serve the purposes of religious conversion. I believe there is a place for religious conversion, but I call the kind of dialogical engagement directed toward conversion "evangelical apologetics." We will return to that topic momentarily. Here, however, our focus is on interreligious dialogue for the many reasons other than that designed to produce religious conversion.)

The academic encounter generally involves experts from both traditions interacting from out of their research and scholarship. The goal at this level, as already mentioned, is to achieve mutual understanding. Academics of course do what they do for many reasons, not the least of which is intellectual curiosity, the love of teaching, or a predisposition to scholarly activity. In each of these cases, then, the purposes of interreligious dialogue

28. Hence the refrain of Hans Küng that that can be "No world peace without peace between the religions" (*Global Responsibility*, xv).

29. Christian theologians like Paul Knitter have thus argued for a liberationist theology of religions for precisely this reason; see Knitter, *One Earth Many Religions*.

between Christian and Buddhist scholars and academics would have as many different rationales as participants.

But there is a specific domain of academic interreligious dialogue that I think needs further comment: that involving the scientific disciplines.[30] While Christians and Buddhists can gather around the dialogue table representing a wide range of perspectives from the humanities, there is a growing realization that their religious perspectives also belong in the dialogue with the natural and human sciences. In this case, I am referring not just to Christians in dialogue with scientists or Buddhists in dialogue with scientists, but rather Christians and Buddhists and scientists interacting in what might be called a "trilogue."[31] Of course, such a trilogue is exponentially more complex than any dialogue because adding a conversation partner to the table multiplies the conversational directions. However, Christians have much to learn from how Buddhists are engaging the sciences and vice versa,[32] even as the sciences have much to benefit from a more inclusive encounter with the world of many religions. And insofar as we live in a world dominated by science, technology, and modern medicine, and inasmuch as there are urgent matters demanding our attention, such as global warming, the environment, and ethical issues surrounding our use (and possible abuse) of science, to that same extent the trilogue between Christianity, Buddhism, and science is not a luxury but a necessity.

The interreligious dialogue also includes, I suggest, the dialogue of spiritual practices. Here I am referring not only to the monastic interreligious dialogue that we have already seen, but also the dialogue between lay practitioners of meditation. In fact, at the lay level, many people who consider themselves Christians are avid advocates of Buddhist meditation practices,[33] even as there are also those who reject either the Christian or Buddhist label but have found much that is valuable in the contemplative traditions of both Christianity and Buddhism. In the latter case, meditators find themselves in group situations in which the interreligious dialogue revolves around the spiritual practices concomitant with, informed by, and supportive of meditation.[34] Here again, the reasons for dialogical

30. Christians have long been involved in the interface of religion and the sciences. Increasingly, Buddhists are making their presence felt in this arena as well; see my "Trinh Thuan and Intersection of Science and Buddhism."

31. I attempt to provide one model for such a trilogue in my "Christian and Buddhist Perspectives." [See also my book *The Cosmic Breath*.]

32. As laid out in Ingram, *Wrestling with God*.

33. As witnessed to in a book that is now a classic: Johnston, *Still Point*.

34. See Gross and Muck, eds., *Christians Talk about Buddhist Meditation, Buddhists Talk about Christian Prayer*.

engagement will vary according to the reasons for embracing the practice, and these range from health and lifestyle concerns to dealing with anxiety to deeply spiritual motivations. Inevitably, however, meditators are less inclined to dwell on doctrinal, theological, or philosophical matters if these fail to illuminate practice in some way.[35] For many of these, interreligious dialogue is both intrapersonal (involving the depths of their own beings) as well as interpersonal (involving other dialogue partners).[36] Many Buddhist practitioners interested in dialogue would consider dialogue itself to be a form of spiritual practice.[37]

This leads to a third level of interreligious dialogue, often the most controversial one: that involving religious ideas, including the doctrines, theologies, and philosophies of both Christian and Buddhist traditions. The reasons for the controversy have something to do with the (alleged) similarities and dissimilarities between Christian and Buddhist traditions. Those concerned about the similarities may be worried about religious syncretism or may just be interested in pursuing the question of how to understand such similarities and what their implications might be.[38] The dissimilarities, however, are just as controversial since they raise the question about how to define Christianity, Buddhism, and religion. Further, they also challenge the sometimes superficial assumptions about the possibility of Christian dialogue with and understanding of Buddhism, and vice versa. Finally, of course, there are the questions of truth claims and the fundamental claims regarding salvation and damnation on the Christian side, and regarding suffering, greed, ignorance, karmic consequences, and enlightenment on the Buddhist side. Which tradition has the greater explanatory power and why? These are very complex matters. I am convinced we are still at the very beginning stages of the Buddhist-Christian dialogue and that we will need much more time before being able to identify the appropriate comparative categories through which we can properly engage these issues.[39]

35. There are also, of course, many other forms of spiritual practices around which Christians and Buddhists might dialogue about. I discuss, for example, the rite of exorcism in Christianity and Buddhism in my "Demonic in Pentecostal-Charismatic Christianity."

36. Panikkar, *Intrareligious Dialogue.*

37. See Rowe, "Zen Presence in America."

38. A recent book with a fascinating title that is on my reading list is Pierce, *We Walk the Path Together.*

39. For sophisticated discussions of the difficulty and yet necessity of identifying appropriate comparative categories in the interreligious conversation, see the various essays on these topics in Neville, *Comparative Religious Ideas Project.*

Finally, I want to discuss what I call the *evangelical* approach to the Buddhist-Christian encounter. By this, I mean a posture that prioritizes evangelizing religious others because of the conviction that the Christian gospel or the Buddhist Four Noble Truths are indeed "good news" (hence: "evangelical") for all people and not only for those who are already Christians or Buddhists. Again, there are at least three aspects of this evangelical approach to the encounter: that related to religious freedom, that related to evangelistic strategies, and that related to apologetics. I will treat these in reverse order.

To begin, evangelical apologetics is but the flip side, I would argue, of interreligious dialogue.[40] By this, I mean that any genuine dialogical encounter must involve religious representatives who have sufficient understanding of and commitment to their own faith tradition so that there is something at stake in the discussion. Without involvement of such individuals, no dialogue ensues; rather a monologue of agreeing voices actually covers up what is really taking place. But given the presence of what I am calling evangelical apologetics, an authentic context of interreligious exchange emerges whereby the explanation of one's religious position at some point in the dialogic process is actually also an apology for that position.[41] Ironically, the greatest interreligious apologists are those who know other faith traditions just as well as their own.[42] In these cases, one is engaged not only in what might be called "negative apologetics" that defend one's position against the criticisms of others, but also "positive apologetics," wherein one critically interacts with the other tradition on its own terms. It should also go without saying, I hope, that evangelical apologetics is a two-way street: Christians who insist on having their turn on the proclamation and apologetic side of the dialogue must also be ready to listen.

A related task of evangelical apologetics is a kind of dialogical engagement that seeks to understand the religious faith of others for the purposes of facilitating smoother interreligious interactions focused on religious conversion. This is what some missiologists have called contextualization or inculturation. The key principle here is that evangelism and mission must be sensitive to the thought forms (world view), practices, and values of the receiving culture in order to minimize misunderstanding and maximize the possibility of reception. This is a part of all interreligious processes designed to establish, sustain, and perpetuate a religious tradition in a foreign context.

40. See Burrows, ed., *Redemption and Dialogue.*

41. See Griffiths, *An Apology for Apologetics.*

42. Here I am thinking about Buddhist apologists like Anagarika Dharmapala (mentioned above) as well as, more recently, Gunapala Dharmasiri, *Buddhist Critique of Christian Concept of God.*

We have seen that Buddhist missionaries, immigrant Buddhist communities, and American converts to Buddhism have wrestled with precisely this set of questions, and it may even be possible that Christians can learn from the experiences of their Buddhist interlocutors on this issue. What I want to warn against, however, is any kind of approach to interreligious dialogue that is not honest about the evangelical motivations for engaging the dialogue. Of course, our dialogue partners are usually able to see through our motivations and identify other purposes that bring us to the dialogue table. I am not saying that dialogue focused on missionization and evangelization is unacceptable. I am simply saying that if that is our objective, it should not be hidden, and that we should not step up to the interreligious dialogue table involving science, academics, monastics, etc., and pretend to be there for the purpose of fostering mutual understanding leading perhaps to mutual transformation, if in fact we are not. There is a time and place for everything, and it is important to be honest about the intentions behind our presence at the dialogue table.

This raises questions about the strategies for evangelical approaches to the interfaith encounter in general and to the Buddhist-Christian encounter in particular. Of course, evangelical apologetics needs to be engaged civilly and respectfully. But there are at least two sides to such an imperative: first, that such respect is earned in the give and take of dialogue borne out of deep commitments, and second, that such respect needs to be accorded up front to the dialogue participant as a matter of common human courtesy. Yet this element of common human courtesy and decency should apply not only in the case of evangelical apologetics but also in any evangelical approach to religious others. Here I have in mind specifically any and all forms of evangelization and missionization that may be deployed in approaching people of other faiths. I would insist that all forms of coercive proselytism—including making promises regarding financial or material reward in exchange for conversion; or the more subtle forms of manipulation that might be applied to people in vulnerable existential situations; or the structural forms of pressure that impinge on refugee populations, etc.—do not respect the integrity of people as religious agents.[43] Evangelical approaches must guard against adopting unfair tactics aimed at generating converts. Of course, this cuts both ways and applies to evangelical agents in all traditions. At the same time, the principle has its own consequences: genuine conversions are usually more lasting, whereas those who convert because of other (nonreligious) motivations do not remain.

43. Here the discussion of Vyver, ed., *Problem of Proselytism in Southern Africa*, is valid, even though the case studies focus on the South African context. See also Witte and Martin, eds., *Sharing the Book*.

But, finally, conversions themselves are certainly appropriate when evangelical approaches respect the religious freedom that the American Constitution protects and upholds. Going back to the 1893 Parliament of World's Religions and beyond, people of all faiths have been free to practice in America. Dharmapala, Soen, and Suzuki were Buddhist "evangelicals" who spread the Dharma far and wide and in the process convinced many Christians (nominal or otherwise) to consider Buddhist beliefs and practices. On the other side, of course, committed Christians have borne witness to the gospel to their Buddhist neighbors, co-workers, and friends; Christian evangelists have held rallies, crusades, and revival meetings inviting people of all or no faith; and Christian denominations have developed specific mission strategies to evangelize Buddhist immigrants to the USA.[44] The nature of religious faith is such that it invites sharing. Christians and Buddhists alike will be driven to share their beliefs and practices if their faith is vibrant. From the perspective of the Buddhist-Christian encounter in America, it would seem that nonrefugee immigrant Buddhists would be the most open to Christian conversion, not only because they have chosen to come to America to begin with, but also because they would be the most committed to assimilating into American life. These social dynamics invite the Christian mission to Asian American Buddhist communities, so long as Christian evangelical agents approach their mission with sensitivity, compassion, and integrity.

Robert A. F. Thurman, Jey Tsong Khapa Professor of Indo-Tibetan Buddhist Studies in the Department of Religion at Columbia University and a longtime Buddhist practitioner, at one point wrote that American Buddhism may be destined to play a key role in the evolution of Buddhism as a world religious tradition.[45] On the one hand, he is convinced that Buddhism must go beyond Buddhism in order to accomplish its American mission, since it should do so precisely in terms of bursting the category of religion altogether in the most pluralistic nation on earth. On the other hand, in the process, American Buddhism will temper the individualism and egocentrism of American life and in that way serve as the therapeutic mechanism that it is. If American Buddhism can do this, then it will continue to be the countercultural force it has been since its emergence in caste "India" in the sixth century BCE.

Similarly, I want to suggest, Christianity can play a number of interesting roles in the ongoing evolution of Buddhism in the American context.

---

44. E.g., Task Force on Christian Witness within a Buddhist Context, *Suffering and Redemption*.

45. Thurman, "Toward an American Buddhism."

On the one hand, Christianity can be a prod that challenges, inspires, and even motivates the transformation of Buddhism on American soil. We have already seen how this might happen in the lives of American converts to Buddhist traditions in America: inevitably, their Christian religious experiences have influenced their Buddhist practices. On the other hand, if Christianity is able to do this in any positive sense for American Buddhism, it will have to be at its best: sensitive to the dynamic complexities that characterize American Buddhism "on the ground" and capable of deploying the wide range of practices needed to engage the varied Buddhist traditions in their various stages of evolution. In these cases, the Christian contribution to the ongoing vitality of Buddhism in America will itself be what is required to sustain the plausibility and vigor of Christianity itself in a world of many faiths. Hence the diversification of Christianity mission practices spells not the waning of Christian faith, but precisely its intensification.

Ironically, then, the Buddhist mission to America would in turn have contributed in its own way to the transformation of American Christianity. In this reading, the Buddhist-Christian encounter in America will have been mutually transformative for both traditions. Such is exactly what happens when religious people are serious about their faith in a pluralistic world.[46]

---

46. A previous version of this paper was presented to the 50th anniversary meeting of Faith and Order, "On Being Christian Together: The Faith and Order Experience in the United States," Oberlin College, July 19–23, 2007. Thanks to Ann Riggs for the invitation to participate in this historic gathering. I am also grateful to my graduate assistant, Doc Hughes, for his feedback on a preconference version of this paper.

CHAPTER 9

The Church and Mission Theology in a Post-Constantinian Era

Soundings from the Anglo-American Frontier

THE CALL FOR A postcolonial missiology has not abated as we peer into the second decade of the twenty-first century.[1] For this we have to thank, at least in part, the honoree of this volume,[2] Professor Lamin Sanneh, for his untiring work in highlighting how the missionary successes of the church have been most spectacular when the gospel has been translated into the vernacular languages of the people. My question as a Malaysian-born, naturalized American but Western educated and situated theologian, however, is what these postcolonial developments mean for the Anglo-American context. More pointedly, what does it mean to fulfill the Great Commission in Anglo-America today, given the postcolonial shifts in the global South?

To ask this question, however, requires a shift from the discourse of postcolonialism to the discourse of post-Constantinianism and post-Christendom. The former (postcolonialism) registers the perspectives and highlights the experiences of the colonialized, especially in the global South; by contrast, the latter pair of terms identifies the situation after those in power particularly in the Anglo-American West have lost their places and spaces of privilege. In other words, to ask about a postcolonial missiology in the Anglo-American sphere invites consideration of a post-Constantinian and post-Christendom theology of mission.

---

1. See, e.g., Dharmaraj, *Colonialism and Christian Mission*, and Robert, ed., *Converting Colonialism*.

2. The volume in reference is Akinade, ed., *A New Day*.

In this essay, I overview the work of John Howard Yoder and Stanley Hauerwas, both of whom have struggled to articulate what they have called a post-Constantinian way of being church. I think both Yoder and Hauerwas can help us identify central theological and ecclesiological issues pertinent to doing mission in a post-Constantinian and post-Christendom (and hence postcolonial) context.[3] In the third part of this essay, I will flesh out aspects of such a post-Constantinian and post-Christendom ecclesial praxis as observed in the emerging church phenomenon in order to identify how the church exists *as* mission (rather than continue to think about how the church *does* mission). In conclusion, I will make correlations between the missionary praxis of these Anglo-American theologians and church movements and that of their postcolonial counterparts in the global South.

THE POLITICS OF MISSION: YODER'S POST-CONSTANTINIAN PROPOSALS

John Howard Yoder (1927–1997) has become one of the most renowned theologians from the Mennonite tradition. While we are unable to do more than scratch the surface of his theological contributions, Yoder's salvos against the heresy of Constantinianism are pertinent for our purposes.[4] Recall that the Roman emperor Constantine (ca. 272–337) converted to Christianity and in effect set in motion a process that eventuated in the Christianization of the Latin world. Along the way, those who before were at the margins of sociopolitical power and persecuted for their faith came to occupy the positions of authority and in turn persecuted others who did not fit into the new world of Christendom. By the time of the Reformation, church and state had been intertwined for a few centuries and the Radical Reformers, including the followers of Menno Simons (1496–1591), proceeded to resist the violence perpetuated by the state, rejected the collusion of the church in and with the affairs of the state, and insisted on a believer's church, with adult rather than infant baptism as the normative path toward membership.

Yoder's indictment of Constantinianism includes each of these elements bequeathed by the Mennonite and broader Radical Reformation and Anabaptist traditions. However, Yoder extends the critique along three

---

3. [Shortly after it was written, the basic thrust of this original festschrift essay was developed and expanded as ch. 5 of my *In the Days of Caesar*.]

4. A summary of Yoder's claims regarding the heresy of Constantinianism can be found in Carter, *Politics of the Cross*, esp. ch. 6.

lines[5]: that Constantinianism (a) affected the church's self-understanding since it collapsed the distinction between the church and the state (and the world); (b) compromised the practices of the church since the power of the church was now interwoven with and into that of the state; and (c) infected Christian discourse since the language of the church was now adopted and transformed by the state and the wider dominant culture. These developments have combined to vernacularize Christianity but in a way that has rendered it indistinguishable from the wider culture and society. Thus Christian ideas are defensible because they are based on a universal rationality; Christian teachings are acceptable because they are founded upon a natural theology; and Christian ways of knowing are comprehensible because they are accessed through a publicly and politically legitimated epistemology. In short, as one of Yoder's commentators has put it, "Constantinianism is the marriage of church and society under the auspices of a political authority."[6]

This should not be, insists Yoder. Instead of capitulating to the demands and rules of the state or the wider public sphere, Christianity provides its own norms, beliefs, and practices through the life of Jesus and the believing community. Yoder grants that in a way, what he is advocating is a sectarian ecclesiological self-understanding—not sectarian in the (by now pejorative) Troeltschean sense, but in the sense that the believer's church assumes the church is catholic (worldwide) and evangelical (focused on the good news of the gospel) and yet also exists as a minority group in terms of its values and commitments amidst and against that of the wider culture and society.[7] At one level, this position allows the church to be a prophetic voice that serves as a critical conscience for society. At another level, the church presents to the world an alternative polis, a countercultural reality that follows after the nonviolent teachings of Jesus.[8] What this requires, of course, is that the church refuses to be co-opted by the reigning powers that be—whether of the state, the culture, or the world—and embodies instead what some have called a diasporic mentality, replete with its own politics and ethics.[9]

Yoder finds models for such a political ethic in the early church. In his reading especially of Luke-Acts, he sees the early Christian community as empowered by the Holy Spirit to organize a public life that involves decision making and implementation, work structures and productive sharing,

5. For details, see Yoder, *Priestly Kingdom*, esp. ch. 7.

6. Heilke, "Yoder's Idea of Constantinianism," 92.

7. This is the gist of Yoder's ecclesiology, expanded on in his *For the Nations*.

8. As articulated in his now-classic text *Politics of Jesus*.

9. See Yoder, *For the Nations*, ch. 3; cf. Rasmussen, "Politics of Diaspora," esp. 103–9.

"ownership" of space and land, and handling of both public and private matters.[10] In all of these areas, the early church as a fellowship of the Spirit deals
with political (public) issues like forgiveness, servanthood, truth telling,
living hopefully, maintaining equal dignity, sharing, etc., and in the process,
relocates the dualism between church and world to that between obedience
(to God) and rebellion.

What are the implications of these ideas for a theology of mission? In
one sense, the answer is simple: the church bears witness to the gospel by
living out and testifying to the teachings of Jesus. Yet such embodiment of
Jesus' teachings is not only a spiritual matter but has concrete historical, social, and political ramifications. Thus, Jesus' way is one of peace in a world of
war; Jesus' ethic is one of forgiveness, reconciliation, and servanthood; and
Jesus' followers are to be salt and light in the world, set apart "on a hill," as it
were, although always seeking the peace of the cities within which they find
themselves.[11] In this sense, Anabaptist "sectarianism" does not constitute
a withdrawal from this-worldly affairs. Instead, the witness and mission of
the church is to be fully engaged with the world—not on the world's terms,
but on the terms established by the gospel—and to that extent the Christian
witness is fully political. This might involve challenges to civil authority,
boycotts of institutions and practices thought to be worldly, demands for
religious tolerance, and enactment of the public rite of believer's baptism as
political practice.[12] Yet, in all cases, Anabaptist witness is pacifistic, combining prophetic critique and nonviolent resistance.

But what about evangelization as traditionally conceived in the history
of Christian mission? What about when we encounter not the secular state
(with a Christian veneer, especially in a Constantinian context) but people
in other faiths? Given a post-Constantinian approach, Yoder has suggested
that Christians engage a pluralistic world in an ad hoc manner.[13] A Radical
Reformation approach to interfaith encounter does not need a fully developed metaphysics (natural theology), system of apologetics (in the modern,
Enlightenment sense), program of social activism (like liberalism), or even
the backing of councilor definitions (like the Roman Catholic Church).
Against all this, a post-Constantinian model starts with repentance (even

10. Yoder sketches what I would call a pneumatological politics in his *For the Nations*, ch. 11.

11. All developed in Yoder, *He Came Preaching Peace*.

12. Biesecker-Mast, "Critique and Subjection in Anabaptist Political Witness." For
other examples of both baptism and Eucharist functioning as rather direct forms of
political practice in the Roman Catholic context, see Cavanaugh, *Torture and Eucharist*.

13. See the chapter titled "Disavowal of Constantine" in Yoder, *The Royal Priesthood*, 242–61.

the repentance of an entire community), invites the telling of stories (testimonies) from the standpoint of the margins, and seeks only to interact honestly and dialogically with others who might be open to such engagements. In the process, Christians will learn from and even be enriched by dealings with their neighbors, even as they will in turn discern how to best translate the uniqueness of their Christian witness into terms intelligible to others.[14]

RESIDENT ALIENS: HAUERWAS AS A COLONY MISSIOLOGIST?

Yoder's work has served as a stimulus for Stanley Hauerwas's thinking, as Hauerwas himself has repeatedly acknowledged.[15] Of course, there are differences between the two, such as Yoder being a member of a marginal Christian community, which connects to his "free church" orientation, and Hauerwas being part of the "mainline," which perhaps explains his more liturgical sensibilities. These ecclesial locations may also explain why Yoder thinks a pluralistic society opens up space for minority voices while Hauerwas thinks that pluralism leads to the illusion of modern liberalism's mantra regarding freedom of choice. Part of the result is that Yoder is more open to the idea of the "translatability" of Christian discourse into other "tongues," while Hauerwas tends to think more in terms of the incommensurability of religious traditions.[16]

Yet these are relatively minor quibbles when it is seen that Yoder's critique of Constantinianism is substantially adopted by Hauerwas. More often than Yoder, Hauerwas uses the language of "Christendom," especially when talking about "Christian America."[17] Yet the points he makes are Yoderian in spirit, even if taken here and there in more philosophic directions. For example, in a collection of essays titled *After Christendom?*, Hauerwas laments that the alignment of the church with the wider American and Western cultures has muted the capacity of Christians to think, talk, and live distinctively as Christians.[18] This is because notions like justice, freedom,

14. For the record, Yoder was at various times in his life engaged in the Jewish-Christian dialogue, and wrestled deeply with the relationship between the two religious traditions; see, e.g., Yoder, *Jewish-Christian Schism Revisited*.

15. One result of this indebtedness is the Yoder festschrift edited by Hauerwas with Harry J. Huebner and Chris K. Huebner, titled *Wisdom of the Cross*.

16. For further discussion of some of these comparisons and contrasts, see Hovey, "Public Ethics of John Howard Yoder and Stanley Hauerwas."

17. See Hauerwas, *Christian Existence Today*, esp. 180–84.

18. Hauerwas, *After Christendom?*

and even democracy have lost their Christian character and content, having now been co-opted by the wider culture. Provocatively (as Hauerwas much more than Yoder tends to be in his writing and speaking), it is claimed that justice is a bad idea because its definition is secularly determined rather than formulated in terms of the gospel narratives and the practices of the believing community; that freedom, even our cherished freedom of religion, is a "subtle temptation" because when we think our religion is protected by the state, we become dependent upon and accomplices of the state and are thereby rendered incapable of speaking to or resisting the state; and that democracy is also a distorted notion since we all now assume there is some generic notion of truth, values, religion, morality, etc., which shapes our democratic institutions when in reality it is global capitalism which drives our nation rather than the God in whom our coins say we trust. In short, not only is the idea of a Christian nation (and of a Christian America in particular) a misleading one, it is downright pernicious since it lulls the nation's citizens and the church's members into a false and untruthful sense of identity.

So what is Hauerwas's concrete proposal for a post-Constantinian and a post-Christendom church? In two books written with William Willimon, Hauerwas has described the church using the metaphors of "resident alien" and "colony."[19] Inspired in part by the Petrine description of the body of Christ as "a chosen race, a royal priesthood, a holy nation" (1 Pet 2:9), the true people of God are imaged as a remnant of faithfulness amidst a wider culture that either ignores or rejects the claims of God. Hence Hauerwas invites Christians to think of their congregational lives as that within a colony assailed from without: "A colony is a beachhead, an outpost, an island of one culture in the middle of another, a place where the values of home are reiterated and passed on to the young, a place where the distinctive language and life-style of the resident aliens are lovingly nurtured and reinforced."[20] In this liminal "place" or space, as resident aliens, Christians are neither sectarian (withdrawn from the world) nor worldly (fully accommodated to the world); rather, they are specially trained—through living apprenticeships as well as emulation of their heroes, otherwise known as the saints—to embody their stories and engage the world, not according to the world's standards (which always involve violence), but according to the loving nonviolence of the gospel. Instead of feeling "at home" in the world, then, Christians are called to be uncomfortable, peculiar, and odd, a contrast that serves as a means to invite the world to another mode of life.

19. Hauerwas and Willimon, *Resident Aliens*.

20. Ibid., 12.

So for the church to be the church, its members are to take their practices of discipleship seriously, to cultivate the Christian virtues, and to nurture the Christian disciplines of joy, selflessness, worship, etc. Such practices contribute to and are also expressions of the communal narrative that provides the substantive Christian content to otherwise abstract philosophic notions (like justice, freedom, and democracy).

In one sense, Hauerwas is suggesting a replacement of the colonial paradigm with a postcolonial or, better, colony paradigm. Instead of the Christian mission proceeding from the center to the margins, he relocates the Christian presence to the margins and, from there, revisions the church's engagement with the center. Like Yoder before him, Hauerwas is advocating a diasporic mentality.[21] Such a mind-set is focused not on showing that Christians have an exclusive copyright on or ownership of practices like forgiveness, healing, praise, friendship, peace, etc., but that Christians have as central to their mission the obligation to remind the world to (re)enact or (re)actualize such practices.[22] Christians who get too entangled with the ways of the world inevitably compromise their distinctive identity and witness. Better to focus on being the church, the distinctive people of God; that in itself is the most productive form of mission that the body of Christ can pursue.[23]

To be sure, Hauerwas's primary "missiological" objective, if we may use that term, is the re-evangelization of a now-secularized "Christian America."[24] However, regardless of where Christians find themselves, their mission is to stand out of and from the world, always gesturing to (rather than coercing) the world in accordance with the nonviolent approaches of Christ. The result will be a post-Constantinian and even post-Christendom form of Christian colony that embodies the "peaceable kingdom" of Jesus.[25]

EMERGENT CHURCH: MISSIONS POST-CHRISTENDOM

It is now time to begin synthesizing the preceding theological and ecclesiological discussions (of Yoder and Hauerwas) in a more explicitly

21. Hauerwas, *The Hauerwas Reader*, 346.

22. Hauerwas, *A Better Hope*, esp. part III.

23. As Vigen Guroian notes, "When the churches set themselves to the task of serving the neighbors and strangers among them in public and private worlds, they do more for the general good than when they draw up programs for fostering public theology and a faith in civility" (*Ethics after Christendom*, 97).

24. Hence also Hauerwas's *Dispatches from the Front*.

25. Hauerwas, *The Peaceable Kingdom*.

missiological key. I have already suggested that the former post-Constantinian ideas are but one (Euro-American and Western) side of a coin that includes postcolonial proposals on the other (global South) side. From this angle, Yoder and Hauerwas might be read as filling out the formal theological and ecclesiological substance derived from existing Christian and missionary practices after Christendom. In this section, I wish to make the case for this reading of Yoder and Hauerwas, with an eye toward reengaging the task of developing a post-Christendom theology of mission.

Missiologists will by now have noticed that the Yoderian and Hauerwasian projects have been articulated, albeit in other words, by theologians of mission. Lesslie Newbigin, for example, has long talked about the need for mission to be delivered from "the cultural captivity of western Christianity."[26] The basic idea is that under the colonial paradigm, the missionary brought the gospel wrapped up in the cultural and ideological garb of the West, and conversion commanded the acceptance of Western culture and civilization. In contrast, once the seductiveness of the colonial (and Christendom) world view has been exposed, we can see the difference between genuine conversion to Christ that invites converts to explore how to live as Christians in their own context, as opposed to proselytism that requires them to give up their inherited cultural identities for another one.[27] While missionaries have often preached conversion, they have usually practiced approaches that demand new believers to fit into a prepackaged script from another culture. One way to minimize confusion of these matters is to empower those being missionized with a greater (if not majority) voice in defining their Christian self-understanding. To do so would be to engage in the Christian mission not from its centers of power, but from the various sites on the periphery.[28] Here, the postcolonial proposals of Newbigin and others would intersect with the post-Constantinian perspectives of Yoder and the "resident aliens" described by Hauerwas.

Other theologians of evangelism and mission, such as Bryan Stone, agree with Yoder and Hauerwas that "the most evangelistic thing the church can do today is to be the church—to be formed imaginatively by the Holy Spirit through core practices such as worship, forgiveness, hospitality, and economic sharing into a distinctive people in the world, a new social option,

---

26. Newbigin, *A Word in Season*; cf. Hall, *End of Christendom and the Future of Christianity*, ch. 4.

27. I get this distinction from Smith, *Mission after Christendom*, 128.

28. See the editor's introduction in Sutherland, ed., *Mission without Christendom*, 9; cf. also the proposals of the dean of pentecostal scholarship, Walter Hollenweger, for a noncolonial form of evangelism—as discussed in Price, *Theology Out of Place*, 110–20.

the body of Christ."[29] In this case, the church would not *have* an evangelistic strategy but would actually *be* such. Evangelism then becomes a core church practice not in terms of being a production oriented toward the achievement of certain goals, but in terms of being the constitutive identification of what it means to be disciples of Christ. Whatever the church does becomes a mode of mission and evangelism. For example, if in the Christendom paradigm the Eucharist was the center out of which mission was generated, in the post-Christendom model, eucharistic practice is precisely about sharing, solidarity, and witness. In this case, there emerges a new politics and economics of evangelism that allows us to see how breaking bread together becomes a site both for embodying and enacting the life of Christ to the world and also for calling the world toward such countercultural fellowship. Thus Stone suggests that, "The economic patterns displayed and enacted in such practices are a necessary condition for inviting the world into a new *oikos* that by its very existence subverts rival ideological claims about family, gender, race, sexuality, or class."[30]

Stone's suggestions invite us to consider the phenomenon of the emerging churches that has captivated the imagination of missiologists, ecclesiologists, and theologians.[31] Although our concerns are predominantly missiological, the post-Christendom discussion has revealed that the church's theology of mission cannot be separated from its ecclesiological self-understanding. This is also the case among leading theorists of the emerging churches. Thus Stuart Murray of the United Kingdom Anabaptist Network published two books in 2004 on the nature of the church post-Christendom, and each is not just replete with missiological implications but also deeply and profoundly missiological at its roots.[32] He notes that the emergent-type churches are not just seeker oriented and purpose driven, but their anti-institutional structures are simply more conducive to outreach and evangelism than those established after the Christendom model. What is appearing are cell or house churches, café gatherings, cyber-churches, community-oriented churches (focused on midweek meetings, etc.), post-church communities, new monastic communities, spirituality oriented groups of practitioners, and congregations in workplaces, pubs, and clubs. These innovations are fundamentally both ecclesiological and missiological, with neither primary over the other.

29. Stone, *Evangelism after Christendom*, 15.

30. Ibid., 202; cf. Bayer, *A Resurrected Church*, ch. 9.

31. See Gibbs and Bolger, *Emerging Churches*, and Pagitt and Jones, *An Emergent Manifesto of Hope*.

32. Murray, *Post-Christendom* and, shortly thereafter (although published in the same year and by the same publisher), *Church after Christendom*.

In Murray's reconceptualization, then, a post-Christendom *ekklesia* means a shift from the center to margins, from the majority to the minority, from an understanding of the church as being constituted by settlers to that constituted by sojourners, from the church considered as an institution to the church considered a movement, from Christian privilege to a plurality of competing interests, from a stance of Christian control to one in which Christians bear witness through serving others, from an emphasis on ecclesial maintenance to one of ecclesial mission.[33] Mission post-Christendom thus requires the church's repentance from hypocrisy and from a lifestyle of comfortableness (and its concomitant vices including cultural imperialism, violence, colonialism, proselytism, interreligious snobbery, rejection of secular agencies, etc.). Instead of missions understood only in terms of proclamation to others, there is a reconception of mission as embodying the gospel in lifestyle and works of service. The church consists not of programs, buildings, or institutions but of people, spiritual practices, and relationships. Further, there is no homogeneity in the worldwide body of Christ; rather, the church embraces pluralism and diversity, deeply informed by the practices of hospitality and welcome. The result is an emphasis on process rather than on documenting convert "decisions."

Yet politically and culturally, there are also new modes of engagement. Besides the church embracing a prophetic stance vis-à-vis society, it also sees the state as consisting of powers, capable of redemption.[34] Yes, there is a separation of church and state, each distinct with its own divine vocation, but this separation does not lead to a quietism with regard to the church's social witness and her concern for justice on behalf of the poor. Instead, the church adopts multiple modes of engagement—reinforcement, retreat, rescue, reform, radicalism, resistance, revolution—all valid in different contexts.[35] This is in part because the church's existence may be revivalistic in some contexts, but is in survival mode in others; in either case, the focus is not on domination, but on serving Christ through serving others. Ultimately, the church's allegiance is to God and the coming kingdom, not to the nation. Since Jesus is Lord, not Caesar, bearing witness and "speaking the truth in love" becomes the church's dominant political strategy.[36]

---

33. Ibid., 20.

34. I present an argument for the redemptability of the powers in my *In the Days of Caesar*, ch. 4.

35. I have argued something similar in terms of the church needing to be discerning about adopting different strategies of mission and engagement depending on the context; see my *Hospitality and the Other*.

36. Murray, *Post-Christendom*, 248.

Clearly Murray's Anabaptist vision connects at various points with Yoder's Mennonite ecclesiology, and maps well onto Hauerwas's exhortations regarding the church as a colony of resident aliens. Murray, however, is first and foremost a missiologist, so in his work, post-Constantinianism and post-Christendom are translated into missiological terms. The concern is on the form of the missional church, not on ecclesiology per se (at least not ecclesiology as traditionally conceived and understood).

In this essay we have explored the contours of what I have called a post-Constantinian and post-Christendom theology of mission in dialogue with North American theologians John Howard Yoder and Stanley Hauerwas, and the emerging church networks in America and the United Kingdom. The preceding discussion has illuminated some of the ways in which such post-Constantinian and post-Christendom thinkers, ideas, and movements parallel what is occurring on the postcolonial soil of the global South. Three sets of comparisons and contrasts are particularly germane in thinking about the church and mission theology as we head into the second decade of the twenty-first century.

First, the post-Constantinian and post-Christendom theologies of mission begin with the nature of the church on the periphery or margins of society. Yoder and Hauerwas thus explicitly call for the church to give up its power at the center and embrace a marginal identity and status. Only in this way, the argument goes, is the church able to present a countercultural witness that shows how the ways of the world and the ways of the gospel are antithetical. But part of the problem with this approach is that in the global South, the church is in many respects already on the margins, and the option of adopting a minority status is generally not available to globally Southern churches. Precisely for this reason, however, the opportunity arises for diasporic exiles, resident aliens, and emerging churches to learn from their brothers and sisters in the majority world about counterculturality. In this respect, postcolonial ecclesiologies and missiologies honed outside the mainstream of their respective centers of power have much to teach Christians seeking to be freed from the privilege and power of Constantinianism and Christendom.

Second, the emphases placed by post-Constantinian and post-Christendom theologians and movements are more on practices rather than on doctrines. More precisely, it is on the core practices of Jesus, especially as emulated by the earliest disciples and messianic followers. Doctrines are not unimportant, but they are clarified and confirmed by the core practices of the church as the living body of Jesus Christ. This emphasis on narrative—the narratives of Jesus and the early believers (especially the Acts of the Apostles), and the narratives of the historical and contemporary church—parallels the role of orality and narrative in the churches of the global South.[37] Not without reason, the churches of Asia, Latin America, and, especially, Africa are marked by a reliance of the narratives of the Hebrew Bible as these recount the stories of the people of God and their relationship with God.[38] Here, Yoder's openness to carefully rereading the Jewish Scriptures provides a bridge over which northern and southern Christians can meet as they explore what it means to be the people of God and what kinds of practices best witness to the world from the margins.

Finally, Yoder's diasporic and exilic mentality along with Hauerwas's resident alien and colony approach combine to highlight the sojourner orientation that marks the missional stance of the contemporary church. What this involves is less a set of missional programs or initiatives than a flexible and dynamic way of being church, and a discerning mode of operation that pays attention to the contextual factors that inevitably shape the church's concrete engagement with the world. Mission thus is less carried out by "outsiders" than emerges as "insiders" discern how best to live out the gospel faithfully from the margins of power and of society. There is an inherent flexibility in such a missional dynamic since it does not have to defend any status quo but can be open to the surprises thrown up by such journeys on the margins.[39]

The challenge for the church in the global South is whether or not there is sufficient resistance to the forces of institutionalization that inevitably and inexorably propel younger churches in their striving for social respectability, cultural assimilation, and political power; the challenge for the church in the West is whether or not prophetic voices like Yoder's or Hauerwas' will be heeded amidst the last gasps of Christendom. Perhaps the colonial, Constantinian, and Christendom forces will yet prevail, or perhaps out of these ashes will arise new forms of Christian faith and life that are only vaguely hinted at in this essay.

37. As Walter Hollenweger has remarked, the vanguard of world Christianity—featuring predominantly pentecostal and charismatic type churches—is characterized by an oral form of theological discourse; see Hollenweger, *Pentecostalism*, part I.

38. See Jenkins, *New Faces of Christianity*, esp. ch. 3.

39. For postcolonial narratives that illuminate precisely this missional orientation a in global context, see Phan and Lee, eds., *Journeys at the Margin*.

PART IV

Systematic Missiology

Notes for a Christian Missiological Theology

CHAPTER 10

Primed for the Spirit

Creation, Redemption, and the *Missio Spiritus*

THE FOCUS OF THIS article is on the pneumatological foundations of Christian mission. Our thesis is that the work of the Holy Spirit in creation, redemption, and eschatological salvation is central to Christian mission theology. Theology of mission is thus approached in terms of the *missio Dei* more generally and the *missio Spiritus* more specifically. This argument for a pneumatological missiology is attentive to recent trends and developments in both theological and missiological literature. In the conclusion, the practical implications of such a pneumatologically oriented theology of mission are explored.

PNEUMATOLOGICAL FOUNDATIONS FOR CHRISTIAN MISSION

Christian theology of mission can be understood in some respects as undergoing a paradigm shift. The older colonial, Enlightenment-based, and Western-motivated approaches have been undergoing convulsions in the last two generations and have slowly given way to postcolonial, post-Enlightenment, and post-Western voices and perspectives. Focus on spiritual or eschatological salvation has shifted toward more holistic emphases that include not only embodiment and materiality but also socioeconomic and political considerations. These various developments have been registered in missiological themes such as *missio Dei*, holistic mission, and transformative mission, as well as in other mission initiatives focused on indigenous agency and local contextualization or inculturation.[1]

Missiological discourse has also been impacted theologically by the emergence of the doctrine of the Trinity and the renaissance of the doctrine of the Holy Spirit (pneumatology) in the last half of the twentieth century.[2] Discussions after Barth have led to an invigoration of thinking about trinitarian theology—e.g., by Pannenberg, Moltmann, and Jenson, among others—and this also has been registered in discussion in theology of mission. Not surprisingly, *missio Dei* perspectives have morphed in a trinitarian direction, not only in terms of emphasizing the divine economic missions of the Son and the Spirit but also in terms of exploring the relevance of trinitarian motifs for missiology.[3]

Alongside developments in Trinitarian theology has been the reemergence of the doctrine of the Holy Spirit.[4] Not surprisingly, such pneumatological reflections have also made their mark in theology of mission.[5] This article endeavors to sketch the pneumatological foundations of such missiological discourse by tracing the implications for the theology of mission of the doctrine of the Spirit in relationship to the doctrines of creation, redemption, and the eschaton. By following out the *missio Spiritus* with regard to these traditional theological and doctrinal loci, we shall see how a pneumatologically founded and funded missiology both reflects and also interfaces with the ongoing paradigm shifts in theology of mission.

1. Representative of this transition is David Bosch's magisterial *Transforming Mission*.

2. As a systematician, I presume the Christian doctrine of the Trinity, but at the same time, I am not unaware of the hazards of reading the Bible from this post-Nicene perspective. The challenges are particularly highlighted when thinking about pneumatology since, as John H. Levison argues—in his *Filled in the Spirit*—the *ruah* of the Hebrew Bible and the *pneuma* of the Christian Testament are not easily translatable into the postconciliar orthodox terms of personal hypostasis regarding the Father and the Son. Nevertheless, this is neither the time nor the place to adjudicate these matters, not to mention that there are space constraints that prohibit how far off the beaten path we can tread in pursuit of this issue. My only recommendation is that readers presuppose neither an unequivocal identity between the biblical references and our received Trinitarian understanding of the Holy Spirit nor a discontinuity between them.

3. The most rigorous development in Trinitarian missiology is Tennent, *Invitation to World Missions*. [Even more robust than Tennent is Sunquist's more recent book, *Understanding Christian Mission*.] See also Chester, *Mission and the Coming of God*, and Seamands, *Ministry in the Image of God*.

4. Much of my work has been devoted to this task; therefore I apologize in advance for the many self-references in the following pages.

5. The classic study is Taylor, *Go-Between God*. Other important works in this area include McConnell, ed., *Holy Spirit and Mission Dynamics*; Kim, *Mission in the Spirit*; and Kärkkäinen, *Toward a Pneumatological Theology*, esp. part IV.

THE SPIRIT OF CREATION: *MISSIO SPIRITUS*—ACT 1

In thinking about pneumatology, pneumatological theology, and pneumatology of mission, we should begin with the doctrine of creation. This not only helps us to ground pneumatological reflection in the doctrine of God, but it also establishes the cosmic, creational, and global scope of the work of the Spirit. Both points are important. Without connection to the doctrine of God as creator, the Spirit may turn out to be less than "holy," perhaps not even related to the God of Judeo-Christian faith at all, or even to monotheistic or theistic sensibilities.[6] There are many spirits indeed, so Christian thinking about pneumatology must be defined, at least initially, as the Spirit of the God who created the heavens and the earth. And without relation to the latter, cosmic compass of the Spirit's work, then we may be tempted to merely interiorize or subjectivize the Spirit's presence and activity.

The role of the Spirit in the Christian doctrine of creation has gradually been recognized.[7] In my own work, I have attempted what I have called a pneumatological reading of the Genesis narratives.[8] This begins with the observation that while "the earth was a formless void and darkness covered the face of the deep," the author of the creation account notes that "a wind from God [*ruah Elohim*] swept over the face of the waters" (Gen 1:2). So while traditional creation theologies have highlighted the creation of the world through the word of God, a pneumatological perspective notices both that the word of God is uttered through the divine breath and that the "history" of the world is "blown" or swept along by the presence and activity of the *ruah Elohim*. The partitioning of the waters from land, the emergence of vegetation, the evolution of life itself—each of these can be understood from this pneumatological vantage point as being propelled by the breath of God that transcendentally hovered over the primordial creation.

But the divine breath is not only transcendent over the creation but also immanent within it. This is because all living creatures have been constituted by Elohim's "breath of life" (Gen 1:30). In particular, human beings have been personally visited by the creator God: "then the Lord God formed man from the dust of the ground, and breathed into his nostrils the breath of life; and the man became a living being" (Gen 2:7). Living creatures, especially human beings, are thus essentially constituted by the divine breath. As

6. There are also possibilities for thinking about the spirit of God in relationship to monotheistic traditions more generally and to the Islamic tradition in particular. I undertake a dialogue with the latter in my *Spirit Poured Out on All Flesh*, ch. 6.

7. The major text so far is Moltmann, *Spirit of Life*. See also Balthasar, *Creator Spirit*; Wallace, *Fragments of the Spirit*; and Edwards, *Breath of Life*.

8. See Yong, "*Ruach*, Primordial Waters, and Breath of Life."

it is said later in the Hebrew Bible: "If he should take back his spirit to himself, and gather to himself his breath, all flesh would perish together, and all mortals return to dust" (Job 34:14–15). Beyond this, however, the Psalmist indicates that the divine breath not only gives life to creatures, but also that through it, the face of the ground is renewed (Ps 104:29–30), just as the prophet Isaiah proclaims that "a spirit from on high is poured out on us, and the wilderness becomes a fruitful field, and the fruitful field is deemed a forest" (Isa 32:15). This suggests that the rhythms of creation itself beat to the drumming of the creator Spirit.[9]

Before going any further, however, it is important to note the missiological implications of a pneumatological theology of creation. If a Logos theology emphasizes that the Word became flesh and, as the true light, "enlightens everyone" in the world (John 1:9), then the doctrine of *creator Spiritus* insists that all life, human life included, exists through the infusion of the divine breath. Thus, as the ancient poets recognized, "In him we live and move and have our being" (Acts 17:28). Human beings meet one another, thereby, on a pneumatological plane. More pointedly, humans interrelate with one another pneumatically, through the breath of life given by the *ruah* of God. Christian mission is thus always and primordially *missio Spiritus*.[10]

But there is one more layer to pneumatological theology of creation that should be lifted up before turning to the doctrine of redemption. Divine redemption is required because although the *ruah Elohim* both hovered over the primordial waters and became the breath of life for all living creatures, nevertheless with the fall of creation, the cosmos and all of its creatures remain alienated from God the Creator. Paradoxically, then, the *ruah Elohim* is simultaneously both present to all creatures—enlivening and vivifying the creation—and yet also absent from them, in the estrangement creatures feel toward other creatures and their Creator. In anticipation of this redemptive work, then, the promise is given in the Hebrew Bible that God will redeem the world pneumatologically through the chosen or elect nation of Israel.

There are two moments constitutive of such a pneumatological promise. First, God pledges to Abraham that, "in you all the families of the earth shall be blessed" (Gen 12:3). Second, however, even the divine promises are insufficient to preserve and ultimately save the people called of God. Rather, God needs to accomplish an internal work, a work of the Spirit: "A

---

9. See also Ellington, "Face of God as His Creating Spirit."

10. Here I apply Lyle Dabney's notion that we begin always and already in the Spirit, except not just in the Christian sense of encountering God through the Holy Spirit but also in the Hebrew sense of being enlivened by the *ruah Elohim*; see in particular Dabney's chs. 1 and 4 in Preece and Pickard, eds., *Starting with the Spirit*.

new heart I will give you, and a new spirit I will put within you; and I will remove from your body the heart of stone and give you a heart of flesh. I will put my spirit within you, and make you follow my statutes and be careful to observe my ordinances" (Ezek 36:26–27). This anticipates the later gift of the Spirit in Christ. But for our purposes at this juncture, it is important to point out that the creational mission of the Spirit not only infuses the dust of the ground with life but also looks ahead to another pneumatic outpouring and infilling. In other words, the creation as a whole, as well as its creatures, is primed to receive the redemptive fullness of the Spirit.

THE SPIRIT OF REDEMPTION: *MISSIO SPIRITUS*—ACT 2

The second moment of the *missio Spiritus* moves us from the universality of the Spirit's presence and activity in the creation to the particularity of the Spirit's historical work in redemption. This redemptive history involves the incarnation of the Son via the power of the Spirit followed by the Son's gift of the Spirit to the people of God. But why are both essential? For at least two reasons, one historical and the other spiritual. Historically, the Son came in order to renew and restore Israel as the people of God, and this renewal and restoration was intended both to serve as a template for the kingdom of God and to inaugurate that kingdom.[11] But God's offer of restoration and renewal in the Son was rejected and he suffered a violent death; yet his death became salvific for his people because he served as a scapegoat that prevented further outbreaks of violence (at least for one generation).[12] Spiritually, the life and death of the Son represented the obedience that served as the basis of reconciliation of human beings in particular and the world as a whole with God; then the resurrection and ascension of the Son confirmed the potentiality of the world's transfiguration in the presence and power of God. Hence, as the ancient church confessed, the Son became human so that human beings might be redeemed as children of God; by extension, the

11. Here, I am in basic agreement with the central thrust of N. T. Wright's interpretation of the mission of Jesus; my own appropriation of Wright's account is in my *In the Days of Caesar*, ch. 3.

12. This historical reading of the significance of Jesus' life and death I find in the persuasive even if controversial thesis of René Girard, who has written many books on mimetic violence and the scapegoat. There is also a growing secondary literature debating the pros and cons of his argument. My own point of entry into Girard's work has been his *I See Satan Fall Like Lightning*.

Son was clothed with the dust of the earth so that the creation itself might be renewed as the dwelling place of God.[13]

But the mission of the Son cannot be divorced from the *missio Spiritus*; in fact, they are inextricably intertwined. The Spirit is the power not just of the Son's breath of life but also of the Son's conception and generation in the womb of Mary; just as the *ruah Elohim* hovered over the structural ordering of the primordial chaos, so also did the Spirit both overshadow and come upon Mary (Luke 1:35). Then, the Spirit descended on the Son at his baptism in the Jordan (Luke 3:22) so that he could be filled with the Spirit for his public ministry, itself launched by his spiritual confrontation with the demonic powers of the world (Luke 4:1, 14). Thus does Jesus pronounce that his mission is that of the Spirit's: "The Spirit of the Lord is upon me, because he has anointed me to bring good news to the poor. He has sent me to proclaim release to the captives and recovery of sight to the blind, to let the oppressed go free, to proclaim the year of the Lord's favor" (Luke 4:18–19). The rest of his public ministry unfolds this agenda according to the power of the Holy Spirit (Acts 10:38).[14]

If Jesus accomplished the saving works of God—proclamation of the gospel to all, in particular to the poor, healing the sick, delivering the oppressed and the captives, and inaugurating the Jubilee year of divine favor and redemption[15]—through the power of the Spirit, then so also did his original disciples. They were initially told to wait in Jerusalem for "power from on high" (Luke 24:49) and then later promised: "you will receive power when the Holy Spirit has come upon you; and you will be my witnesses in Jerusalem, in all Judea and Samaria, and to the ends of the earth" (Acts 1:8). So as the Gospel of Luke narrates the saving works of the Spirit impelling the life and ministry of Christ, so the book of Acts tells, in turn, of Jesus' sending from the right hand of the Father the promised redemptive power of the Spirit to the lives and ministries of the apostolic believers (Acts 2:33).

13. The preceding only outlines a few important trajectories for a theology of the atonement. A more in-depth discussion can be found in my *Spirit Poured Out on All Flesh*, ch. 2. For greater elaboration of a pneumatological soteriology in dialogue with disability perspectives, see my *Theology and Down Syndrome*, chs. 6–8.

14. This is the basis for a Spirit-Christology, not one that dispenses with Logos-Christology but that recognizes the "from above" model to insufficiently capture the historicity and humanity of the life and ministry of the Son through the Spirit. I unpack the Spirit-empowered ministry of Jesus as Savior/deliverer, sanctifier, Spirit-Baptizer, healer, and coming king in my *In the Days of Caesar*, part II.

15. There is a virtual scholarly consensus that "year of the Lord's favor" cited by Jesus from the Isaianic scroll refers to the ancient Israelite year of Jubilee, in which economic justice was reestablished throughout the land. See, e.g., Laseto, *Nazareth Manifesto*. A contemporary expansion is Lord, *Spirit-Shaped Mission*.

Whereas Jesus came first to renew and restore Israel, with forays into Samaria, the Spirit-filled ministry of the earliest followers of Jesus took them to the ends of the earth.[16]

The outpouring of the Spirit at Pentecost brings to historical fulfillment two promises made to ancient Israel. First, if ancient Israel had been disobedient to the covenant with Yahweh due to hardness of heart, the newly reconstituted people of God were no longer merely bound externally by law but were empowered internally by transformed hearts that had been touched by the Spirit. This is one of the central messages of New Testament: that the Hebraic law provided for sacrifices for sins but the gift of the Spirit enables the evangelical obedience that produces sanctified and holy lives (see Heb 9:13–14 and passim). In other words, the divine breath of life in every person as a result of the creative work of the Spirit is now, potentially, the divine breath of holiness as a result of the redemptive work of the Spirit unleashed on the Day of Pentecost.

Secondly, the Pentecost outpouring of the Spirit inaugurates the promised redemption of the nations derived from the covenant made with Abraham. This occurred in two ways: through the presence at Jerusalem at the Pentecost feast of "devout Jews [and proselytes] from every nation under heaven living in Jerusalem" (Acts 2:5, 10), and through the apostolic missionary movement that not only went from Jerusalem to Rome (as recounted in Acts) but that also commissioned others to take the gospel in other directions (i.e., as did the Ethiopian eunuch in Acts 8).[17] There are innumerable cultural and religious implications here in the Pentecost narrative for the Christian mission (to which I return to comment on at the end of this essay), but the root of the issue is that the promises made to Abraham are now available to the Gentiles, which together with the Jews constitute the church as the people of God. This was a point of tumultuous contention among the earliest followers of Jesus as the Messiah, primarily because most of them were uneducated Jews who could not understand why the covenant promises were now being extended to their Gentile oppressors. The *missio Spiritus* thus generates ongoing surprises that involve the crossing of borders so that agents of mission continually find a blurring of the lines between "insiders" and "outsiders"—at least on this side of the

16. For my own commentary (not quite in the traditional scholarly commentary genre but consisting certainly of my own exegetically based analyses) on Acts, see Yong, *Who is the Holy Spirit?*

17. Pentecostal missiologists who have made this argument include Pomerville, *Third Force in Mission*; York, *Mission in the Age of the Spirit*; and Anderson, *Spreading Fires*.

eschaton during which time we all see through a glass dimly—in the divine scheme of things.

The lack of formal closure to the book of Acts invites readers in every place and time since to participate in the work and witness of the spirit of God in Christ as part of the book's twenty-ninth chapter, as it were. The Spirit who empowered the Son and who was poured out upon and filled the apostles is the same Spirit who continues to accomplish the redemptive work of God in Christ and through the church in this post-apostolic period. This ongoing work in history, however, leads us to the third and concluding act of the *missio Spiritus*.

THE SPIRIT OF THE ESCHATON: *MISSIO SPIRITUS—* ACT 3

We began with the work of the Spirit in creation and have in the preceding discussed the Spirit's redemptive work in Christ and the Pentecost outpouring that constituted the church. Now we turn to the eschatological work of the Spirit anticipating the final renewal and restoration of the creation as a whole. This eschatological work, however, was inaugurated in the redemptive work of the Spirit in the life, death, and resurrection of Christ. As the Apostle Peter said (quoting the prophet Joel, at least as recorded by Luke the evangelist): "*In the last days* it will be, God declares, that I will pour out my Spirit upon all flesh . . . " (Acts 2:17, citing Joel 2:28; italics added).[18] Again, there are two dimensions to this eschatological work of the Spirit: the christological and the ecclesiological.

Christologically, the eschatological work of the Spirit is most clearly revealed in Jesus' proclamation regarding the coming kingdom and his accomplishing the signs of the kingdom. These latter include his miraculous deeds, his healings, and his exorcisms of evil spirits.[19] These are signs of the coming kingdom precisely because they can be understood either as enacted by suspensions of the present order of things (i.e., the "laws of nature" as currently conceived) or as anticipations of the ways in which the coming world will operate.[20] The Spirit enables Christ to accomplish the works that bring about the shape of the coming kingdom, in the process announcing the end of the present cosmic order.

18. Pentecostal mission has by and large been motivated by this eschatological impulse; see, e.g., Goff Jr., *Fields White unto Harvest*, and Faupel, *The Everlasting Gospel*.

19. E.g., Williams, *Signs, Wonders, and the Kingdom of God*, and Irvin, *Healing*.

20. I make these arguments in my *The Spirit of Creation*, chs. 3–4; see also my article "How Does God Do What God Does?"

Most importantly, however, the Spirit announces the arrival of the kingdom in the resurrection of Jesus. If death is the most ubiquitous sign of the world as we know it, resurrection life provides us with a foretaste of the world to come. The apostles noted that Jesus was "put to death in the flesh, but made alive in the spirit" (1 Pet 3:18b)—alternatively: "He was revealed in flesh, vindicated in spirit . . . " (1 Tim 3:16)—and "declared to be Son of God with power *according to the spirit of holiness by resurrection from the dead*" (Rom 1:4, italics added). So whereas sin, condemnation, and death reign in the present dispensation, holiness, justification, righteousness, and resurrection life are signs of the coming kingdom. Hence, "If the Spirit of him who raised Jesus from the dead dwells in you, he who raised Christ from the dead will give life to your mortal bodies also through his Spirit that dwells in you" (Rom 8:11). Yet even christologically, the fullness of the Spirit is not yet manifest; that awaits the Parousia and the return of the anointed Messiah who will finally and fully establish the coming reign of God. As the author of the first Johannine epistle writes: "when he is revealed, we will be like him, for we will see him as he is" (1 John 3:2).

But again, the work of the Spirit in the life, death, and resurrection of Jesus is now available to the followers of Christ, the church—the body of Christ and the fellowship of the Spirit. We now also have received the Spirit as well as the gifts of the Spirit that are given liberally for the edification of all and for the common good (1 Cor 12:7–11).[21] Empowerment by the Spirit thus also enabled the apostles to work miraculous signs and wonders, including healing the sick, exorcising demons, and even raising the dead. These continued the pronouncement regarding the imminence of the coming kingdom even while precipitating its arrival. Delivered by people of the eschatological Spirit, the apostolic message was proclaimed "not with plausible words of wisdom, but with a demonstration of the Spirit and of power" (1 Cor 2:4). In this sense, then, the church as the people of the Spirit glimpses through the eschatological mirror dimly (1 Cor 12:13), even now enacting the works of the kingdom in anticipation of the full glory that is to be revealed. There is a fundamental sense, then, in which the Spirit is both present (already having introduced the coming reign of God) and yet also absent (still to fully establish the righteousness of God).

Yet the eschatological work of the Spirit is not merely anthropocentric but has a cosmic scope. The Apostle Paul wrote: "We know that the whole creation has been groaning in labor pains until now; and not only the creation, but we ourselves, who have the first fruits of the Spirit, groan inwardly

---

21. For more on my pneumatological theology of the charisms, see *Spirit of Love*, ch. 7.

while we wait for adoption, the redemption of our bodies" (Rom 8:22–23). On the one hand, the outpouring of the Spirit upon all flesh has already begun the final transfiguration, to the point that the sun, the moon, and the heavenly elements have also begun to anticipate the great and coming Day of the Lord (Acts 2:19–20); on the other hand, the gift of the Spirit in Act 2 has done no more than initiate the apocalyptic conditions under which the fullness of redemption—the third Act—will be fully accomplished in the coming reign of God. In the meanwhile, there will be fleeting signs of the Spirit's presence and activity, following after the works of the Spirit manifest in Christ and the charismatic experiences of the apostolic believers, works which are a prelude to the fullness of the Spirit's work in the future. While Easter Sunday has occurred in the resurrection of Christ and in the regenerating work of the Spirit (the "already" of the Spirit's presence), yet the world nevertheless remains also amidst the Holy Saturday of the present fallen order, betwixt and between the times, anticipating the resurrection of all flesh (the "not yet" of the Spirit's eschatological activity).

But beyond the resurrection of dead bodies, this final eschatological revelation of the Spirit signals the completion of the divine work begun in the creation of the world and brings to fruition what was set in motion in the hovering of the *ruah Elohim* over the primordial waters.[22] All of creation is destined to be reconciled to the Creator: not only human beings but also the entire cosmic order. This is so that all things may be reconciled to God in Christ (Col 1:15–20) and that "God may be all in all" (1 Cor 15:28b): "For from him and through him and *to him* are all things" (Rom 11:36, italics added). The dynamic engine driving this eschatological reconciliation, however, is the Spirit. In other words, the Spirit of creation and redemption is also the coming Spirit, the one who enables the renewal and restoration of all things to the image of God in Christ. So if in Act 2 the redemptive work of the Spirit enables her inhabitation of human flesh—first the flesh of Jesus and then that of all flesh—then in Act 3, the eschatological work of the Spirit transforms and transfigures all creation as the dwelling place of the Spirit of the living God.[23]

PNEUMATOLOGICAL PROLEPSIS AND CHRISTIAN MISSION

This paper has attempted to survey the pneumatological foundations of Christian missiology by identifying the mission, role, and work of the Spirit

22. See Yong, *In the Days of Caesar*, ch. 8.3.

23. This is the brilliant thesis of Macchia, *Justified in the Spirit.*

in creation, redemption (in Christ and through the church), and the eschaton. I proffer that such a pneumatological emphasis is essential for a fully Trinitarian mission theology precisely because most have an anemic theology of the Holy Spirit. Without a robust pneumatology, allegedly Trinitarian theological constructs inevitably reduce to binitarian formulations (at best). But a sturdy pneumatological foundation that understands the *missio Spiritus* as both related to but also distinct from the economy of the Son will result in an enriched patrology and Christology while simultaneously comprehending the full scope—both the cosmic across space and the diachronic across time (past, present, and future)—of God's redemptive work.

There is one more set of implications for a *missio Spiritus* understood in three acts—that concerning the scope of the Spirit's presence and activity. If the Spirit's creative reach stretches across the cosmos, and if the Spirit's redemptive work covers, at least potentially, all flesh, then a pneumatological theology of mission includes at least also the following domains:

- a theology of culture that sees the cultural dimension of human life already imbued with the Spirit's presence and activity, thereby enabling the inculturation and contextualization of the gospel message;[24]

- a political theology that sees the Spirit is already at work in the public, social, and economic spheres of human life, thereby enabling the redemption and transfiguration of these dimensions of human existence according to the gospel of Christ;[25]

- a theology of religions that views the religious dimension of human life as pointing to and awaiting fulfillment in the gospel of Jesus Christ;[26]

- a theology of the environment or an ecological theology that sees the en-Spirited nature of the creation and all creatures as anticipating the renewal of the cosmos as the dwelling place or inhabitation of the Holy Spirit.[27]

---

24. [For a sketch of what I have called a hermeneutics of culture, see my *Spirit-Word-Community*, 300–305.]

25. I suggest (in *In the Days of Caesar*, §2.2.3 and passim), following Abraham Kuyper's notion of sphere sovereignty, that these are prelapsarian dimensions of human experience, the powers of which are judged and redeemed by the gospel.

26. My own work has focused on the implications for the pentecostal narrative for interreligious encounter, relations, and dialogue—e.g., *Discerning the Spirit(s)*, *Beyond the Impasse*, and *Hospitality and the Other*.

27. Aside from their many other important contributions to pneumatology, this has been one of the significant legacies of feminist theologies of the Spirit—e.g., Prichard, *Sensing the Spirit*; Victorin-Vangerud, *Raging Hearth*; and Marshall, *Joining the Dance*.

Each of these domains is not necessarily devoid of demonic aspects. Mission in the Spirit, however, enables the discernment of spirits so that what is impure can be identified and exorcised in order that what remains can be redeemed to bear witness—through the many tongues of the Spirit—to the wondrous works of God in Christ (Acts 2:11).

This tripartite pneumatological missiology also suggests that while we live in the world (the cosmos) even as we are not of it, we also abide in the present as informed by the past but yet anticipate the future. More precisely, the eschatological Act 3 of the Spirit has already arrived in a real sense in the life, death, and resurrection of Christ. This means that the present is now primed for transfiguration according to the power of the Spirit whose kingdom is both here (Luke 17:21) but also paradoxically yet to come. In other words, our present era is also the time of God's proleptic revelation. The future time of the Spirit is now present, at least in part, in and through the body of Christ. Hence we experience the resurrection life of the Spirit even while we hasten the soon arrival of the kingdom.[28] Life in the Spirit is thus received in faith, experienced in love, and anticipated in hope. And the *missio Spiritus* is less driven by the forces of history than drawn forward by the pull of the eschaton. If that is the case, then the Christian mission is less about what we do—as important as that is—than about our participation in the last days' work of the Spirit to renew, restore, and redeem the world. Come, Holy Spirit . . .[29]

---

28. See Cho, *Spirit and Kingdom in the Writings of Luke and Paul.*

29. Thanks to Dr. Jooseop Keum of the World Council of Churches Committee on World Mission and Evangelism for his invitation to participate in this Working Group on Mission and Spirituality. My graduate assistant Timothy Lim read and commented on a prior version of this paper. The ideas represented, however, are my own.

CHAPTER 11

Christological Constants in Shifting Contexts

Jesus Christ and the *Missio Spiritus* in a Pluralistic World

RECENT DEVELOPMENTS IN CHRISTIAN theology of religions have included a turn to pneumatology.[1] Yet these developments have drawn forth various reservations regarding how to understand the relationship between the work of Christ and the Spirit in a pluralistic world; whether it is possible to bracket christological commitments, however momentarily (as some have urged), in the interfaith dialogue and encounter; and what the implications of such a pneumatological prioritization are for Christian self-understanding.[2] Although various responses to these concerns have been articulated,[3] questions persist about how to understand the mission of and in the Holy Spirit (*missio Spiritus*) in a world of many faiths.[4]

This essay pursues the christological questions related to a pneumatological theology of religions. It is motivated by the sense that christological concerns in this area reflect anxieties about how to understand the

1. I have been one at the forefront of this discussion, with a number of books on the topic, including *Discerning the Spirit(s)* and *Beyond the Impasse*.

2. These are the major questions posed by critics such as Merrick, "Spirit of Truth as Agent in False Religions?"; Miles, *A God of Many Understandings?*, ch. 6; and Johnson, *Rethinking the Trinity and Religious Pluralism*, ch. 4.

3. See, for instance, Richie, "Spirit of Truth as Guide into All Truth." My own responses include "A P(new)matological Paradigm for Christian Mission in a Religiously Plural World" [ch. 3 in this volume] and "Jesus, Pentecostalism, and the Encounter with Religious Others."

4. On the *missio spiritus*, see my "Primed for the Spirit" [ch. 10 this volume].

fundamental reality of Christian faith and mission in a pluralistic world. Hence, I argue two interrelated theses: that although there is one Christ, there are many understandings of that Christ and these are intrinsically related to the contexts of Christian mission as well as to the encounter with those in other faiths that occurs in mission;[5] and that such a multifarious and dynamic Christology both presumes a robust pneumatology in general and is supported by pneumatological or Spirit-Christology in particular. While we will not in what follows engage at any length with the details of the interreligious encounter, the discussion is both informed by as well as undergirds an openness to those in other faiths that respects and honors the differences of their particularities.

The essay is structured triadically according to three central and interrelated categories related to the work of Christ embedded deep within the Christian tradition: of Christ as king, prophet, and priest.[6] Each section, however, will unfold the two mutual theses in two steps: by approaching each christological theme from a pneumatological perspective, and by following up on the opportunities and challenges opened up by such a pneumatologically understood Christology for the interfaith encounter. The considerations of Christ as king and prophet will also trace out the pneumatological trajectories toward their eschatological horizons in relationship to this discussion. In the end, we shall see that such a pneumatological Christology empowers Christian mission not just of lips (and words) but of hands and hearts as well, and it may well be that the latter witnesses ultimately do more for Christian mission in a pluralistic world than might have been anticipated. More precisely, what emerges is a dialogical posture of openness to those in other faiths on the one hand and, on the other hand, a prophetic stance toward engaging such others from out of a committed Christian identity.

CHRIST THE KING: THE SPIRIT ENABLES PROCLAMATION AND CONFESSION OF JESUS

The Philippian hymn indicates that Christ's kenosis or humiliation was precisely the reason for his subsequent ascension and exaltation. "Therefore," St. Paul writes, "God also highly exalted him and gave him the name that is above every name, / so that at the name of Jesus every knee should bend, in heaven and on earth and under the earth, / and every tongue should confess that Jesus Christ is Lord, to the glory of God the Father" (Phil 2:9–11). This

5. Here I am helped by Bevans and Schroeder, *Constants in Context*.

6. E.g., Letham, *The Work of Christ*, and Sherman, *King, Priest, and Prophet*.

image of Christ's enthronement is comprehensive, cosmic, and eschatological. Christ's kingship is already established, but not yet actually fully realized by every knee and tongue.

And how shall this realization unfold? Historically, it has been believed, through Christian obedience to the Great Commission of going to the ends of the earth, bearing witness to Christ, and making disciples of all people (Matt 28:19, Acts 1:8). St. Paul also indicated as such:

> But how are they to call on one in whom they have not believed? And how are they to believe in one of whom they have never heard? And how are they to hear without someone to proclaim him? And how are they to proclaim him unless they are sent? As it is written, "How beautiful are the feet of those who bring good news!" But not all have obeyed the good news; for Isaiah says, "Lord, who has believed our message?" So faith comes from what is heard, and what is heard comes through the word of Christ (Rom 10:14–17).

The logic of this regal Christology suggests that each person will either acknowledge Christ as king freely in response to the gospel message or that even those who do not do so in the present life will, regretfully, do so in the world to come. The implications for Christian mission and evangelism are clear: that followers of Christ ought to be motivated to proclaim him to all nations before the end arrives (cf. Matt 24:14). Failure to do so will mean that there will be more who bend their knee and confess the name reluctantly (while in the process of being consigned to eternal damnation) than willingly (the prerequisite for their joyous acceptance into eternal bliss).

There are two further implications for the preceding with regard to Christian mission in a pluralistic world. First, people in other faiths bow to and worship other (false) deities. Hence, second, unless they are converted to Christ in this life, they will, belatedly and amidst the suffering of everlasting retribution, acknowledge Christ as king. Such conclusions seem inexorable when considered within the logic of Christian faith understood in this way. They do not, however, take into account what religiosity involves for others, or consider how the faith without which "it is impossible to please God" (Heb 11:6) might be otherwise manifest or expressed.

Such a classical "exclusivist" position, as it has come to be known—which basically insists that salvation in the world to come is found exclusively in bending the knee to and confessing Christ in the present life "for there is no other name under heaven given among mortals by which we must be saved" (Acts 4:12)[7]—nevertheless founders on the question concerning the

---

7. I use "exclusivism" as a catchall phrase since it is the more traditional designation

status of those who are unevangelized: is Christ's kingship eschatologically begrudging for those who have never heard the gospel? More pointedly, it overlooks the fact that Scripture is basically silent about this issue. The famous John 3:16 text, for instance, is followed by the assertions that "God did not send the Son into the world to condemn the world, but in order that the world might be saved through him. Those who believe in him are not condemned; but those who do not believe are condemned already, because they have not believed in the name of the only Son of God" (John 3:17–18). Yet "those who do not believe" are neither logically nor actually equivalent to those who have never heard the gospel.[8] The latter do not believe not because they have rejected the gospel but because they have never been in the position to believe and confess. In fact, this raises a series of questions: what does it mean to be adequately evangelized? At what point can Christian missionaries or evangelists be assured that what they have communicated to their audiences is sufficient for their believing? How do we know all of the factors on the recipients' side that may facilitate their believing unto redemption or hinder their unbelief unto damnation? What if, for instance, we spoke of God the Father who loves us all so that he sent the Son to die for us, and our hearers include those who have been abused by their fathers? How do we know that our message may actually inhibit reception of Christ?

Other questions persist. What if people are evangelized first by Oneness pentecostals, Jehovah's Witnesses, or Mormons, all of whom affirm Christ's substitutionary atonement but otherwise have a variant understanding of the person of Christ from that of classical Christianity? Or what if people are first witnessed to by, and accept the testimonies of Nestorian, or Apollinarian, or Arian Christians, all of whose christologies have been rejected by the mainstream of the Christian faith? Is their bended knee to and confession of the Arian, etc., Jesus valid in God's sight? Or when exactly did the Christian dispensation begin, in which salvation is bestowed according to knowledge and confession of Christ's name? On the Day of Pentecost? At the moment of Christ's ascension? His resurrection? His death? His baptism? His birth? Let us assume, for the moment, that the answer to this is Pentecost and it can be dated. Then another series of questions arise: Did this moment—of "before" and "after" Christ—apply to all who were alive during this period? Only to all who were born after this moment? Only to those who died before this moment? In other words, if a new soteriological dispensation was

---

for the position sketched here, even though "particularism" has become more *en vogue* in recent times; see, e.g., Geivett and Phillips, "A Particularist View."

8. These are contested matters, especially among evangelical Christians—e.g., Fackre et al., *What about Those Who Have Never Heard?*, and Crockett and Sigountos, eds., *Through no Fault of Their Own?*.

inaugurated at Pentecost so that salvation after this related to confession of Christ, then did this requirement apply only to all living at that moment? To only those born after that moment? Or to those "evangelized" (which is not easily definable, per above) after that moment? Does "before" or "after" Christ apply to Christ's person and work apart from hearers or receivers of the gospel or does it apply only when the latter are evangelized?[9]

I think that these questions are basically unanswerable both scripturally and theologically, and that this is in part why many evangelicals have moved from an exclusivist position to a more inclusive one that does not minimize the kingship of Christ but is less dogmatic about how to understand the exaltation of Christ, now and eschatologically, among those who are (properly or not) evangelized. The exclusive position's strength is its emphasis on the cognitive content of knowing Christ, but this strength is also its weakness for the unevangelized, which include those unevangelizable (those who die as infants or those with severe and profound intellectual disabilities).[10]

My approach is to emphasize not only Christ as Logos, "the way, and the truth, and the life" (John 14:6), but also as the one whom God anointed "with the Holy Spirit and with power" (Acts 10:38a). Such a Spirit-christological perspective recognizes also that Christ is the "true light, which enlightens everyone" (John 1:9) and that "no one can say 'Jesus is Lord' except by the Holy Spirit" (1 Cor. 12:3b). The cosmic Christ (of John's Prologue) is the anointed one of God's Spirit even as confession of Christ's lordship occurs under the work of the same Spirit. Normally this occurs through evangelism and conversion as classically conceived. However, due to inadequate or nonevangelization—whether due to constraints of space and time or due to inhibitions related to biology (i.e., cognitive disabilities), psychology (i.e., lack of capacity to adequately comprehend or translate the gospel), culture (i.e., a culture of shame rather than that of sin), or the political (i.e., in a Muslim country where it is illegal to convert to Christianity)—faith in Christ can be pneumatologically generated even if not expressed according to traditional manifestations.

In a pluralistic world, such Christ-following can be genuinely enabled by the Holy Spirit but be covert rather than overt as in the various forms of hidden or cultural rather than ecclesial (as in Hindu Christians or Muslim followers of Isa) Christians. Alternatively, understandings of Christ can be mediated in different categories more relevant to diverse religious contexts

9. For elaboration of these difficult questions, see my article "Spirit, Christian Practices, and the Religions," esp. 14–16.

10. I take up the theological questions related to intellectual disability in my book *Theology and Down Syndrome*.

(as in Christ the guru in South Asia, the awakened one in Buddhist environments, as ancestor in Africa, etc.). These are not to be considered statically or absolutistically. Rather, they reflect the dynamic horizons of mission and evangelism, simply recognizing that sometimes people come into relationship with Christ through certain pathways, but that neither ends nor precludes further christological development.

This is in part because what people (of any other or no faith) encounter is not just a set of doctrines (the Nicene or Chalcedonian Christ, for instance, as important as these symbols are for Christian orthodox self-understanding), but the living Christ. Indeed, the Christ who came is also the Christ who is coming, who we "now we see in a mirror, dimly, but then we will see face to face" (1 Cor 13:12). And knowing this Christ is not just articulating a set of propositions but being transformed into his living image: "We are God's children now; what we will be has not yet been revealed. What we do know is this: when he is revealed, we will be like him, for we will see him as he is. And all who have this hope in him purify themselves, just as he is pure" (1 John 3:2–3).

A Spirit-Christology neither denies nor displaces a Logos-Christology. Rather, a pneumatological approach recognizes that the eternal Son and Word of God nevertheless became flesh, thus taking on human form in all of its concreteness, contextuality, and particularity, and hence that human beings encounter the living Word amidst their historicity, sociality, linguisticality, and even perhaps even cultural-religiosity. None of this embraces the worlds of the religions as is or only on their own terms. It is to say that insofar as God is in the redemptive business, and insofar as there are elements of truth, goodness, and beauty in the cultural and religious traditions of the world, then for Christians, these anticipate and are finally and eschatologically fulfilled only in Christ.[11]

Christ the king, hence, rules not by lording it over the improperly-, under-, or unevangelized. Rather, the king is also the servant who meets human beings in their own tongues, idioms, and realities. Confession of Christ is not imposed but emerges out of a living testimony to a personal relationship with Christ in the Holy Spirit. Discernment of Christ's enthronement in a pluralistic world can only be eschatological, but even that can be anticipated in the present by hints in the lives of people of faith, however implicit these may be. How else then might we discern the presence of Christ through his Spirit in the world? Thus while there is kerygmatic proclamation in any authentically Christian approach to and interaction with those

---

11. See the pentecostal and evangelical Indian theologian Satyavrata, *God Has Not Left Himself without Witness.*

in other faiths, such ought to be carried out conversationally with humility as well, and herein we anticipate the prophetic and yet dialogical posture to be more clearly delineated below.

PROPHETIC CHRIST: THE SPIRIT EMPOWERS THE HANDS OF THE BODY OF CHRIST TO ANTICIPATE THE REIGN OF GOD

The clearest way to discern the shape of Christ is to identify the works of Christ. Here, a Spirit-Christology also emerges to the fore, one which empowers the prophetic message and even prophetic actions. At the beginning of his ministry, Jesus said of his own vocation, drawing from the prophet Isaiah:

> The Spirit of the Lord is upon me,
> because he has anointed me
> to bring good news to the poor.
> He has sent me to proclaim release to the captives
> and recovery of sight to the blind,
> to let the oppressed go free,
> to proclaim the year of the Lord's favor (Luke 4:18–19; cf. Isa 61:1–2).

The rest of Jesus' life and ministry, as recorded in the Gospel of Luke, manifests this prophetic way of life under the charismatic anointing of the Spirit. The good news of the prophetic Christ resonates with the poor, is liberative for those oppressed and captive in whatever respects, includes the healing of those afflicted or impaired, and involves proclamation of the Jubilee year of redemption.[12] Note then that the gospel comes not as a set of abstract proclamations but as engaging, remedying, and transforming specific historical situations. These include the Holy Spirit empowering life amidst poverty, bringing healing to human bodies, and transforming socioeconomic conditions. Yes, there is a spiritual and perhaps even psychological dimension to these works of Christ, but these are not merely to be spiritualized or psychologized. Rather the word of Christ is good news precisely because it addresses not just human heads but lives in all their specificity and complexity.

The disciples seemed to have "got it" in terms of living out the Spirit-filled life in the footsteps of Jesus.[13] They did not shrink back from pro-

12. See Prior, *Jesus the Liberator.*

13. I elaborate on this claim and those of this paragraph in my book *Who is the Holy Spirit?*; cf. Yong, *In the Days of Caesar*, ch. 3.

claiming the name of Christ (note Acts 4:12 cited above), yet did so not in the abstract but in the concreteness of daily life. For them, the Pentecostal baptism of the Spirit that empowered witness to the living Christ involved baptism into his name and embodiment of his way of life. So,

> All who believed were together and had all things in common; they would sell their possessions and goods and distribute the proceeds to all, as any had need. Day by day, as they spent much time together in the temple, they broke bread at home and ate their food with glad and generous hearts, praising God and having the goodwill of all the people. And day by day the Lord added to their number those who were being saved (Acts 2:44–47).

Notice then that the confession of Christ involved acceptance of and obedience to his message. If Jesus proclaimed the Jubilee message of full human redemption, then apostolic preaching would also need to be confirmed by liberation according to the Jubilee paradigm. Hence confession of Christ's name brought with it acknowledgment of his lordship, even over their personal possessions. The boldness of life in the Spirit here enabled not only pronouncement of a prophetic message but also embodiment of a countercultural way of life. In fact, Christian witness to the unbelieving world is here seen to flow out of rather than foreground Christian community. The disciples did not make evangelism of those outside the community their priority; rather, they focused on living out the liberative dimensions of a prophetic life and "day by day the Lord added to their number those who were being saved"!

My claim is that in a pluralistic world, actions speak louder than words. In fact, turning up the amplifier on traditional evangelistic activities without preceding or following with a holistic Christian witness is counterproductive. A prophetic message about Christ without a prophetic Spirit-empowered mode of community engagement and transformation undermines the Christian witness. In that sense, Jesus himself challenged the Jews to heed the prophetic parable of the good Samaritan. Whereas the lawyer's self-concern for inheriting eternal life blinded him to the way of life manifest in the teacher he was addressing, the Samaritan's concern for others reflected the fruit of eternal life without knowledge of the "Teacher."[14] This is not to say that people—whether of other or no faith—are saved by works. It is to say that while works on their own are not salvific, the fruits of the Spirit are expressions of the work of the Spirit perhaps even where the name of Christ is either unknown or unconfessed.

14. See further my discussion of this parable vis-à-vis the interfaith encounter in my *Spirit Poured Out on All Flesh*, 240–44.

It is here that I think Christ the prophet requires not merely a repetition of prophetic discourse but embodiment of the prophetic message of liberation for the poor, justice for the oppressed, and deliverance of all in captivity. In part for this reason, theologians of the religions like Paul Knitter think it inconceivable that we focus only on what religions (including Christianity) teach and neglect what they may or may not do to inspire missionary collaboration toward making the world a better place.[15] Knitter's point is that any message that does not prophetically engage the destructive powers of this world is a pseudogospel, and that Christians thus should look for opportunities to work with other religionists toward a more just world. For me, Christ the prophet thus challenges the conventions, systems, and structures of the world, especially those which perpetuate the death and destruction brought on by the Satan (cf. John 10:10). Toward this end, any Christian theology of religions or any evangelical approach to other faiths that does not encourage mutual social witness when possible fails to heed the prophetic message of Christ.[16] As such, then, the prophetic stance in the footsteps of Christ is relational—even dialogical (as will be explicated momentarily)—in interacting mutually with those of other religious paths.

In the end, Christ the prophet judges the world in accordance to whether they have embodied his prophetic way of life. While there is much debate about how to understand the parable of the sheep and the goats in Matthew 25—with some arguing that those who are poor, naked, hungry, sick, and in prison are not people in general but missionaries of the gospel more specifically[17]—sometimes I think that this amounts to Christians looking for excuses to focus only on their own rather than on the non-Christians around them. The fact of the matter is that the telling of this parable, unique to Matthew, is yet consistent with the telling of the parable of the good Samaritan, unique to Luke. In both cases, the discussion is on attaining eternal life, and in each case, inheritors of such life are not those "in the know" but those who live out the heart of the gospel, in particular its concerns for the poor, the hurting, and the oppressed. In the case of the good Samaritan, it is precisely those "in the know" who are in most danger of forfeiting life everlasting, and this is consistent also with the Matthean warnings that:

> Not everyone who says to me, "Lord, Lord," will enter the kingdom of heaven, but only one who does the will of my Father in heaven. On that day many will say to me, "Lord, Lord, did we

15. See especially Knitter, *One Earth Many Religions* and *Jesus and the Other Names.*

16. I make this argument in my book *Hospitality and the Other*, esp. ch. 5.

17. See my discussion of this passage in *Bible, Disability, and the Church*, 136–41.

not prophesy in your name, and cast out demons in your name, and do many deeds of power in your name?" Then I will declare to them, "I never knew you; go away from me, you evildoers" (Matt 7:21–23).

In fact, how followers of Christ respond to the poor and hurting of the world can be considered as the fruit of their confession. Such "work" will in the day of judgment "be revealed with fire, and the fire will test what sort of work each has done. If what has been built on the foundation survives, the builder will receive a reward. If the work is burned, the builder will suffer loss; the builder will be saved, but only as through fire" (1 Cor 3:13b–15). Human beings will eventually be judged according to what they have done (Rev 20:12), and this includes how they have responded to the message and life of Christ the prophet. It is the work of the Spirit to enable not just a verbal confession of Christ but the sanctified and missional life on behalf of others that Christ exemplified.

In a pluralistic world, this dimension of Christ the prophet is important since it highlights that we have to be concerned not only with the teachings of the religions but also with their practices.[18] To the degree that other faiths inspire liberative actions by their adherents and urge initiatives of justice to address social, structural, and systemic inequalities, followers of Jesus as Messiah ought to partner with their coreligionists to address these latter realities that oftentimes can only be confronted with coalitions across ideological (and religious) lines. To the degree that other cultural and religious traditions perpetuate unjust practices, to that same degree, concomitantly, living out the prophetic message of Christ should urge Christian opposition to and confrontation of such as well as provision for an alternative Jubilee-type future.[19] Christ the Spirit-filled prophet hence becomes an exemplar for a Spirit-empowered prophetic mode of interaction with people in other faiths.

CHRIST THE PRIEST: THE SPIRIT DIALOGICALLY ENGAGES HUMAN HEARTS AND LIVES WITH THE LIVING CHRIST

Christ is, finally, also priest. As priest, Christ is the "one mediator between God and humankind . . . who gave himself a ransom for all" (1 Tim 2:5–6). Christ's priesthood is often considered as central to the doctrine

18. See Yong, "Inviting Spirit."

19. For more on prophetic mission, see Bevans and Schroeder, *Prophetic Dialogue*.

of the atonement of Christ, especially its substitutionary character, which, however many other (nonsubstitutionary) facets there are, should not be minimized. Christ the mediator between deity and humanity includes his intercessory work. In the exclusivist model, this means knowledge of Christ that confesses his having bridged the chasm between God and creation opened up by sin.

However, in considering Christ as mediator, I would like to suggest also Christ as a dialogical pathway between divinity and humanity. The Greek for "mediator" is *mesites*, which also means "go-between," analogous in many ways to the etymology of dialogue, or *dialogos*, as a between space enabling two (or more) to meet and converse. St. Paul himself, the model apostolic missionary, utilized dialogical approaches in his evangelistic work. At Thessalonica, Corinth, and Ephesus it is said that he engaged in dialogue and in reasoned discussion (*dialegato*) on a regular basis (Acts 17:2, 18:4, 19). The dialogues at Athens, especially at the Areopagus (Acts 17:27–28), reflected Paul's engagement with and drawing upon pagan sources familiar to his audience to make his points.[20] In Lystra, earlier, Paul similarly resorted to what might be called natural theological arguments in urging that God "has not left himself without a witness in doing good—giving you rains from heaven and fruitful seasons, and filling you with food and your hearts with joy" (Acts 14:17). Throughout, Paul showed himself to be the consummate missionary, always holding fast to his commitment to Christ but yet sensitive to his audience, appreciative of his status as guest in the presence of others,[21] and alert to a more mediating mode of interacting with others. This is nowhere more palpably expressed when on the isle of Malta, amidst "barbarians" (*barbaroi* from Acts 28:2), where we find Paul being the recipient of Maltese hospitality and yet also purveyor of divine generosity in healing the father of the islanders' chief official, all without any indication that kerygmatic proclamation was the *modus operandi*. This suggests that while the Christian encounter with those in other faiths can never defer indefinitely the evangelical moment of lifting up the name and person of Christ, this can also be done in ways other than verbal ones. Christ as mediator can be present by the power of the Spirit in many forms and interactions, each of which can be charismatic moments of significance in the interfaith encounter.

My claim is that a Spirit-Christology empowers witness to Christ in many tongues and according to many modes of receptivity, at least as forecasted in the Day of Pentecost narrative. If the Pentecostal miracle was

20. See Gärtner, *Areopagus Speech and Natural Revelation*.

21. The theme of being guests of religious others is a challenging but important one; I have addressed its implications variously, e.g., "Spirit of Hospitality" and "Guests, Hosts, and the Holy Ghost."

both that of speech (in unknown and unlearned languages) and of hearing (as the crowd in Jerusalem queried in surprise: "how is it that we hear, each of us, in our own native language?"—Acts 2:8), then why ought not the Christian witness amidst the interfaith encounter also be mediated by a multiplicity of modes of communication? More precisely, the Pentecost model suggests that every encounter involves a two-way dialogue between the evangelist and his or her audience, one mediated by the translatability of the gospel into a diversity of tongues or cultural-linguistic, if not also religiously refracted, forms.[22] This is because languages never exist only in the abstract but are always carried by cultural realities and the latter are also never absolutely separable from religious beliefs and practices.

Concretely, we can see how the Spirit inspires a dialogical witness to the living Christ in Peter's encounter with Cornelius.[23] There is no de-emphasizing the fact that Peter declares and proclaims "Jesus Christ—he is Lord of all . . . judge of the living and the dead" (Acts 10:36b and 42b) to Cornelius and his household. He is also clear about Jesus' death and resurrection (10:39–40), and that "everyone who believes in him receives forgiveness of sins through his name" (10:43b). The result is that Cornelius and all who were with him received the Holy Spirit, began "speaking in tongues and extolling God" (10:46), and were "baptized in the name of Jesus Christ" (10:48).

On the other hand, it also ought not be minimized that through his encounter with Cornelius, Peter himself was also transformed. Whereas previously he considered himself an observant Jewish worshiper of the one true God who separated himself from unclean Gentiles and pagans, this episode brought about a change of perspective: "God has shown me that I should not call anyone profane or unclean" (10:28). More pointedly, Peter came to see that "God shows no partiality, but in every nation anyone who fears him and does what is right is acceptable to him" (10:34–35). Thus was Cornelius characterized, even before his conversion, as a "devout" (or "godly," from the Greek *eusebes*), "upright" (or "righteous," from the Greek *dikaois*), and "God-fearing man" (10:2 and 22). Not only did Peter come to a new estimation of Gentiles like Cornelius, he also came to see that the way of Jesus was wider than previously understood: "Can anyone withhold the water for baptizing these people who have received the Holy Spirit just as we have?" (10:47). Later Peter would become an apologist for accepting and receiving such unclean or profane people (10:14–15, 11:8–9) into baptismal

---

22. I make this argument in many places, but most succinctly in my article "A P(new)matological Paradigm for Christian Mission" [ch. 3 of this volume].

23. Richie, *Toward a Pentecostal Theology of Religions*, esp. ch. 1.

faith to other Jews who questioned such activity: "If then God gave them the same gift that he gave us when we believed in the Lord Jesus Christ, who was I that I could hinder God?" (11:17). My point is to highlight the dialogical nature of the encounter between Peter and Cornelius. Both were transformed as a result of meeting. We might say that while Cornelius was converted to Christ, Peter was also converted in his relationship with the God of Jesus Christ. Herein we find Christ revealed through the Spirit not only as dialogical priest (enabling the mutual transformation of Cornelius and Peter) but also prophetic king (inviting the repentance of Cornelius toward a deeper commitment to the God of Jesus Christ).

We see such a dialogical—and yet prophetic and regal—model of encountering others also in the life and ministry of Jesus.[24] Matthew (15:21–28) and Mark (7:24–30) tell of Jesus' meeting with a Greek-speaking Canaanite (Matthew) or Syro-Phoenicean (Mark) woman who wanted him to deliver her daughter from demonic oppression and possession. Matthew's account indicates that she was rebuffed thrice: first through Jesus' ignoring her cries and pleas; second through his affirming to his disciples, and to her through them, that "I was sent only to the lost sheep of the house of Israel" (Matt 15:24); and finally, directly to her, while she was kneeling before him: "it is not fair to take the children's food [meant for the house of Israel] and throw it to the dogs [an accepted euphemism in first century Palestine for Gentiles]" (15:26). Yet despite this triad of rejections, she persists, finally with this result: "She said, 'Yes, Lord, yet even the dogs eat the crumbs that fall from their masters' table.' Then Jesus answered her, 'Woman, great is your faith! Let it be done for you as you wish.' And her daughter was healed instantly" (15:27–28). What seems clear especially in the Matthean telling is that this woman's perseverance and determination brought about a change in Jesus' intentions and actions. In a similar account regarding Jesus' interactions with a centurion who had a paralyzed servant and came to Jesus for healing on behalf of the servant, Jesus not only performs the healing but also comes to an unexpected new awareness: "When Jesus heard him, *he was amazed* and said to those who followed him, 'Truly I tell you, *in no one in Israel have I found such faith*'" (Matt 8:10, emphases added). In this case, the centurion finds confirmation in Jesus' healing and saving power even as Jesus comes to recognize that a greater measure of faith existed in this pagan centurion than could be found within the house of Israel. Here, as with the Canaanite/Syro-Phoenicean woman, there is a dialogical mutuality: both Jesus and these Gentiles undergo transformations of belief and behavior as a result of the encounter. Simultaneously, of course, these Gentiles evince a

---

24. Alonso, *The Woman Who Changed Jesus*; cf. Jackson, *'Have Mercy on Me.'*

deep faith in Christ as Lord (Matt 8:8, 15:22). From a pneumatological perspective it might be said that the Spirit accomplishes dialogical interaction while prophetically and regally inviting acknowledgment of the lordship of Christ.

My claim is that a Spirit-Christology both emphasizes that Jesus accomplishes the will of God in the power of the Spirit even as it provides a window into how Jesus was also surely "a man attested to you by God" (Acts 2:22). As divine, Jesus bears iconic witness to God's message, glory, and being (Heb 1:3), but as human, he does so in the relational mode within which human beings existing in the Trinitarian image of God participate. The Spirit who is the bond of love between the Father and the Son is also the matrix within which human beings interact and through which creatures relate to and with God.[25] Jesus himself becomes the paradigmatic exemplar of such dialogical relationality and it is therefore not surprising to see the apostolic community also embodying such virtues.

In the interfaith encounter then, such a dialogical approach enables authentic exchange. Christians can testify out of the depths of their experience of the living Christ.[26] But as with any dialogical encounter, they ought also to be open to the religious lives of others. The challenge here is more existential than dogmatic or doctrinal, since the latter only has meaning within communities of practice. It is therefore the case that any interreligious dialogue is also an intrareligious dialogue, that is, a conversation taking place within believers as they wrestle with what it means to be people of faith bearing witness to others while simultaneously receiving the witness of others.[27] It is surely the case that sometimes, Christian conversion in the interfaith encounter will be toward other faith commitments; more often, however, through such relationships Christians will convert more deeply to the living God of Jesus Christ, as was the case with Peter in his encounter with Cornelius.

MISSIO SPIRITU CHRISTI IN A PLURALISTIC WORLD

At one level, "Jesus Christ is the same yesterday and today and for ever" (Heb 13:8). At another level, as he is the living Christ, words can ever exhaust the reality of Christ. This does not mean that words are unimportant, but that coming to know Christ is not only a matter of the head but also of the hands and of the heart. Christ as king, prophet, and priest is the constant

---

25. As I elaborate in my book *Spirit of Love*.

26. As argued by Richie, *Speaking by the Spirit*.

27. See Panikkar, *Intrareligious Dialogue*.

amidst history's shifting contexts, but the communication of Christ will take on various forms—cognitive, missional, and relational—depending on such contexts. Faith in Christ surely involves the intellect, but its full expression involves expression in human behaviors, practices, and ways of life, and the heads and the hands can only be in sync if the heart is involved.

Thus the interfaith encounter will feature, at its foundations, the encounter of human hearts with horizons of transcendence. Propositional apologetics should not be rejected wholesale, although their effectiveness will be muted apart from a holistic approach that involves hands and hearts. Purely social justice engagement is essential but will also be incomplete apart from heads introduced to the words of Christ and hearts directed toward his person. Last but not least, human hearts in all of their complexity—including human hopes, loves, aspirations, affections, etc.—ought to be engaged on the interfaith front. If religions do not concern our hearts, then they may be ideologies or philosophies but they are not matters of ultimate concern, as Paul Tillich suggested. But if they are matters of ultimate concern, then they have to be adjudicated at the existential depths of the human gut, which will include both heads and hands as well.

A pneumatological approach to the interfaith encounter can facilitate such dialogical and holistic interchange even while prophetically and regally lifting up Jesus as the Christ and Messiah.[28] If knowing Christ is not merely cognitive (urging recognition and acknowledgment of his kingship) but also practical (embodying his prophethood) and even affective (embodying his dialogical and mediating relationality), then what is helpful is a pneumatological Christology that insists we understand and discern not just the doctrines of other faiths but also their practices, and even their aspirations. Learning about other religious traditions therefore will include becoming vulnerable as hosts to and guests of not only the ideas but also the practices at the heart of other faiths. From a Christ-centered point of view, this may open up to recognition, through the Holy Spirit who leads into all truth (not to mention goodness and beauty), of the "seeds of the Logos" that are within other traditions. Such may be aspects of Christian faith that have been neglected or even which are complementary to the truth, goodness, and beauty of Christ. However, they will not contradict the revelation of the triune God, even if sometimes their initial manifestation will lead to a period of (prolonged) discernment and also disputation (as the various conciliar processes in history well depict). Such is the nature of life in the

---

28. For instance, as displayed in my *Pneumatology and the Christian-Buddhist Dialogue*.

Spirit, whose "wind blows where it chooses, and you hear the sound of it, but you do not know where it comes from or where it goes" (John 3:8).[29]

29. The first version of this essay was presented as a plenary paper at the 2013 meeting of the Society for Vineyard Scholars. Thanks to Caleb Maskell for the invitation, to Jason Clark for his dialogical response, and for the SVS members who engaged with my paper during the conference, asked helpful questions, and made suggestive and encouraging comments. I appreciate also Vince Le, my former graduate assistant, for proofreading the article. Enoch Charles, my present graduate assistant, also proofread a revised version of the essay and produced the bibliography. Last but not least, I am grateful to Steve Bevans and Cathy Ross for inviting my contribution to this volume [*Mission as Prophetic Dialogue*] and for their helpful editorial feedback.

CHAPTER 12

God, Christ, Spirit

Christian Pluralism and Evangelical Mission in the Twenty-First Century

THE FOLLOWING SKETCHES IN broad strokes a Trinitarian theology of mission for a pluralistic world, especially its relational, shalomic, and transformational aspects. This proposal supports a generous evangelical approach to the Christian engagement with other faiths. In the process, Christians bear witness to the living God of Jesus Christ in the power of the Spirit, even while they are also open to being transformed through encounter with those in other faiths.

This essay is written as a tribute to the work of Roswith Gerloff. Roswith embodies in her life, scholarship, and work the kind of border crossing—between "North" and "South," between the "West" and the "rest," between "white" and "black"—that has long inspired my own thinking about Christian theology of religions and theology of interfaith encounter. While my own proposal is resolutely Trinitarian in its character, I do not believe it is inconsistent with the predominantly Oneness and yet triadic thrust of Roswith's own work.[1] Some might wonder how that might be possible since it would seem that Oneness and Trinitarian thinking are at odds. I would suggest that this is the case only if the tripersonal conceptions lead to three deities, which I reject, or if the triadic shape of the New Testament witness— i.e., to Father, Son, and Spirit—is denied, which Roswith does not deny.[2] The

---

1. Going back to her PhD thesis, published as *A Plea for British Black Theologies*.

2. For my own constructive treatment of Oneness theology in Trinitarian

hope that has animated her scholarship all along, however, is precisely the kind of hospitality between Oneness and Trinitarian believers that leads to mutual transformation as well as transformation of society into a more just world. This is in line with the basic thrusts of this article as well, and I trust that its ideas can contribute something small toward, and motivate others to build on, her body of work.

TRINITARIAN THEOLOGY AND CHRISTIAN MISSION IN A PLURALISTIC WORLD

A generous Christian pluralism is robustly theological and missional. This is because the scriptural revelation depicts a triune God—Father, Son, and Holy Spirit—who has created all things and who works to redeem all of the creation and its full potential. Christian monotheism is thus also Trinitarian, neither absolutely one without qualifier but yet also neither three in any conventional sense. Rather, there is one God revealed as Father, Son, and Spirit, who works variously to redeem the world.[3]

The one God is revealed in the Scriptures of ancient Israel as being jealous over his people. At the same time, this one God also promises through his various covenants that the divine blessings are intended for all the peoples of the earth. God has chosen Abraham to be the father of many nations so that the entirety of the human race can be blessed.[4] All of this is representative of the divine graciousness. God chooses Israel not meritoriously but unconditionally. Israel's election is thus not for herself but for the world.

The Father then sends the Son at the appointed time to carry out the plan for making Israel a blessing to the nations. The mission of the Son is to mediate the fulfillment of the promises of God to save the world through Israel. In effect, the Son himself arrives in the flesh, as part of the divine mission of reconciling the world to God. Karl Barth identified this as the Son of God's journey into a far country,[5] a sojourn into the world of creatures and of creatureliness. The one through whom all things were created is now also part of the divine mission to renew, restore, and redeem the world. He became human, taking on the dust of the world, in order that he might elevate and deify the world, as the ancient church fathers believed. Achievement of this soteriological goal required that the Son descend into the very depths

---

perspective, see Yong, *Spirit Poured Out on All Flesh*, ch. 5.

3. See Tennent, *Invitation to World Missions*.

4. Martin-Achard, *A Light to the Nations*.

5. Barth, *Church Dogmatics*, vol. 4, part 1, §59.1.

of the human condition so that he may overcome death and make possible reconciliation with God. As such, the incarnational mission of the Son takes up the historicity, particularity, and specificity of the human condition. The mission of the Son is not abstract, but concrete—not as generically human but as male, as Jew, as carpenter, etc.—so as to declare God's intention to save real people in space-time, culture, and language.

Yet the sending of the Son and the accomplishment of the work of redemption through the Son was also made possible through the wind or breath of God. The spirit of God that hovered over the formlessness and voidness of the creaturely chaos also brought life into the womb of the "Mother of God"; raised up the Son from the dead; and then was poured out by the Son upon all flesh. Hence the mission of the Father and the Son also includes, and is constituted by, the mission of the Spirit.[6] If the mission of the Son declares God's intention to save to actual flesh and blood, then the mission of the Spirit announces the universal horizons of the triune deity's saving plan. The Day of Pentecost narrative thus suggests that the curse of Babel is redeemed: the many tongues and languages now no longer divide but are capable, through the Spirit, of declaring the wonders of God. Insofar as languages are not disembodied but are cultural expressions and realities, to that degree also does the pentecostal mission of the Spirit herald the divine intention to redeem humanity in and through its cultural horizons. And last but not least, inasmuch as the cultural dimensions of human life are intertwined with the religious domains, this raises the question about how the mission of the Spirit not only confronts and pronounces judgments on the religions in the light of Word (*Logos*) of God, but also sanctifies their aspirations and redeems them according to the fullness of Christ.[7]

On the one hand, the religions—including the Christian religion in its institutionalized and conventionalized traditions—are a mixture of truth and falsity, of beauty and ugliness, and of good and bad. In fact, aspects of human religiosity are demonic and need to be identified and exorcised as such.[8] In these cases, a pneumatological theology, because of its attentiveness to how the spiritual dimensions of religious forms of life can be distorted, disoriented, and even demonized, may be more adept at enabling discernment of what is at stake. On the other hand, a pneumatological and Trinitarian theology of religions also invites Christians and provides them with explicitly Christian theological warrant to recognize that there are

6. See my article, "Primed for the Spirit" [ch. 10 of this volume].

7. See also my "As the Spirit Gives Utterance . . . ," [ch. 2 of this volume] and "A P(new)matological Paradigm for Christian Mission" [ch. 3 of this volume].

8. See the nuanced and sophisticated argument by McDermott, *God's Rivals*; cf. my *Discerning the Spirit(s)*.

multiple facets to religious traditions, even as there are to the Christian faith. This might open up to a Trinitarian theology of religions that provides, for Christians, a differentiated set of perspectives on the non-Christian faiths.[9] Alternatively, it might also suggest that Trinitarian faith in God as Father, Son, and Spirit invites a diversity of approaches to missional faithfulness in a pluralistic world. The variety of modes with which Christians engage with those in other faiths would thus reflect the redemptive generosity of the triune God. The remainder of this essay sketches three dimensions—of mission as relational, shalomic, and transformational—as flowing out of the Trinitarian logic of Christian faith.

MISSION AS RELATIONAL: INTERFAITH OPPORTUNITIES AND CHALLENGES

The triune God is believed, according to the main lines of the Christian theological tradition, to subsist as three interpersonal relations. This ancient conviction—also known in Greek as *perichoresis* and in Latin as *circumincessio*—highlights both that the Trinity is not "three gods" as conventional notions of triune persons might suggest, but that they are, perhaps paradoxically, distinct and yet interrelated. The point is that God is one, albeit constituted as Father, Son, and Spirit.

This triune character also illuminates God's relationship to the world. Albeit revealed roughly as creator (Father), redeemer (Son), and sanctifier (Spirit), God nevertheless relates to the world in ways consistent with the triune nature. Hence, while distinct from the world, God yet invites the world's participation in the divine life and activity. The world is dependent on God but still has been created for relationship with God. Human beings, in particular, are intended to experience friendship and union with God, precisely the goal of divine redemption.

God hence enters into such dialogical relationality with the world. The world is given a degree of freedom to respond to God. God reveals himself as one who invites relationship with others. Christian mission is also about proclaiming and manifesting such a God-desiring friendship with

9. Three examples are Kärkkäinen, *Trinity and Religious Pluralism*, which provides a broadly evangelical orientation that opens up the discussion; Heim, *Depth of the Riches*, which suggests that the three faces of God fulfills the various traditions in many ways; and Panikkar, *Trinity and Religious Experience of Man*, which suggests that there is a mystical and even Trinitarian dimension to all religious life so that this notion does not belong only to Christian faith. This essay ought to be considered a development of the theological pathway charted by Kärkkäinen's work.

humanity. Christ becomes the model of interpersonal relationality, mediating between the triune God and humankind.

In a pluralistic world, Christian mission does not cease dialogical engagement with people of other or no faith. Such dialogue is characterized by interpersonal reciprocity, mutual give-and-take, and authentic hospitality. Our scriptural models for these are Jesus' interactions with the Canaanite woman, St. Paul's missionary model, and Peter's encounter with Cornelius.[10]

Matthew (15:21–28) and Mark (7:24–30) tell of Jesus' meeting with a Greek-speaking Canaanite (Matthew) or Syro-Phoenicean (Mark) woman who wanted him to deliver her daughter from demonic oppression and possession. Matthew's account indicates that she was rebuffed thrice: first through Jesus' ignoring her cries and please; second through his affirming to his disciples, and to her through them, that "I was sent only to the lost sheep of the house of Israel" (Matt 15:24); and finally, directly to her, while she was kneeling before him: "it is not fair to take the children's food [meant for the house of Israel] and throw it to the dogs [an accepted euphemism in first-century Palestine for gentiles]" (15:26). Yet despite this triad of rejections, she persists: "She said, 'Yes, Lord, yet even the dogs eat the crumbs that fall from their masters' table.' Then Jesus answered her, 'Woman, great is your faith! Let it be done for you as you wish.' And her daughter was healed instantly" (15:27–28). What seems clear especially in the Matthean telling is that this woman's perseverance and determination brought about a change in Jesus' intentions and actions. In a similar account regarding Jesus' interactions with a centurion who had a paralyzed servant and came to Jesus for healing on behalf of the servant, Jesus not only performs the healing but also comes to an unexpected new awareness: "When Jesus heard him, *he was amazed* and said to those who followed him, 'Truly I tell you, *in no one in Israel have I found such faith*'" (Matt 8:10, emphases added). In this case, the centurion finds confirmation in Jesus' healing and saving power even as Jesus comes to recognize that a greater measure of faith existed in this pagan than could be found within the house of Israel. Here, as with the Canaanite/Syro-Phoenicean woman, there is an interpersonal reciprocity: both Jesus and these Gentiles undergo transformation of belief and behavior through their encounter.

St. Paul himself, the model apostolic missionary, utilized dialogical approaches in his evangelistic work. At Thessalonica, Corinth, and Ephesus it is said that he engaged in reasoned give-and-take (*dialegato*) on a regular basis (Acts 17:2, 18:4, 19). The discussions at Athens, especially at

---

10. I develop these ideas more extensively in my "Christological Constants in Shifting Contexts" [ch. 11 of this volume].

the Areopagus, reflected Paul's engagement with and drawing upon pagan sources familiar to his audience to make his points (Acts 17:27–28). In Lystra, earlier, Paul similarly resorted to what might be called natural theological arguments in urging that God "has not left himself without a witness in doing good—giving you rains from heaven and fruitful seasons, and filling you with food and your hearts with joy" (Acts 14:17). Paul never compromises on declaring the redemptive work of God now available in Christ. Yet such declaration also does not ignore engagement with his audience in terms recognizable and even appreciable by them.

Last but not least, authentic hospitality is manifest in Peter's encounter with Cornelius.[11] There is no de-emphasizing the fact that Peter declares and proclaims "Jesus Christ—he is Lord of all . . . judge of the living and the dead" (Acts 10:36b and 42b) to Cornelius and his household, and that "everyone who believes in him receives forgiveness of sins through his name" (10:43b). On the other hand, it also ought not be minimized that through his encounter with Cornelius, Peter himself was also transformed. Whereas previously he considered himself an observant Jewish worshipper of the one true God who separated himself from unclean gentiles and pagans, this episode brought about a change of perspective: "God has shown me that I should not call anyone profane or unclean" (10:28). More pointedly, Peter came to see that "God shows no partiality, but in every nation anyone who fears him and does what is right is acceptable to him" (10:34–35). Thus was Cornelius characterized, even before his conversion, as a "devout" (or "godly," from the Greek *eusebes*), "upright" (or "righteous," from the Greek *dikaios*), and "God-fearing man" (10:2 and 22). Not only did Peter come to a new estimation of Gentiles like Cornelius, he also came to see that the way of Jesus was wider than previously understood: "Can anyone withhold the water for baptizing these people who have received the Holy Spirit just as we have?" (10:47). My point is to highlight the hospitality expressed in the encounter between Peter and Cornelius. The latter was host to the former but the former also represented the divine hospitality extended to the latter; hence, both were simultaneously guests and hosts, giving and receiving. While Cornelius was converted to Christ, Peter was also converted in his relationship with the God of Jesus Christ.

Such relational approaches reflect evangelical instincts to befriend their neighbors. At the same time, they also potentially open up a level of vulnerability that will be challenging for interfaith relations. We will return to this important matter at the end of this article.

---

11. See also Richie, *Toward a Pentecostal Theology of Religions*, esp. ch. 1.

MISSION AS SHALOMIC: MULTI-RELIGIOUS IDEALS AND REALITIES

Evangelical mission in the twenty-first century is not only relational but also shalomic. This reflects the revelation of the triune deity as a God of blessing, of peace, and of justice.[12] Jesus himself indicated that his ministry, under the power of the Spirit, was "to bring good news to the poor . . . to proclaim release to the captives and recovery of sight to the blind, to let the oppressed go free, to proclaim the year of the Lord's favor" (Luke 4:18–19). The reference to "the year of the Lord's favor" anticipates the freedom and flourishing of the ancient Israelite ideal of Jubilee.[13]

The disciples, filled with the same Spirit who anointed Jesus, also went forth proclaiming the forgiveness of sins and debts (central to the Jubilee message and ideal) and then organizing a community of sharing so that the poor would not be in need (see Acts 2:42–47). For the earliest followers of the Messiah, then, the gospel was indeed good news to the poor. Divine salvation had socioeconomic ramifications for the believing community. Bodies were literally healed, so why would not the poor and the oppressed also be economically, rather than merely spiritually, delivered?[14]

In a pluralistic world, this shalomic dimension of the gospel ought not be minimized. Poverty is no respecter of religious identity: there are poor and oppressed people in all faith traditions and communities. This suggests that the emphases on holistic mission gaining ground in many evangelical circles are on the mark.[15] A holistic missiology in a pluralistic world recognizes that people in other faiths are evangelized best perhaps not verbally (kerygmatically) but through works of service and of love: feeding the hungry, clothing the naked, visiting those in prison, providing shelter, etc. People become open to the gospel when they are touched by the love of God manifest by those who bear his name.

However, while the Christian mission should never desist from these concrete acts of service, the systematic and structural factors that perpetuate poverty, disease, and crime also should not be neglected. Particularly in pentecostal and charismatic renewal circles, the palpable sense of divine presence manifest in healings and in the hearts of many powerfully warmed and touched is sometimes taken as the final panacea to the ills of the human condition. But this means that Christian spirituality and the life of faith

---

12. See Yoder, *Shalom*, and Grassi, *Jesus is Shalom*.
13. See Ringe, *Jesus, Liberation, and the Biblical Jubilee*.
14. See Yong, *Who is the Holy Spirit?*, ch. 4; cf. also part III of this book.
15. A recent articulation of this is by Lord, *Spirit-Shaped Mission*.

are "not really addressing the root cause of the deep alienation that people experience, *but only the feeling* of alienation."[16] The result is that if Christian mission is focused only on meeting the immediate physical needs of the poor, then the root causes of oppression remain untouched.

It is in part for this reason that some Christian theologians have called for a liberationist approach to the interfaith encounter.[17] If the shalomic reign of God will indeed cover the earth, then Christians ought to work toward such a vision in faith, even if they recognize that its full realization will have to await God's future timing. At the same time, since the impediments to the divine shalom are systemic and structural, such will require the collaborative efforts of all human beings of good will. Some issues cannot be addressed except by large coalitions consisting of groups of people that work together across ideological (and religious) lines. Even if there was a distinctively "Christian nation," the globalizing realities of our time mean that Christian efforts will need to be complemented by, if not also inform, the efforts of those in non-Christian countries. Christians on their own cannot work toward the peace and justice of the Jubilee ideal. They need the contributions of all concerned about the common good. This is part of the reality of globalization in our time.

Toward this end, the Christian mission needs to join hands with others to address the "powers of destruction" that beset human flourishing.[18] A generous Christian approach to a pluralistic world recognizes that people of all faiths can contribute to the common good, at least in part based on principles and ideals in their own religious tradition. For Christians, such is motivated by the vision of the triune God, including the incarnational mission of the Son to meet the needs of the poor and the oppressed, and the empowering work of the Holy Spirit who only can make a difference in a world otherwise mired in poverty and injustice.[19] If lived out following the lead of the Holy Spirit of Jesus, such shalomic postures, commitments, and related practices will prove missional for those in other faiths even as they transform Christian faith as well.

16. Brandner, "Premillennial and Countercultural Faith," 23 (italics added).

17. See especially Knitter, *One Earth Many Religions*, and *Jesus and the Other Names*.

18. Here I am thinking about Wink, *The Powers that Be*; cf. Gingerich and Grimsrud, eds., *Transforming the Powers*.

19. As I argue in *Hospitality and the Other*, esp. ch. 5.

MISSION AS TRANSFORMATIONAL: TOWARD A NEW "US" AND "THEM"

This leads to the transformational dynamic of the interfaith encounter. Both the relational and shalomic dimensions lead inexorably to consideration of this issue. A Christian missiological orientation will surely anticipate the transformative power of the Christian way of life in a pluralistic world, and there is no question that this happens. People of other faiths sometimes experience healing in their bodies as a result of interactions with Christians and this in itself is life transformative at a certain level. In other cases, non-Christians will learn about Christian faith and gradually come to be disabused of their stereotypes and misunderstandings, and this itself leads to a certain degree of intellectual conversion on their part. Most fundamentally, some convert to and become disciples of Jesus Christ, and followers of Christ rejoice on these occasions of life-revolutionizing decisions and actions.

While a generous Christian perspective will celebrate these fruits of the Christian mission, it cannot rest here. Christians can only be faithful in their bearing witness to the risen Christ, and if and how others come into Christian faith lies in some respects beyond their control and rests in the hands of God. Yet Christians can and ought to be responsible to ask and consider this question: how is the Christian encounter with other faiths in the twenty-first century also potentially transformative for Christian self-understanding?

I can think of at least three levels of self-transformation Christians can potentially experience on the interreligious pathway. First, relationally, Christians can come into new awareness of other faiths. Having neighbors and perhaps friends who are members of other traditions goes a long way toward dispelling our ignorance about others. Those in other faiths are no longer merely objects to be described but are subjects that invite us as guests into their homes. Our understanding of other faiths thus becomes firsthand, and this means that what is "head knowledge" about other religions will begin to become a kind of "heart knowledge"—or at least "interpersonal knowledge"[20]—about other religious commitments, sensibilities, and ways of life. This kind of relational encounter with religious others hence transforms us personally.

At a second level, working with those in other faiths for the common good, among other relational and collaborative ventures across faith lines, can also transform our understanding of the ideals of these faith traditions.

---

20. Here of course I am playing off Michael Polanyi's *Personal Knowledge*.

Here we come to a deeper understanding of not only what motivates other religionists personally, but also of how they are responding to core teachings of their faith traditions. In the process, we come to understand the deeper logic of other faiths, including how their beliefs and practices are intertwined. This may include the opportunity to wrestle with appreciating how other religious ways of life are informed by their teachings, so that we may even begin to "experience" other faiths from their perspective. When Christians invite non-Christians into their spaces of worship, etc., they are also inviting others to begin to experience Christian faith on its own terms. I am suggesting that the transformative dimension of the interfaith encounter actually works both ways: that non-Christians are altered by their exposure to Christianity even while Christians can also undergo changes of perspective if they are open to such in their interactions with those in other faiths.

But there is potentially a third level of more radical transformation that can happen in the interfaith encounter. Most drastically, people can convert to other faiths, and this happens also to those who before considered themselves Christians. In other instances, people will adopt dual religious identities, believing that they are not leaving behind their Christian commitments but working these out in ways that they believe are compatible with the fundamental commitments of another faith tradition.[21] Sometimes, people will adopt "spiritual-but-not-religious" identities, insisting that their spiritual lives can be informed by one or more faith perspectives without any institutional participation in those faith traditions. In each of these ways, the journey across faith lines leaves people transformed in ways that are often unrecognizable by those in the original faith tradition. Just as people of other faiths sometimes fully convert to become followers of Christ, so also is there a risk in the interfaith encounter that those who start out as Christ followers might find themselves converting variously to other allegiances. The vulnerability and risk involved at these interfaith crossroads cannot be artificially managed in any fully relational approach.

However, there is another type of radical transformation that occurs in the interfaith encounter that does not involve departure from the home faith, but instead results in an even deeper immersion in it, one opened up, paradoxically perhaps, by crossing over to and returning from another faith.[22] In these cases, one does not reinhabit the home tradition in exactly the same way as one did prior to encountering the religious other. But what happens is that engagement with the other transforms the self so that one

21. I discuss some aspects of dual religious belonging in the context of the comparative theological project in the article "Francis X. Clooney's 'Dual Religious Belonging'" [reprinted in *The Dialogical Spirit* as ch. 10].

22. As elaborated by Cobb Jr., *Beyond Dialogue*.

now sees and lives out the Christian faith differently. Perhaps one observes elements neglected in the home tradition that were lifted up in the other faith (i.e., some Christian rediscover the contemplative streams in their own ranks after being exposed to meditative practices in Eastern religious traditions). Alternatively, one comes to appreciate elements in the other that are believed to be compatible with and become a source of enrichment of Christian faith and practice (e.g., Confucian filial piety and Buddhist ontology of becoming are seen as complementary to Christian faith). In these cases, Christian life and mission is itself revitalized, unexpectedly, through the interfaith encounter.

Evangelical missiology is already increasingly relational, shalomic, and transformational. In this article, I have only made a few suggestions about how such funds a generous Christian approach to interfaith relations that remains evangelical and missiological, while recognizing that Christians do little more than participate in the redemptive mission of the triune God. Such a Trinitarian missiology and theology of the interfaith encounter enables Christians to be confident in being guests of those in other faiths while also being hopeful that these are occasions when they can mediate the shalomic, transformative, and redemptive hospitality of God.[23]

23. Thanks to the organizers of the Missio Alliance conference for their invitation to present these ideas at a workshop alongside Gary Black in April 2013. I appreciate my graduate assistant, Vince Le, for his proofreading help. Last but not least, I am grateful to Armin Triebel for organizing this festschrift [*Roswith Gerloff*] and including me in it.

CONCLUSION

Christian Mission Theology

Toward a Pneumato-Missiological Praxis for the Third Millennium

IT IS NOW TIME to quickly review where we have come from in order to situate where we have arrived and to anticipate next steps. The preceding has attempted to envision Christian theology of mission (Christian beliefs and practices related to its missional identity) and mission theology (Christian theological self-understanding fundamentally informed by mission) at the beginning of the third millennium. I have also shown that the movement back and forth between these tasks is theologically funded by a pneumatological imagination as manifested particularly in the Acts narrative. Further, such a pneumatologically inspired mission theology is uniquely suited to enable navigation of our contemporary postmodern, postcolonial, post-secular, and pluralistic landscape. This is not to say that other approaches are impotent in this era; it is to say that for those wondering if Christian faith is up to the task of the present time, a pneumatological imagination is one candidate charting the missiological path forward.

In these last few pages, however, I want to attend more systematically to such a pneumatological mission theology. If before and elsewhere I have elaborated at length on the ontological, epistemological, hermeneutical, and dialogical aspects of the pneumatological imagination,[1] here I want to provide a summary sketch of a theology of mission and a mission theology, make explicit the pneumatological correlates, and then specify their present

1. See Yong, *Spirit-Word-Community* and *Dialogical Spirit*.

contextual environments and performative character. The following builds on but also clarifies the preceding discussion. In many respects it makes explicit what the chapters of this book indicate, while in some respects it will also illuminate the lacunae in the preceding pages.

THE *MISSIOLOGICAL* SPIRIT

The major threads of this volume bring together two theological domains: Christian theology of mission and Christian mission theology. The former focuses on the theological framework for thinking about Christian mission, and the latter on the missional dimensions of Christian theology. In thinking about the *missiological* spirit, I want to briefly clarify the central elements of these complementary theological tasks, beginning with the latter.

What then does it mean to talk about a Christian mission theology? Two aspects of this question invite comment and consideration. First, what kind of Christian theology, if any, is not missional? Some might say that there are various forms of Christian theological reflection—speculative, philosophical, or metaphysical; comparative; dogmatic; historical; systematic; etc. At one level, then, mission theology is one among any number of theological undertakings. Those working in this vein are, perhaps, missiologists, theologians of culture, practical theologians, and pastoral agents, among others, who would be less likely to spend as much time in some of the other domains we have identified. On another level, if theology is understood at least in part as being by the church and for the church's mission, then it may also be argued that in that sense, any other theological effort also has this missional aspect. One might write a Christian systematics, for instance, but yet structure the discussion all the way through so as to address as least the missional implications, if not also foundations, of the classical doctrinal or theological loci.[2] The missiological spirit in this case would provide missional perspectives on the Christian theological task, as broadly or narrowly conceived as it might be.

This would be possible because, second, when talking about Christian theology (as opposed to Jewish or Islamic theology, for instance),[3] we are also talking about the good news of God revealed in Jesus through the Holy Spirit. This gospel is at the heart of the Christian self-understanding and re-

2. I attempt something along these lines in my book, with Jonathan A. Anderson, *Renewing Christian Theology*.

3. Islam also has missiological commitments; see Faruqi, "On the Nature of Islamic Da'wah." For a comparative study with Christian mission commitments and practices, see Sanneh, "Christian Experience of Islamic Da'wah."

flects the Christian revelation and message about God reconciling the world to himself through Christ, in the Spirit. The Christian mission is thus about communicating, in whatever way possible, this message of reconciliation with God, which involves reconciliation with others and even with the world around us. If so, then, Christian theological reflection ultimately attempts to comprehend and enable this reconciliation—which is precisely what it means to talk about Christian theology as mission theology.

But if Christian theology is hence missional in this way, then a Christian mission theology will at least include or interface with a Christian theology of mission. If the Christian message is about the good news of creation's reconciliation with God in Christ by the Holy Spirit, then any theology of mission will attempt to think through the theological warrants for the church's mission practices and activities. The preceding chapters have delineated at least three major missional initiatives: proclamation, justice and compassion ministries, and dialogue.[4] The Christian mission proceeds with each uniquely engaging with specific places, times, and opportunities. At some point, one form of these missional practices will dominate, but at other times, one of the other two will come to the fore. The missiological spirit discerns when is the time for whom to embody or communicate the gospel message in which way.

Who does what and when depends in part on many variables. The church as guest or as host, as discussed throughout this book, requires in some instances more of just being in the presence of others and in other cases more of actively engaging with the missional task. The Christian mission unfolds as much through the people of God "being" the church as it does through followers of Jesus "doing" missionary works. Hence we ought not to think of the Christian mission merely terms of what the church does.[5]

To be sure, any full theology of mission will involve at some level a more thorough biblical reconsideration and some historical perspective. The former involves perhaps a kind of systematic scriptural assessment of the major themes of salvation history, divine revelation, reconciliation at its various levels, and Spirit-empowered witness. The latter includes not only a history of Christian expansion but also critical analyses of the *how* and the results of Christian mission over the centuries. Historical considerations

4. This is not to exhaust the many forms of missional praxis; as the alert reader will realize, I use these more as placeholders for three kinds of missional sensibilities and orientations, than to be reductive about just what kind of activities it is that missionaries carry out or about what constitutes missionary practice.

5. In fact, I have argued elsewhere—i.e., *Theology and Down Syndrome*, ch. 7, and *The Bible, Disability, and the Church*, ch. 4—that even people with severe and profound disabilities who are dependent on others may have a ministerial and missional charism.

provide concrete case studies from which to learn what to do and what to avoid, while biblical reflection shapes our normative values, commitments, and practices. This book has attempted neither a biblical nor a historical theology of mission, and in that sense, it remains incomplete.[6]

Yet we have made some progress in this volume by triangulating around pentecostal perspectives, theology of mission tasks, and mission theological considerations. The missiological spirit that has emerged is fundamentally informed by a set of pneumatological intuitions. The Christian mission theological project unfolded across this volume is inspired by a pneumato-theological imagination while the Christian theology of mission is driven by a pentecostal (in the Acts 2 sense) vision of the Spirit empowering the church's witness. Hence the missiological spirit is not only a sentiment or sensibility, but is also theologically pneumatic.

THE MISSIOLOGICAL *SPIRIT*

What then is the theological and pneumatological nature of the missiological spirit? If all theology is in some respect missiological, and if missiology is pneumatological in the respects explicated in this book, then what is the character of this pneumatic reality? How can we understand the Spirit who inspires, enables, and accomplishes God's mission of reconciliation? This section triangulates around an ecclesiological, christological, and theological response.

Ecclesiologically, the Holy Spirit given at Pentecost is also the Spirit of the church, the body of Christ. Yet put alternatively, the body of Christ is what it is precisely through the Spirit. St. Paul writes: "For in the one Spirit we were all baptized into one body—Jews or Greeks, slaves or free—and we were all made to drink of one Spirit" (1 Cor 12:13). Hence the body of Christ is also the "communion of the Holy Spirit" (2 Cor 13:13). Missionally speaking, then, God reconciles the world to himself through the body of Christ and the fellowship of the Spirit.

The question then is how to understand the nature of the people through whom the mission of God is being accomplished. One christological type of response defines the matter sacramentally and institutionally through apostolic succession: the true church over which Christ is the head includes all those who have been baptized into the community through legitimately appointed ministers. In this case, access to the sacraments becomes the

---

6. If I were to make recommendations, at the top of my list of theologies of mission would be Bosch's *Transforming Mission*; Skreslet, *Comprehending Mission*; Sunquist, *Understanding Christian Mission*; and Julie C. Ma and Wonsuk Ma, *Mission in the Spirit*.

most important missiological criterion to achieve God's reconciliation with the world. Another more Protestant version de-emphasizes the liturgical aspects of the baptismal ritual in favor of the evangelical proclamation of the gospel via missionaries; in this case, access to, understanding of, and reception of the good news becomes the indispensable missiological criterion to experience reconciliation with God. Either approaches defines the missiological spirit ecclesiologically, the former via the sacraments (through priestly activity) and the latter via the kerygmatic declaration of the gospel (through missionary agency).

But what if ecclesiology were defined pneumatologically instead? Without minimizing the liturgical and proclamatory aspects of the gospel's advance and of the church's practices, perhaps we can understand the Spirit's presence and activity in the world as irreducible to the church's activities. The work of the body of Christ can be acknowledged as the normal modality of God's reconciling work, but where the church fails, is disobedient, or simply has not "arrived" (whatever this may mean), the Holy Spirit is nevertheless at work, drawing hearts into the coming reign of God where their ecclesial "membership" may finally be unveiled.[7]

Christologically, the Holy Spirit is given at Pentecost precisely by Jesus the exalted and ascended Christ, from the right hand of the Father (Acts 2:33). As such, the witness of the Spirit as the spirit of Christ is always unmistakably and ultimately to Jesus. God's self-revelation is concretely in Jesus (Col 1:15; Heb 1:3), and God's way of reconciling the world to himself is through Jesus (2 Cor 5:19). Whatever testimony is inspired by the Spirit, then, is finally about Jesus. In fact, "no one can say 'Jesus is Lord' except by the Holy Spirit" (1 Cor 12:3b).

Similarly to thinking about the missiological Spirit in ecclesiological terms, however, is the question of how to think about the Spirit christologically, that is, how to understand the living Christ encountering human beings in and through the Spirit. Is Christ mediated only through either baptism or evangelistic proclamation? Or is Christ's saving presence and activity carried by the spirit of Jesus perhaps through other means? Again, I would suggest, without minimizing the liturgical and proclamatory

---

7. This is different than Karl Rahner's "anonymous Christianity" thesis, since Rahner wants to say that people are Christian or part of the body of Christ without knowing it; my claim is that people may be encountered by the spirit of God apart from the church and hence may yet be drawn into the eschatological people of God, but this does not make them anonymous Christians. While my view may be seen as less optimistic than Rahner's, I simply want to acknowledge the integrity of Christian ecclesiological self-understanding, albeit while also explore possible pneumatological implications and explications. Compare this with my previous discussion of Rahner in *Discerning the Spirit(s)*, 71–77.

witnesses to Christ, perhaps we can understand Christ's saving presence and activity in the world in terms irreducible to the church's activities. These sacramental and evangelical aspects of witness to Christ can be acknowledged as the normal modality of God's reconciling work, but where the church fails, is disobedient, or simply has not "arrived" (whatever this may mean), the spirit of Jesus is nevertheless at work, drawing hearts into the coming reign of God where they may recognize and acknowledge Jesus' lordship.

This is because the living Christ is nevertheless also the "true light, which enlightens everyone" (John 1:9). Further, the living Christ is sometimes incognito, not only because even his followers are incapable of recognizing his resurrected body (e.g., Luke 24:13–32, John 20:10–14) but because that remains in part his chosen mode of ambiguous presence in and through the sick, the poor, the hungry, and even those in prison (see Matt 25:31–46). Last but not least, the living Christ is also the coming Christ, one who "now we see in a mirror, dimly, but then we will see face to face" (1 Cor 13:12); in fact, "when he is revealed, we will be like him, for we will see him as he is" (1 John 3:2b). Hence the missiological Spirit is the Spirit who points to the coming Christ. God's eschatologically reconciling work happens finally through Christ and in the Spirit.

Theologically, then, the missiological Spirit is also the spirit of God. More expansively, the Holy Spirit is the spirit of the Trinitarian or triune God. The God of Jesus Christ is also the creator of the world, revealed initially as the God of Israel. The spirit of the church and the spirit of Jesus is thus also the Spirit of Creator Yahweh, the one whose breath or wind "swept over the face of the [primordial] waters" (Gen 1:2).[8] The Christ who poured out his Spirit upon all flesh also repeatedly witnessed, under the unction of that same Spirit, to the coming reign of God; hence, the spirit of Christ is also the spirit of God who inspired the prophets of Israel to testify to the eschatological deliverance of Israel.

The people of God now—the body of Christ, in this time between his first and second coming—are hence both distinct from the covenant people of Israel and yet also continuous of them. From a Christian theological perspective, I can only affirm in faith that Christ fulfills the aspirations of Israel through the work of the Spirit; I cannot proclaim with similar certainty that God's covenant with Israel no longer holds.[9] The point is that the Spirit will continue to inspire witness to Christ to Jew and Greek, and that is part of the privilege and responsibility related to Christian self-understanding.

8. See also my *Spirit of Creation*, 151–62, for a pneumatological reading of the creation narratives (Gen 1–2).

9. See ch. 8 of my *In the Days of Caesar* for further discussion of my theology of Israel.

Christians can only bear witness to Jews, even as Jews can also do nothing less than bear witness to Christians; eschatologically, the spirit of God and the spirit of Christ will harmonize their testimonies in ways that will in all likelihood exceed our comprehension.

That the spirit of Christ is also the spirit of God suggests that the missiological Spirit both points to Christ and also reconciles the world to God, in tandem, even if the connections between the two remain fuzzy on this side of eternity. Such a pneumatological missiology is both similar to and different from previous theological paradigms in ways that can illuminate its distinctiveness. The Roman Catholic natural law tradition suggests that the Spirit works at two levels: naturally to sustain life and supernaturally to reveal Christ and provide the beatific vision. The Reformed tradition similarly identifies the work of the Spirit in giving life to humanity in terms of common grace, and associates the salvific work of the Spirit with special grace. Finally, Wesleyans understand the Spirit's presalvific work as prevenient grace, which is followed by saving grace.

The pneumatological missiology advocated herein can accept each of these delineations but then also doubts if the lines can be drawn as sharply as suggested in these classical accounts. As detailed in the preceding chapters (and hence not needing to be repeated extensively here), a pneumatological theology approaches the revealing, saving, and reconciling works of God in the world more dynamically than other paradigms. God, Christ, and church are all fundamentally central to the gift of salvation, but the Spirit inspires, enables, and empowers the witness of creation and its creatures to the coming reign of God in mysterious ways. This does not undermine the Christian mission of proclamation, social justice, compassion ministries, and interpersonal relationship and dialogue. But it does nevertheless insist that before Christian missionaries arrive and even long after they leave, God "has not left himself without a witness" (Acts 14:17); "but in every nation anyone who fears him and does what is right is acceptable to him" (Acts 10:35).

PNEUMATO-MISSIOLOGICAL PRAXIS FOR THE TWENTY-FIRST CENTURY

So far in this concluding chapter, we have focused on the nature or spirit of Christian missiology and on the who—the Holy Spirit—of the missiological task. In this final section, I want to tie the many threads of this book together by asking about the context of Christian mission and complementary mission sensibilities in the twenty-first century. How does a pneumato-missiological praxis facilitate Christian response to the missional vocation amidst the complexities of this present world? I suggest that the Spirit simultaneously, if in different respects, empowers a witness to the coming reign of God that is affective, imaginative, and narrative; that is multivocal, pluriform, and polysemous; and that is harmonious, expansive, and beautiful—all of which combine to ensure its relevance to the distinctive contextual challenges of our contemporary age.

Our context is characterized first by a postmodern, post-Enlightenment, and post-Western sensibility. By this I am referring to the feeling that modern rationality pushed to its limits leads science to scientism, reduces humanity to materialism, and explicates the world in mechanistic, mathematical, and naturalistic terms. To the degree that the modern mind has defined universal human reason, to that same degree we have lost the capacity to think by our feelings, our affections, our imaginations, and our stories. A pneumatological imagination emphasizes the affective, imaginative, and narrative aspects of human rationality.[10] A pneumato-missiological praxis therefore does not ignore discursive modes of cognition and communication but recognizes the embodied, communal, and dynamic nature of human reason. Hence the gospel witness has to be lived out, not just proclaimed. Christian mission is thus manifested by transformed hearts, not just preached by information-filled heads. Pneumatic mission is thereby relational, interpersonal, and even intersubjective, enabling people to touch each other in the core of their beings, through the power of the Spirit.

Our world is also, if we believe the pundits, in a postcolonial, postsecular, and post-European era. Here I am talking less about moving beyond the Western epistemological paradigm (which we just discussed) and more about our trying to find our way in a truly pluralistic public square. If our postcolonial space foregrounds indigenous languages, cultures, and traditions, our postsecular mentality encourages, even demands, that each of these voices belong in the public domain. Eurocentric policies and practices are no longer privileged, even if what we have is more cacophony than intelligible conversation in the public arena. Into this vortex, a pentecostal and pneumatological imagination conceives of the possibility that the many tongues and perspectives might yet be redemptively orchestrated to accomplish divine purposes. If so, then a pneumato-missiological praxis emerges

10. Again, see also Yong, *Spirit-Word-Community*, part II; for cognitive scientific explication in the context of considering intellectual disability and moral formation, see my essay "Virtues and Intellectual Disability." My colleague James K. A. Smith has also done extensive work in this area, beginning with his *Thinking in Tongues*, ch. 3; see also Smith's *Desiring the Kingdom* and *Imagining the Kingdom*, for the phenomenological epistemology that I call the pneumatological imagination.

that does not seek to create a unified (Babelian) language, but that derives resources from out of the many to envision a flourishing and shalomic common world. Such an approach features and invites what I have else-where called many tongues and many practices,[11] precisely what is needed to address the many ills that plague our pluralistic and multifarious global situation.

Perhaps the biggest challenge for Christians, relatedly, is that ours is also a post-Christendom and even post-Christian time. This is not to deny that at least nominally Christianity is the largest of the world religions, even growing especially in the majority world. It is to say that the historic politi-cal, institutional, and social fabric of a "Christian society" may be waning. Certainly that is the case in Europe, and increasingly also in America, which has always insisted on the separation of church and state. More pointedly, if the church in the West before wielded political influence and authority, today's postdenominational world observes informal, dynamic, and chaotic networks of congregations, movements, and relationships that—so it ap-pears—do not hold together long enough to make a political impact.[12] In this context, however, a pneumatological imagination enacts divine possi-bilities from the countercultural and cruciform margins of society. As such, a pneumato-missiological praxis emerges that relies not on Christians having or exercising political authority but on their capacity to promote the healing and reconciliation essential to a peaceful, just, and beautiful world order. This is not the abandonment of the church as institution for the church as charismatic; it is to enable the renewal of the church—institutional and otherwise—according to the many charismatic giftings of the Spirit poured out on all flesh.

While my theological journey was initiated by what I felt then to be the intractable questions related to Christian faith in a pluralistic world,[13] twenty years later I am convinced that thinking through challenges related to theology of religions, interfaith encounter, and comparative theology from a pentecostal and pneumatological perspective remains relevant for Christian self-understanding and mission in the third-millennium global context. A pneumatological approach to theological reflection opens up not only to neglected theological ideas but sustains a more dynamic modality of theological reflection than perhaps otherwise possible. As importantly,

11. What I argued in *In the Days of Caesar*.

12. The corresponding ecclesiology for such a postdenominational time is rhizo-mic, as articulated by Lord, *Network Church*.

13. I took up this question during my second master's course of study at Portland State University (1993–1995), where I studied Buddhist traditions and explored pro-cess thought mediating the Christian-Buddhist dialogue, among other topics.

a pneumato-missiological vision of Christian faith embraces a pluralistic model of missional engagement even as it welcomes the challenges of pluralism across all fronts—religious, cultural, political, economic, social, etc.—that will persist through the twenty-first century and beyond. What is needed for Christian faith and practice is an appreciation of not only right thinking (orthodoxy) but also right feeling (orthopathy) and right acting (orthopraxis), and how each of these inform the other rather than any being subordinated to the other.[14] A pneumatological theology provides such a grounding precisely through its robust christological and Trinitarian framework, and this in turn contributes to theology of mission even as it also returns to inform a Christian mission theology.

To the degree that our present context—one that is, as indicated: postmodern, post-Enlightenment, post-Western, postcolonial, postsecular, post-European, post-Christendom, even post-Christian—persists, to that same degree the vision of Christian self-understanding and mission elaborated in these pages can potentially invigorate Christian life and witness into the middle of the twenty-first century. If our times change, even then, a pneumatological theology of mission will be discerning about what is emerging and enable adjustment and adaptation to the new realities. In any and all cases, the work of the Holy Spirit is to accomplish the reconciliation of the world to God through Jesus Christ, and toward that end, Christians live in humility and confidence amidst a pluralistic world, in anticipation of the coming reign of God.

14. See also my book *Spirit of Love*, which attempts to weave together an orthopathic, orthopraxic, and orthodoxic theological vision.

Bibliography

Abe, Masao. *Zen and Western Thought*. Edited by William R. LaFleur. Honolulu: University of Hawaiʻi Press, 1985.

Akinade, Akintunde, ed. *A New Day: Essays on World Christianity in Honor of Lamin Sanneh*. New York: Peter Lang, 2010.

Albrecht, Daniel. *Rites in the Spirit: A Ritual Approach to Pentecostal/Charismatic Spirituality*. Journal of Pentecostal Theology Supplement Series 17. Sheffield: Sheffield Academic Press, 1999.

Alexander, Loveday. "The Acts of the Apostles as an Apologetic Text." In *Apologetics in the Roman Empire: Pagans, Jews, and Christians*, edited by Mark Edwards, et al., 15–44. New York: Oxford University Press, 1999.

Alexander, Paul. *Peace to War: Shifting Allegiances in the Assemblies of God*. The C. Henry Smith Series 9. Telford, PA: Cascadia, 2009.

Allen, Roland. "Pentecost and the World." In *The Ministry of the Spirit: Selected Writings of Roland Allen*, edited by David M. Paton, 1–62. Grand Rapids: Eerdmans, 1960.

Alonso, Pablo. *The Woman Who Changed Jesus: Crossing Boundaries in Mk 7, 24–30*. Biblical Tools and Studies 11. Leuven: Peeters, 2011.

Anderson, Allan H. "Global Pentecostalism in the New Millennium." In *Pentecostals after a Century: Global Perspectives on a Movement in Transition*, edited by Alan Anderson and Walter J. Hollenweger, 209–23. Sheffield: Sheffield Academic Press, 1999.

———. *An Introduction to Pentecostalism: Global Charismatic Christianity*. Cambridge: Cambridge University Press, 2004.

———. "Introduction: World Pentecostalism at a Crossroads." In *Pentecostals after a Century: Global Perspectives on a Movement in Transition*, edited by Alan Anderson and Walter J. Hollenweger, 19–31. Sheffield: Sheffield Academic Press, 1999.

———. *Spreading Fires: The Missionary Nature of Early Pentecostalism*. London: SCM, 2007.

———. *To the Ends of the Earth: Pentecostalism and the Transformation of World Christianity*. Oxford: Oxford University Press, 2013.

———. "Towards a Pentecostal Missiology for the Majority World." *Asian Journal of Pentecostal Studies* 8:1 (2005) 29–47.

Anderson, Gerald H., and Thomas F. Stransky, eds. *Faith Meets Faith*. Mission Trends 5. Grand Rapids: Eerdmans, 1981.

Anderson, James B. *A Vatican II Pneumatology of the Paschal Mystery: The Historical-Doctrinal Genesis of Ad Gentes I, 2–5*. Rome: Editrice Pontificia Universita Gregoriana, 1988.

Arterbury, Andrew E. "The Custom of Hospitality in Antiquity and Its Importance for Interpreting Acts 9:43—11:18." PhD diss., Baylor University, 2003.

Arweck, Elisabeth, and Martin D. Stringer, eds. *Theorizing Faith: The Insider/Outsider Problem in the Study of Ritual*. Birmingham, UK: University of Birmingham Press, 2002.

Ateek, Naim. "Pentecost and the Intifada." In *Reading From This Place*, vol. 2: *Social Location and Biblical Interpretation in Global Perspective*, edited by Fernando F. Segovia and Mary Ann Tolbert, 69–81. Minneapolis: Fortress, 1995.

Baird, Robert D. *Category Formation and the History of Religions*. The Hague: Mouton, 1971.

Baker, James T. *Religion in America: Primary Sources in U.S. History*. 2 vols. Belmont, CA: Thomson Wadsworth, 2006.

Balthasar, Hans Urs von. *Explorations in Theology*, vol. 3: *Creator Spirit*. Translated by Brian McNeil. San Francisco: Ignatius, 1993.

Barclay, John M. G. *Jews in the Mediterranean Diaspora: From Alexander to Trajan (323 BCE–117 CE)*. Edinburgh: T & T Clark, 1996.

Barnhart, Bruno, and Joseph Wong, eds. *Purity of Heart and Contemplation: A Monastic Dialogue between Christians and Asian Traditions*. New York: Continuum, 2001.

Barreto, Eric Daniel. "Reading in Black and White: The Ethiopian Eunuch, Acts, and Constructs of Race." Unpublished paper presented to the southeast regional meeting of the American Academy of Religion, Atlanta, GA, March 10–12, 2006.

Barrett, William, ed. *Zen Buddhism: Selected Writings of D. T. Suzuki*. New York: Doubleday/Image, 1996.

Barrows, John Henry, ed. *The World's Parliament of Religions*. 2 vols. Chicago: Parliament Publishing, 1893.

Bartchy, S. Scott. "*Agnōstos Theos*: Luke's Message to the 'Nations' about Israel's God." In *Society of Biblical Literature 1995 Seminar Papers*, edited by Eugene H. Lovering Jr., 304–20. Atlanta: Scholars, 1995.

Barth, Karl. *Church Dogmatics*, vol. 4, part 1. Translated by G. W. Bromiley. London: T & T Clark, 1956.

Bartleman, Frank. *Azusa Street: The Roots of Modern-Day Pentecost*. Plainfield, NJ: Logos International, 1980.

Batchelor, Stephen. *Buddhism without Beliefs: A Contemporary Guide to Awakening*. New York: Riverhead, 1997.

Bayer, Charles H. *A Resurrected Church: Christianity after the Death of Christendom*. St. Louis: Chalice, 2001.

Bays, J. Daniel. *From Every People and Nation: A Biblical Theology of Race*. New Studies in Biblical Theology 14. Downers Grove, IL: InterVarsity, 2003.

Bechard, Dean Philip. *Paul Outside the Walls: A Study of Luke's Socio-Geographical Universalism in Acts 14:8–20*. Analecta Biblica 143. Rome: Editrice Pontificio Istituto Biblico, 2000.

Berkhof, Hendrikus. *Christ and the Powers*. Translated by John H. Yoder. Scottsdale, PA: Herald, 1962. Reprint, Waterloo, ON: Mennonite Publishing House, 1977.

Berryhill, Carisse Mickey. "From Dreaded Guest to Welcome Host: Hospitality and Paul in Acts." In *Restoring the First-century Church in the Twenty-first Century:*

Essays on the Stone-Campbell Restoration Movement, edited by Warren Lewis and Hans Rollman, 71–86. Eugene, OR: Wipf and Stock, 2005.

Bevans, Stephen. "God Inside Out: Notes toward a Missionary Theology of the Holy Spirit." *International Bulletin of Missionary Research* 22:3 (1998) 102–5.

Bevans, Stephen B., and Roger P. Schroeder. *Constants in Context: A Theology of Mission for Today*. Maryknoll, NY: Orbis, 2004.

————. *Prophetic Dialogue: Reflections on Christian Mission Today*. Maryknoll, NY: Orbis, 2011.

Biesecker-Mast, Gerald. "Critique and Subjection in Anabaptist Political Witness." In *Exiles in the Empire: Believers Church Perspectives on Politics*, edited by Nathan E. Yoder and Carol A. Scheppard, 45–59. Studies in the Believers Church Tradition 5. Kitchener: Pandora, 2006.

Bilaniuk, Petro B. T. *Theology and Economy of the Holy Spirit*. Placid Lecture Series 2. Bangalore: Dharmaram, 1980.

Blaising, Craig A., and Darrell L. Bock, eds. *Dispensationalism, Israel and the Church: The Search for Definition*. Grand Rapids: Zondervan, 1992.

Blossom, Jay S. F. "Evangelists of Destruction: Missions to Native Americans in Recent Film." In *The Foreign Missionary Enterprise at Home: Explorations of North American Cultural History*, edited by Daniel H. Bays and Grant Wacker, 237–50. Tuscaloosa, AL: The University of Alabama Press, 2003.

Boer, Harry R. *Pentecost and Missions*. Grand Rapids: Eerdmans, 1962.

Bond, Edward L. "Colonial Virginia Mission Attitudes toward Native Peoples and African-American Slaves." In *Remembering Jamestown: Hard Questions about Christian Mission*, edited by Amos Yong and Barbara Brown Zikmund, 69–90. Eugene, OR: Pickwick, 2010.

Borgen, Peder. *Early Christianity and Hellenistic Judaism*. Edinburgh: T & T Clark, 1996.

Bosch, David J. *Transforming Mission: Paradigm Shifts in Theology of Mission*. Maryknoll, NY: Orbis, 1991.

Bossey Consultation organized by the World Council of Churches networks of Faith and Order, Conference on World Mission and Evangelism, and the Office on Interreligious Relations and Dialogue. "Religious Plurality and Christian Self-Understanding." *Current Dialogue* 45 (2005) 4–12. Available at http://wcc-coe.org/wcc/what/interreligious/cd45–01.html.

Boyd, Gregory A. *Trinity and Process: A Critical Evaluation and Reconstruction of Hartshorne's Di-Polar Theism towards a Trinitarian Metaphysics*. New York: Peter Lang, 1992.

Braaten, Carl. *No Other Gospel! Christianity among the World's Religions*. Minneapolis: Fortress, 1992.

Brandner, Tobias. "Premillennial and Countercultural Faith and Its Production and Reception in the Chinese Context." *Asian Journal of Pentecostal Studies* 14:1 (2011) 3–26.

Brewer, Teri. "Touching the Past, Teaching Ways Forward: The American Indian Powwow." In *Indigenous Religions: A Companion*, edited by Graham Harvey, 255–68. New York: Cassell, 2000.

Brouwer, Steve, Paul Gifford, and Susan D. Rose. *Exporting the American Gospel: Global Christian Fundamentalism*. New York: Routledge, 1996.

Brown, Robert McAfee. *Unexpected News: Reading the Bible with Third World Eyes*. Philadelphia: Westminster, 1984.

Bruce, F. F. "Philip and the Ethiopian." *Journal of Semitic Studies* 34:2 (1989) 377–86.

Bulgakov, Sergius. *The Bride of the Lamb.* Translated by Boris Jakim. Grand Rapids: Eerdmans, 2002.

Bundy, David. "Hollenweger, Walter Jacob." In *The New International Dictionary of Pentecostal and Charismatic Movements,* edited by Stanley M. Burgess and Eduard M. Van Der Maas, 729. Grand Rapids: Zondervan, 2002.

———. "Missiological Reflections on Nestorian Christianity in China during the Tang Dynasty." In *Religion in the Pacific Era,* edited by Frank K. Flinn and Tyler Hendricks, 14–30. New York: Paragon House, 1985.

———. "Problems and Promises: Pentecostal Mission in the Context of Global Pentecostalism." Unpublished plenary paper presented at the 29th Annual Meeting of the Society for Pentecostal Studies, Kirkland, WA, March 16–18, 2000.

Burn, Geoffrey. "Hospitality and Incarnational Vulnerability in Luke 10:1–12." *Theology* 103 (2000) 445–46.

Burrows, William R. "Moving beyond Christian Imperialism to Mission as Reconciliation with all Creation." In *Remembering Jamestown: Hard Questions about Christian Mission,* edited by Amos Yong and Barbara Brown Zikmund, 69–90. Eugene, OR: Pickwick, 2010.

Burrows, William R., ed. *Redemption and Dialogue: Reading Redemptoris Missio and Dialogue and Proclamation.* Maryknoll, NY: Orbis, 1993.

Byrne, Brendan. *The Hospitality of God: A Reading of Luke's Gospel.* Collegeville, MN: Liturgical, 2000.

Cadge, Wendy. *Heartwood: The First Generation of Theravada Buddhism in America.* Chicago: The University of Chicago Press, 2005.

Caird, G. B. *Principalities and Powers: A Study in Pauline Theology.* Oxford: Clarendon, 1956.

Calvin, John. *Institutes of the Christian Religion.* 2 vols. Edited by John T. McNeill. Translated by Ford Lewis Battles. Philadelphia: Westminster, 1965.

Carson, Cottrell R. "'Do You Understand What You are Reading?' A Reading of the Ethiopian Eunuch Story Acts 8.26–40 from a Site of Cultural Marronage." PhD diss., Union Theological Seminary, 1999.

Carter, Craig A. *The Politics of the Cross: The Theology and Ethics of John Howard Yoder.* Grand Rapids: Brazos, 2001.

Carter, J. Kameron. *Race: A Theological Account.* Oxford: Oxford University Press, 2008.

Cartledge, Mark J. *Testimony in the Spirit: Rescriptive Ordinary Pentecostal Theology.* Burlington, VT: Ashgate, 2013.

Cavanaugh, William T. *Torture and Eucharist: Theology, Politics, and the Body of Christ.* Oxford: Blackwell, 1998.

Chapman, Thomas Gregory. "A Phenomenological Method of Post-Dialogue within a World of Religious Pluralism." PhD diss., Southern Baptist Theological Seminary. Ann Arbor, MI: University Microfilms International, 1992.

Chester, Tim. *Mission and the Coming of God: Eschatology, the Trinity and Mission in the Theology of Jürgen Moltmann and Contemporary Evangelicalism.* Milton Keynes, UK: Paternoster, 2006.

Cho, Youngmo. *Spirit and Kingdom in the Writings of Luke and Paul: An Attempt to Reconcile These Concepts.* Eugene, OR: Wipf & Stock, 2007.

Clapsis, Emmanuel. "What Does the Spirit Say to the Churches? Missiological Implications of the Seventh Assembly of the WCC." *International Review of Mission* 80:319/320 (1991) 327–38.

Clarke, Clifton. "Dialogue or Diatribe: Toward a Renewal Approach to Interreligious Conversation." In *Global Renewal, Religious Pluralism, and the Great Commission: Toward a Renewal Theology of Mission and Interreligious Encounter*, edited by Amos Yong and Clifton Clarke, 17–42. Asbury Theological Seminary Series in World Christian Revitalization Movements in Pentecostal/Charismatic Studies 4. Lexington, KY: Emeth, 2011.

Collins Winn, Christian T., and Amos Yong. "The Apocalypse of Colonialism, Colonialism as Apocalyptic Mission; Or, Notes towards a Postcolonial Eschatology." In *Evangelical Postcolonial Conversations: Global Awakenings in Theology and Praxis*, edited by Kay Higuera Smith, Jayachitra Lallitha, and L. Daniel Hawk, 139–51. Downers Grove, IL: IVP Academic, 2014.

Coakley, John W., and Andrea Sterk, eds. *Readings in World Christian History*, vol. 1: *Earliest Christianity to 1453*. Maryknoll, NY: Orbis, 2004.

Cobb, John B., Jr. *Beyond Dialogue: Toward the Mutual Transformation of Christianity and Buddhism*. Philadelphia: Fortress, 1982.

Cobble, James F. *The Church and the Powers*. Peabody, MA: Hendrickson, 1988.

Collins, John J. *Between Athens and Jerusalem: Jewish Identity in the Hellenistic Diaspora*. New York: Crossroad, 1983.

Copleston, F. C. *Religion and the One: Philosophies East and West*. New York: Crossroad, 1982.

Corrie, John, ed. *Dictionary of Mission Theology*. Downers Grove, IL: InterVarsity, 2007.

Cox, Harvey G. *Fire from Heaven: The Rise of Pentecostal Spirituality and the Reshaping of Religion in the Twenty-first Century*. Reading, MA: Addison-Wesley, 1995.

Crockett, William V., and James G. Sigountos, eds. *Through No Fault of Their Own? The Fate of Those Who Have Never Heard*. Grand Rapids: Baker, 1991.

Dabney, D. Lyle. "*Pneumatologia Crucis*: Reclaiming *Theologia Crucis* for a Theology of the Spirit Today." *Scottish Journal of Theology* 53 (2000) 511–24.

Das, Lama Surya. "Emergent Trends in Western Dharma." In *Buddhism in America*, edited by Al Rapaport and Brian D. Hotchkiss, 543–54. Boston: Charles E. Tuttle, 1998.

Dempster, Murray W., et al., eds. *Called and Empowered: Global Mission in Pentecostal Perspective*. Peabody, MA: Hendrickson, 1991.

Dharmaraj, Jacob S. *Colonialism and Christian Mission: Postcolonial Reflections*. Delhi: Indian Society for Promoting Christian Knowledge, 1993.

Dharmasiri, Gunapala. *A Buddhist Critique of the Christian Concept of God*. Antioch, CA: Golden Leaves, 1988.

Diamond, Sara. *Spiritual Warfare: The Politics of the Christian Right*. Boston: South End, 1989.

Dollar, Harold E. *A Biblical-Missiological Exploration of the Cross-Cultural Dimensions in Luke-Acts*. San Francisco: Mellen Research University Press, 1993.

Dombrowski, Kirk. *Against Culture: Development, Politics, and Religion in Indian Alaska*. Lincoln, NE: University of Nebraska Press, 2001.

Dumm, Demetrius R. "Luke 24:44–49 and Hospitality." In *Sin, Salvation, and the Spirit: Commemorating the Fiftieth Year of The Liturgical Press*, edited by Daniel Durken, 231–39. Collegeville, MN: Liturgical, 1979.

Dupuis, Jacques. *Toward a Christian Theology of Religious Pluralism*. Maryknoll, NY: Orbis, 1997.

Duraisingh, Christopher. "Mission and the Holy Spirit, Transforming Energy." *International Review of Mission* 80:17 (1991) 1–6.

Edwards, Denis. *Breath of Life: A Theology of the Creator Spirit*. Maryknoll, NY: Orbis, 2004.

Ellington, Scott A. "The Face of God as His Creating Spirit: The Interplay of Yahweh's *panim* and *ruach* in Psalm 104:29–30." In *The Spirit Renews the Face of the Earth: Pentecostal Forays in Science and Theology of Creation*, edited by Amos Yong, 17–29. Eugene, OR: Pickwick, 2009.

Eppsteiner, Fred, ed. *The Path of Compassion: Writings on Socially Engaged Buddhism*. 2nd rev. ed. Berkeley: Parallax, 1988.

Fackre, Gabriel, Ronald H. Nash, and John Sanders. *What about Those Who Have Never Heard? Three Views on the Destiny of the Unevangelized*. Downers Grove, IL: InterVarsity, 1995.

Falola, Toyin. *Violence in Nigeria: The Crisis of Religious Politics and Secular Ideologies*. Rochester, NY: University of Rochester Press, 1998.

Faruqi, Isma'il al-. "On the Nature of Islamic Da'wah." In *Christian Mission and Islamic Da'wah: Proceedings of the Chambésy Dialogue Consultation*, edited by Emilio Castro, et al., 33–42. Leicester, UK: The Islamic Foundation, 1982.

Fasholé-Luke, Edward W. "Ancestor Veneration and the Communion of Saints." In *New Testament Christianity for Africa and the World: Essays in Honour of Harry Sawyerr*, edited by Mark E. Glasswell and Edward W. Fasholé-Luke, 209–21. London: SPCK, 1974.

Faupel, D. William. *The Everlasting Gospel: The Significance of Eschatology in the Development of Pentecostal Thought*. Journal of Pentecostal Theology Supplement series 10. Sheffield: Sheffield Academic Press, 1996.

———. "Glossolalia as Foreign Language: An Investigation of the Early Twentieth Century Pentecostal Claim." *Wesleyan Theological Journal* 31 (1996) 95–109.

Fields, Rick. *How the Swans Came to the Lake: A Narrative History of Buddhism in America*. Boulder, CO: Shambhala, 1981.

Finger, Reta Halteman. *Of Widows and Meals: Communal Meals in the Book of Acts*. Grand Rapids: Eerdmans, 2007.

Fitzmyer, Joseph A. *The Acts of the Apostles: A New Translation with Introduction and Commentary*. The Anchor Bible 31. New York: Doubleday, 1998.

Folkemer, Lawrence D. "Dialogue and Proclamation." *Journal of Ecumenical Studies* 13:3 (1975) 420–39.

Foster, John. *The Church of the T'ang Dynasty*. London: SPCK, 1939.

French, Talmadge L. *Our God is One: The Story of Oneness Pentecostals*. Indianapolis: Voice & Vision, 2001.

Gallagher, Robert L. "The Holy Spirit in the World: In Non-Christians, in Creation, and Other Religions." *Asian Journal of Pentecostal Studies* 9:1 (2006) 17–33.

Gärtner, Bertil E. *The Areopagus Speech and Natural Revelation*. Acta Seminarii Neotestamentici Upsaliensis 21. Uppsala: C. W. K. Gleerup, 1955.

Geivett, R. Douglas, and W. Gary Phillips. "A Particularist View: An Evidentialist Approach." In *More than One Way? Four Views on Salvation in a Pluralistic World*, edited by Dennis L. Okholm and Timothy R. Phillips, 211–45. Grand Rapids: Zondervan, 1995.

Gelpi, Donald L. *The Conversion Experience: A Reflective Process for RCIA Participants and Others*. New York: Paulist, 1998.

———. *The Divine Mother: A Trinitarian Theology of the Holy Spirit*. Lanham, MD: University Press of America, 1984.

Gerloff, Roswith. *A Plea for British Black Theologies: The Black Church Movement in Britain in Its Transatlantic Cultural and Theological Interaction with Special References to the Pentecostal Oneness (Apostolic) and Sabbatarian Movements*. Studies in the Intercultural History of Christianity 77. Eugene, OR: Wipf & Stock, 2010.

Gibbs, Eddie, and Ryan K. Bolger. *Emerging Churches: Creating Christian Community in Postmodern Cultures*. Grand Rapids: Baker Academic, 2005.

Gifford, Paul. *The New Crusaders: Christianity and the New Right in Southern Africa*. Rev. ed. London: Pluto, 1991,

Gill, David W. J., and Bruce W. Winter. "Acts and Roman Religion." In *The Book of Acts in Its First Century Setting*, vol. 2: *The Book of Acts in Its Graeco-Roman Setting*, edited by David W. J. Gill and Conrad Gempf, 79–103. Grand Rapids: Eerdmans, 1994.

Gingerich, Ray C., and Ted Grimsrud, eds. *Transforming the Powers: Peace, Justice, and the Domination System*. Minneapolis: Fortress, 2006.

Girard, René. *I See Satan Fall Like Lightning*. Translated by James G. Williams. Maryknoll, NY: Orbis, 2001.

Goddard, Dwight, ed. *A Buddhist Bible*. 1938. Reprint, Boston: Beacon, 1994.

Goff, James R., Jr. *Fields White Unto Harvest: Charles Fox Parham and the Missionary Origins of Pentecostalism*. Fayetteville, AR: University of Arkansas Press, 1988.

———. "Initial Tongues in the Theology of Charles Fox Parham." In *Initial Evidence: Historical and Biblical Perspectives on the Pentecostal Doctrine of Spirit Baptism*, edited by Gary B. McGee, 57–71. Peabody, MA: Hendrickson, 1991.

———. "Parham, Charles Fox." In *The New International Dictionary of Pentecostal and Charismatic Movements*, edited by Stanley M. Burgess and Eduard M. Van Der Maas, 955–57. Grand Rapids: Zondervan, 2002.

González, Justo L. *Acts: The Gospel of the Spirit*. Maryknoll, NY: Orbis, 2001.

Gordon, A. J. *The Holy Spirit in Missions*. New York: Revell, 1893.

Gort, Jerald D., et al. *Dialogue and Syncretism: An Interdisciplinary Approach*. Grand Rapids: Eerdmans, 1989.

Gowler, David B. *Host, Guest, Enemy and Friend: Portraits of the Pharisees in Luke and Acts*. Emory Studies in Early Christianity 2. New York: Peter Lang, 1991.

Grassi, Joseph A. *Jesus is Shalom: A Vision of Peace from the Gospels*. New York: Paulist, 2006.

Griffin, David Ray, ed. *The Reenchantment of Science: Postmodern Proposals*. SUNY Series in Constructive Postmodern Thought. Albany: State University of New York Press, 1988.

Griffiths, Nicholas, and Fernando Cervantes, eds. *Spiritual Encounters: Interactions between Christianity and Native Religions in Colonial America*. Lincoln, NE: The University of Nebraska Press, 1999.

Griffiths, Paul J. *An Apology for Apologetics: A Study in the Logic of Interreligious Dialogue*. Maryknoll, NY: Orbis, 1991.

Gross, Rita M. "The International Buddhist-Christian Theological Encounter: Twenty Years of Dialogue." *Buddhist-Christian Studies* 25 (2005) 3–7.

Gross, Rita M., and Terry C. Muck, eds. *Buddhists Talk about Jesus, Christians Talk about the Buddha.* New York: Continuum, 2000.

———. *Christians Talk about Buddhist Meditation, Buddhists Talk about Christian Prayer.* New York: Continuum, 2003.

Guroian, Vigen. *Ethics after Christendom: Toward an Ecclesial Christian Ethic.* Grand Rapids: Eerdmans, 1994.

Haar, Francis, and Masao Abe. *A Zen Life: D. T. Suzuki Remembered.* New York: Weatherhill, 1986.

Hackett, Rosalind I. J. "Devil Bustin' Satellites: How Media Liberalization in Africa Generates Religious Intolerance and Conflict." In *Religious Dimensions of Conflict and Peace in Neoliberal Africa*, edited by Rosalind I. J. Hackett and James H. Smith, 163–208. Notre Dame, IN: University of Notre Dame Press, 2012.

———. "Discourses of Demonization in Africa and Beyond." *Diogenes* 50:3 (2003) 61–75.

———. "Managing or Manipulating Religious Conflict in the Nigerian Media." In *Mediating Religion: Conversations in Media, Religion and Culture*, edited by Jolyon Mitchell and Sophia Marriage, 47–63. London: T & T Clark, 2003.

———. "Radical Christian Revivalism in Nigeria and Ghana: Recent Patterns of Intolerance and Conflict." In *Proselytization and Communal Self-Determination in Africa*, edited by Abdullahi Ahmed An-Na'im, 246–67. Maryknoll, NY: Orbis, 1999.

Haenchen, Ernst. *The Acts of the Apostles: A Commentary.* Translated by Bernard Noble and Gerald Shinn. Revised by R. McL. Wilson. Philadelphia: Westminster, 1971.

Hall, Douglas John. *The End of Christendom and the Future of Christianity.* Valley Forge, PA: Trinity, 1997.

Hanh, Thich Nhat. *Interbeing: Fourteen Guidelines for Engaged Buddhism.* 3rd ed. Berkeley: Parallax, 1998.

Hauerwas, Stanley. *After Christendom? How the Church Is to Behave If Freedom, Justice, and a Christian Nation are Bad Ideas.* Nashville: Abingdon, 1991.

———. *A Better Hope: Resources for a Church Confronting Capitalism, Democracy, and Postmodernity.* Grand Rapids: Brazos, 2001.

———. *Christian Existence Today: Essays on Church, World, and Living In Between.* 1988. Reprint, Grand Rapids: Brazos, 2001.

———. *Dispatches from the Front: Theological Engagements with the Secular.* Durham, NC: Duke University Press, 1994.

———. *The Hauerwas Reader.* Edited by John Berkman and Michael Cartwright. Durham, NC: Duke University Press, 2001.

———. *The Peaceable Kingdom: A Primer in Christian Ethics.* Notre Dame, IN: University of Notre Dame Press, 1983.

Hauerwas, Stanley, et al., eds. *The Wisdom of the Cross: Essays in Honor of John Howard Yoder.* Grand Rapids: Eerdmans, 1999.

Hauerwas, Stanley, and William H. Willimon. *Resident Aliens: Life in the Christian Colony.* Nashville: Abingdon, 1989.

———. *Where Resident Aliens Live: Exercises for Christian Practice.* Nashville: Abingdon, 1996.

Hawkins, Thomas R. *Shearing the Search: A Theology of Christian Hospitality.* Nashville: Upper Room, 1987.

Heilke, Thomas. "Yoder's Idea of Constantinianism: An Analytical Framework Toward Conversation." In *A Mind Patient and Untamed: Assessing John Howard Yoder's Contributions to Theology, Ethics, and Peacemaking*, edited by Ben C. Ollenburger and Gayle Gerber Koontz, 89–126. Scottdale, PA: Herald, 2004.

Heim, S. Mark. *The Depth of the Riches: A Trinitarian Theology of Religious Ends*. Grand Rapids: Eerdmans, 2001.

Heston, Edward L. *The Spiritual Life and the Role of the Holy Ghost in the Sanctification of the Soul, as Described in the Works of Didymus of Alexandria*. Rome: Pontificiae Universitas Gregoriana, 1938.

Hobbs, Maurice. "Our Lord's Approach to People of Other Cultures." In *Jesus Christ the Only Way: Christian Responsibility in a Multicultural Society*, edited by Patrick Sookhdeo, 37–42. Exeter: Paternoster, 1978.

Hodges, Melvin L. *The Indigenous Church*. Springfield, MO: Gospel Publishing House, 1953.

———. *A Theology of the Church and Its Mission: A Pentecostal Perspective*. Springfield, MO: Gospel Publishing House, 1977.

Hollenweger, Walter. "Black Roots of Pentecostalism." In *Pentecostals after a Century: Global Perspectives on a Movement in Transition*, edited by Alan Anderson and Walter J. Hollenweger, 33–44. Sheffield: Sheffield Academic Press, 1999.

———. "Critical Issues for Pentecostals." In *Pentecostals after a Century: Global Perspectives on a Movement in Transition*, edited by Alan Anderson and Walter J. Hollenweger, 176–91. Sheffield: Sheffield Academic Press, 1999.

———. *Pentecostalism: Origins and Developments Worldwide*. Peabody, MA: Hendrickson, 1997.

———. *The Pentecostals: The Charismatic Movement in the Churches*. Translated by R. A. Wilson. Minneapolis: Augsburg, 1972. Reprint, Peabody, MA: Hendrickson, 1988.

Hooker, Roger, and Christopher Lamb. *Love the Stranger: Christian Ministry in Multi-Faith Areas*. London: SPCK, 1986.

Horton, Stanley M. *What the Bible Says About the Holy Spirit*. Springfield, MO: Gospel Publishing House, 1992.

Hovey, Craig R. "The Public Ethics of John Howard Yoder and Stanley Hauerwas: Difference or Disagreement?" In *A Mind Patient and Untamed: Assessing John Howard Yoder's Contributions to Theology, Ethics, and Peacemaking*, edited by Ben C. Ollenburger and Gayle Gerber Koontz, 205–45. Scottdale, PA: Herald, 2004.

Hughes, Ray H. *Church of God Distinctives*. Cleveland, TN: Pathway, 1989.

Humphrey, Peggy. *J. H. Ingram: Missionary Dean*. Church of God World Missions Missionary Series. Cleveland, TN: Pathway, 1966.

Hütter, Reinhard. *Suffering Divine Things: Theology as Church Practice*. Grand Rapids: Eerdmans, 2000.

Ingram, Paul O. *Wrestling with God*. Eugene, OR: Cascade, 2006.

Irvin, Dale T. *Christian Histories, Christian Traditioning: Rendering Accounts*. Maryknoll, NY: Orbis, 1998.

———. "'Drawing All Together in One Bond of Love': The Ecumenical Vision of William J. Seymour and the Azusa Street Revival." *Journal of Pentecostal Theology* 6 (1995) 25–53.

———. "Review of *Beyond the Impasse: Toward a Pneumatological Theology of Religions*, by Amos Yong." *Journal of Pentecostal Theology* 12:2 (2004) 277–80.

Irvin, Dale T., and Scott W. Sunquist. *History of the World Christian Movement*, vol. 1: *Earliest Christianity to 1453*. Maryknoll, NY: Orbis, 2001.

Irvin, Howard M. *Healing: A Sign of the Kingdom* Peabody, MA: Hendrickson, 2002.

Isasi-Diaz, Ada María. *Mujerista Theology: A Theology for the Twenty-First Century*. Maryknoll, NY: Orbis, 1996.

Ives, Christopher, ed. *Divine Emptiness and Historical Fullness: A Buddhist-Jewish-Christian Conversation with Masao Abe*. Valley Forge, PA: Trinity, 1995.

Jackson, Glenna S. *'Have Mercy on Me': The Story of the Canaanite Woman in Matthew 15.21–28*. Journal for the Study of the New Testament Supplement series 228. London: Sheffield Academic Press, 2002.

Jenkins, Philip. *The New Faces of Christianity: Believing the Bible in the Global South*. New York: Oxford University Press, 2006.

Jennings, Willie James. *The Christian Imagination: Theology and the Origins of Race*. New Haven: Yale University Press, 2010.

Jervell, Jacob. "The Church of Jews and Godfearers." In *Luke-Acts and the Jewish People: Eight Critical Perspectives*, edited by Joseph B. Tyson, 11–20. Minneapolis: Augsburg, 1988.

Johns, Cheryl Bridges. "Partners in Scandal: Wesleyan and Pentecostal Scholarship." *Pneuma: The Journal of the Society for Pentecostal Studies* 21:2 (1999) 183–97.

Johnson, Keith E. *Rethinking the Trinity and Religious Pluralism: An Augustinian Assessment*. Downers Grove, IL: IVP Academic, 2011.

Johnston, William. *The Still Point: Reflections on Zen and Christian Mysticism*. New York: Fordham University Press, 1970.

Jongeneel, J. A. B., ed. *Pentecost, Mission, and Ecumenism: Essays on Intercultural Theology—Festschrift in Honour of Professor Walter J. Hollenweger*. Frankfurt: Peter Lang, 1992.

Kalu, Ogbu U. "Estranged Bedfellows? The Demonisation of the Aladura in African Pentecostal Rhetoric." *Missionalia* 28:2/3 (2000) 121–42.

———. *Power, Poverty and Prayer: The Challenges of Poverty and Pluralism in African Christianity, 1960–1996*. Studies in the Intercultural History of Christianity 122. Frankfurt: Peter Lang, 2000.

———. "Sharia and Islam in Nigerian Pentecostal Rhetoric, 1970–2003." *Pneuma: The Journal of the Society for Pentecostal Studies* 26:2 (2004) 242–61.

Kaplan, Steven. "The Africanization of Missionary Christianity: History and Typology." In *Indigenous Responses to Western Christianity*, edited by Steven Kaplan, 9–28. New York: New York University Press, 1995.

Kärkkäinen, Veli-Matti. "*Dukkha* and *Passio*: A Christian Theology of Suffering in the *Theravāda* Buddhist Context." In *Global Renewal, Religious Pluralism, and the Great Commission: Toward a Renewal Theology of Mission and Interreligious Encounter*, edited by Amos Yong and Clifton Clarke, 97–116. Asbury Theological Seminary Series in World Christian Revitalization Movements in Pentecostal/Charismatic Studies 4. Lexington, KY: Emeth, 2011.

———. "How to Speak of the Spirit among Religions: Trinitarian 'Rules' for a Pneumatological Theology of Religions." *International Bulletin of Missionary Research* 30:3 (2006) 121–27.

———. *An Introduction to the Theology of Religions*. Downers Grove, IL: InterVarsity, 2003.

————. "Pentecostal Theology of Mission in the Making." *Journal of Beliefs and Values* 25:2 (2004) 167–76.

————. *Pneumatology: The Holy Spirit in Ecumenical, International and Contextual Perspective*. Grand Rapids: Baker Academic, 2002.

————. "A Response to Tony Richie's 'Azusa-Era Optimism: Bishop J. H. King's Pentecostal Theology of Religions as a Possible Paradigm for Today.'" *Journal of Pentecostal Theology* 15:2 (2007) 263–68.

————. *Toward a Pneumatological Theology: Pentecostal and Ecumenical Perspectives on Ecclesiology, Soteriology and Theology of Mission*. Edited by Amos Yong. Lanham, MD: University Press of America, 2002.

————. "Toward a Pneumatological Theology of Religions: A Pentecostal-Charismatic Inquiry." *International Review of Mission* 91:361 (2002) 187–98.

————. *Trinity and Religious Pluralism: The Doctrine of the Trinity in Christian Theology of Religions*. Burlington, VT: Ashgate, 2004.

————. "'Truth on Fire': Pentecostal Theology of Mission and the Challenges of a New Millennium." *Asian Journal of Pentecostal Studies* 3:1 (2000) 33–60.

Kärkkäinen, Veli-Matti, et al., eds. *Interdisciplinary and Religio-Cultural Discourses on a Spirit-Filled World: Loosing the Spirits*. New York: Palgrave Macmillan, 2013.

Kee, Howard Clark. *Good News to the Ends of the Earth: The Theology of Acts*. Philadelphia: Trinity, 1990.

Keener, Craig S. *Gift and Giver: The Holy Spirit for Today*. Grand Rapids: Baker Academic, 2001.

Keightley, Alan. *Into Every Life a Little Zen Must Fall: A Christian Philosopher Looks at Alan Watts and the East*. London: Wisdom/Elements, 1986.

Kerr, David. "'Come Holy Spirit—Renew the Whole Creation': The Canberra Assembly and Issues of Mission." *International Bulletin of Missionary Research* 15:3 (1991) 98–105.

Khodr, Georges. "Christianity in a Pluralistic World—The Economy of the Holy Spirit." *Ecumenical Review* 23 (1971) 118–28.

Kim, Kirsteen. *Mission in the Spirit: The Holy Spirit in Indian Christian Theologies*. Delhi: ISPCK, 2003.

————. "Theologies of Religious Pluralism: Pneumatological Foundations and Conversion in India." In *Global Renewal, Religious Pluralism, and the Great Commission: Toward a Renewal Theology of Mission and Interreligious Encounter*, edited by Amos Yong and Clifton Clarke, 117–36. Asbury Theological Seminary Series in World Christian Revitalization Movements in Pentecostal/Charismatic Studies 4. Lexington, KY: Emeth, 2011.

King, Sallie B. *Being Benevolence: The Social Ethics of Engaged Buddhism*. Honolulu: University of Hawai'i Press, 2005.

Klauck, Hans-Josef. *Magic and Paganism in Early Christianity: The World of the Acts of the Apostles*. Translated by Brian McNeil. Minneapolis: Fortress, 2003.

Klaus, Byron D. "The Holy Spirit and Mission in Eschatological Perspective: A Pentecostal Viewpoint." *Pneuma: The Journal of the Society for Pentecostal Studies* 27:2 (2005) 322–42.

Klaver, Miranda. "In Search of a Pentecostal-Charismatic Theology of Religions: A critical investigation of the work of Clark H. Pinnock and Amos Yong." MA thesis, Free University Amsterdam, 2004.

Klimkeit, Hans-J. "Christian-Buddhist Encounter in Medieval Central Asia." In *The Cross and the Lotus: Christianity and Buddhism in Dialogue*, edited by G. W. Houston, 9–24. Delhi: Motilal Banarsidass, 1985.

Knitter, Paul F. *Jesus and the Other Names: Christian Mission and Global Responsibility*. Maryknoll, NY: Orbis, 1996.

———. "A New Pentecost? A Pneumatological Theology of Religions." *Current Dialogue* 19 (1991) 32–41.

———. *No Other Name? A Critical Survey of Christian Attitudes toward the World Religions*. Maryknoll, NY: Orbis, 1985.

———. *One Earth Many Religions: Multifaith Dialogue and Global Responsibility*. Maryknoll, NY: Orbis 1995.

Koenig, John. *New Testament Hospitality: Partnership with Strangers as Promise and Mission*. Overtures to Biblical Theology 17. Philadelphia: Fortress, 1985.

Kraft, Charles. *Christianity and Culture*. Maryknoll, NY: Orbis, 1979.

Küng, Hans. *Global Responsibility: In Search of a New World Ethic*. Translated by John Bowden. New York: Continuum, 1993.

Lai, Whalen, and Michael von Brück. *Christianity and Buddhism: A Multicultural History of Their Dialogue*. Maryknoll, NY: Orbis, 2001.

Land, Steven J. *Pentecostal Spirituality: A Passion for the Kingdom*. Journal of Pentecostal Theology Supplemental Series 1. Sheffield: Sheffield Academic Press, 1993.

Langdon, Adrian. "Review of *Beyond the Impasse: Toward a Pneumatological Theology of Religions*, by Amos Yong." *ARC: The Journal of the Faculty of Religious Studies at McGill University* 31 (2003) 227–29.

Laseto, Razouselie. *Nazareth Manifesto: Theology of Jubilee and Its Trajectories in Luke to Acts*. Delhi: ISPCK, 2006.

Learman, Linda. "Introduction." In *Buddhist Missionaries in the Era of Globalization*, edited by Linda Learman, 1–22. Honolulu: University of Hawai'i Press, 2005.

Lee, Robert. "A Response to: Why Jesus Instead of the Buddha?" In *How Wide is God's Mercy? Christian Perspectives on Religious Pluralism*, edited by Dale W. Little, 84–91. Tokyo: Hayama Seminar Annual Report and Tokyo Mission Research Institute, 1993.

Lee, Sung Hyun. *The Philosophical Theology of Jonathan Edwards*. Princeton, NJ: Princeton University Press, 1988.

Letham, Robert. *The Work of Christ*. Downers Grove, IL: InterVarsity, 1993.

Levinskaya, Irina. *The Book of Acts in Its Diaspora Setting*. Grand Rapids: Eerdmans, 1996.

Levison, John H. *Filled in the Spirit*. Grand Rapids: Eerdmans, 2009.

Lie, Henry E. "Open Particularism: An Evangelical Alternative to Meet the Challenge of Religious Pluralism in the Asian Context." PhD diss., Trinity Evangelical Divinity School, 1998.

Lindbeck, George. *The Nature of Doctrine: Religion and Theology in a Postliberal Age* Philadelphia: Westminster, 1984.

Lord, Andrew. *Network Church: A Pentecostal Ecclesiology Shaped by Mission*. Global Pentecostal and Charismatic Studies 11. Leiden: Brill, 2012.

———. "The Pentecostal-Moltmann Dialogue: Implications for Mission." *Journal of Pentecostal Theology* 11:2 (2003) 271–87.

———. "Principles for a Charismatic Approach to Other Faiths." *Asian Journal of Pentecostal Studies* 6:2 (2003) 235–46.

————. *Spirit-Shaped Mission: A Holistic Charismatic Missiology.* Carlisle, UK: Paternoster, 2005.

Lyotard, Jean-François. *The Postmodern Condition: A Report on Knowledge.* Translated by Geoff Bennington and Brian Massumi. Minneapolis: University of Minneapolis Press, 1984.

Ma, Julie C. *When the Spirit Meets the Spirits: Pentecostal Ministry among the Kankana-ey Tribe in the Philippines.* Studies in the Intercultural History of Christianity 118. Frankfurt: Peter Lang, 2000.

Ma, Julie C., and Wonsuk Ma. *Mission in the Spirit: Towards a Pentecostal/Charismatic Missiology.* Oxford: Regnum International, 2013.

Macchia, Frank D. *Baptized in the Spirit: A Global Pentecostal Theology.* Grand Rapids: Zondervan, 2006.

————. "Discerning the Spirit in Life: A Review of *God the Spirit* by Michael Welker." *Journal of Pentecostal Theology* 10 (1997) 3–28.

————. *Justified in the Spirit: Creation, Redemption, and the Triune God.* Grand Rapids: Eerdmans, 2010.

————. "Revitalizing Theological Categories: A Classical Pentecostal Response to J. Rodman Williams's *Renewal Theology.*" *Pneuma: The Journal of the Society for Pentecostal Studies* 16:2 (1994) 293–304.

————. "The Tongues of Pentecost: The Promise and Challenge of Pentecostal/Roman Catholic Dialogue." *Journal of Ecumenical Studies* 35:1 (1998) 1–18.

Maimela, Simon S. "Practice of Mission and Evangelism." *LWF [Lutheran World Federation] Report* 13–14 (1983) 43–58.

Mann, Barbara Alice. "A Failure to Communicate: How Christian Missionary Assumptions Ignore Binary Patterns of Thinking within Native-American Communities." In *Remembering Jamestown: Hard Questions about Christian Mission*, edited by Amos Yong and Barbara Brown Zikmund, 29–48. Eugene, OR: Pickwick, 2010.

Marshall, Molly T. *Joining the Dance: A Theology of the Spirit.* Valley Forge, PA: Judson, 2003.

Marshall-Fratani, Ruth. "Mediating the Global and Local in Nigerian Pentecostalism." In *Between Babel and Pentecost: Transnational Pentecostalism in Africa and Latin America*, edited by Andre Corten and Ruth Marshall-Fratani, 80–105. Bloomington, IN: Indiana University Press, 2001.

Martin-Achard, Robert. *A Light to the Nations: A Study of the Old Testament Conception of Israel's Mission to the World.* Translated by John Penney Smith. London: Oliver and Boyd, 1962.

McClendon, James Wm., Jr. *Biography as Theology: How Life Stories Can Remake Today's Theology.* Nashville: Abingdon, 1974.

————. *Systematic Theology.* 3 vols. Nashville: Abingdon, 1986–1994.

McClung Jr., L. Grant, ed. *Azusa Street and Beyond.* Gainesville, FL: Bridge-Logos, 2006.

————. *Globalbeliever.com: Connecting to God's Work in Your World.* Cleveland, TN: Pathway, 2000.

McConnell, C. Douglas, ed. *The Holy Spirit and Mission Dynamics.* Evangelical Missiological Society 5. Pasadena, CA: William Carey Library, 1997.

McCutcheon, Russell T., ed. *The Insider/Outsider Problem in the Study of Religion: A Reader.* London: Cassell, 1998.

McDermott, Gerald R. *Can Evangelicals Learn from World Religions? Jesus, Revelation and Religious Traditions.* Downers Grove, IL: IVP Academic, 2000.

———. *God's Rivals: The Challenge of Other Religions in the Bible and the Early Church.* Downers Grove, IL: InterVarsity, 2007.

———. "What If Paul Had Been from China? Reflections on the Possibility of Revelation in Non-Christian Religions." In *No Other Gods Before Me? Evangelicals and the Challenge of World Religions,* edited by John G. Stackhouse Jr., 17–36. Grand Rapids: Baker, 2001.

McDonald, J. Ian H. "Alien Grace: Luke 10:30–36." In *Jesus and His Parables: Interpreting the Parables of Jesus Today,* edited by V. George Shillington, 177–90. Edinburgh: T & T Clark, 1997.

McDowell, Josh, and Don Stewart. *Understanding the Occult.* San Bernardino, CA: Here's Life, 1982.

McGee, Gary B. "Hodges, Melvin Lyle." In *The New International Dictionary of Pentecostal and Charismatic Movements,* edited by Stanley M. Burgess and Eduard M. Van Der Maas, 723–74. Grand Rapids: Zondervan, 2002.

———. "Pentecostal and Charismatic Missions." In *Toward the 21st Century in Christian Mission: Essays in Honor of Gerald H. Anderson,* edited by James M. Philips and Robert T. Coote, 41–56. Grand Rapids: Eerdmans, 1993.

———. "Pentecostal Missiology: Moving beyond Triumphalism to Face the Issues." *Pneuma: The Journal of the Society for Pentecostal Studies* 16:2 (1994) 275–81.

———. "The Radical Strategy in Modern Missions: The Linkage of Paranormal Phenomena with Evangelism." In *The Holy Spirit and Mission Dynamics,* edited by C. D. McDonnell, 69–95. Pasadena, CA: William Carey Library, 1997.

———. *This Gospel Shall Be Preached: A History and Theology of Assemblies of God Foreign Missions.* 2 vols. Springfield, MO: Gospel Publishing House, 1986, 1989.

Méndez-Moratalla, Fernando. *The Paradigm of Conversion in Luke.* Journal for the Study of the New Testament Supplemental series 252. London: T & T Clark, 2004.

Merrick, James R. A. "The Spirit of Truth as Agent in False Religions? A Critique of Amos Yong's Pneumatological Theology of Religions with Reference to Current Trends." *Trinity Journal* 29:1 (2008) 107–25.

Metzger, Paul Louis. *Connecting Christ: How to Discuss Jesus in a World of Diverse Paths.* Nashville: Nelson, 2012.

Meyer, Birgit. "Beyond Syncretism: Translation and Diabolization in the Appropriation of Protestantism in Africa." In *Syncretism/Anti-syncretism: The Politics of Religious Synthesis,* edited by Charles Steward and Rosalind Shaw, 44–68. New York: Routledge, 1994.

———. "'Make a Complete Break with the Past': Memory and Post-Colonial Modernity in Ghanaian Pentecostalist Discourse." *Journal of Religion on Africa* 28:3 (1998) 316–49.

———. "The Power of Money: Politics, Occult Forces, and Pentecostalism in Ghana." *African Studies Review* 41:3 (1998) 15–37.

Miles, Todd. *A God of Many Understandings? The Gospel and Theology of Religions.* Nashville: B & H Academic, 2010.

Miller, Robert J. "Christianity, American Indians, and the Doctrine of Discovery." In *Remembering Jamestown: Hard Questions about Christian Mission,* edited by Amos Yong and Barbara Brown Zikmund, 51–68. Eugene, OR: Pickwick, 2010.

Mitchell, Donald W., and James Wiseman, OSB, eds. *The Gethsemani Encounter: A Dialogue on the Spiritual Life by Buddhist and Christian Monastics*. New York: Continuum, 1999.

Mittelstadt, Martin. "Reimagining Luke-Acts: Amos Yong and the Biblical Foundation of Pentecostal Theology." In *The Theology of Amos Yong and the New Face of Pentecostal Scholarship: Passion for the Spirit*, edited by Wolfgang Vondey and Martin W. Mittelstadt, 25–43. Global Pentecostal and Charismatic Studies 14. Leiden: Brill, 2013.

Moltmann, Jürgen. *The Coming of God: Christian Eschatology*. Translated by Margaret Kohl. Minneapolis: Fortress, 1996.

———. *The Spirit of Life: A Universal Affirmation*. Translated by Margaret Kohl. London: SCM, 1992.

Morales, José F., Jr. "Babel, Mount Sinai, Pentecost: Charismatic Punctuations in Luke's Covenantal History." In *Toppling the Tower: Essays on Babel and Diversity*, edited by Theodore Hiebert, 34–47. Chicago: McCormick Theological Seminary, 2004.

Moran, Gabriel. *Uniqueness: Problems or Paradox in Jewish and Christian Traditions*. Maryknoll, NY: Orbis, 1992.

Moshay, G. J. O. *Who is This Allah?* Bucks, UK: Dorchester House, 1994.

Muck, Terry, and Frances S. Adeney. *Christianity Encountering World Religions: The Practice of Mission in the Twenty-first Century*. Grand Rapids: Baker Academic, 2009.

Murphy, Nancey. *Anglo-American Postmodernity: Philosophical Perspectives on Science, Religion, and Ethics*. Boulder, CO: Westview, 1997.

Murray, Stuart. *Church after Christendom*. Carlisle, UK: Paternoster, 2004.

———. *Post-Christendom*. Carlisle, UK: Paternoster, 2004.

Nañez, Rick M. *Full Gospel, Fractured Minds? A Call to Use God's Gift of the Intellect*. Grand Rapids: Zondervan, 2005.

Neely, Alan. "Religious Pluralism: Threat or Opportunity for Mission?" In *Mission at the Dawn of the 21st Century: A Vision for the Church*, edited by Paul Varo Martinson, 32–47. Minneapolis: Kirk House, 1999.

Neville, Robert Cummings, ed. *The Comparative Religious Ideas Project*. 3 vols. Albany: State University of New York Press, 2001.

Newbigin, Lesslie. *Trinitarian Faith in Today's Mission*. Richmond, VA: John Knox, 1964.

———. *A Word in Season: Perspectives on Christian World Missions*. Grand Rapids: Eerdmans, 1994.

Oden, Thomas. *After Modernity . . . What? Agenda for Theology*. Grand Rapids: Zondervan, 1992.

Ojo, Matthews A. "American Pentecostalism and the Growth of Pentecostal-Charismatic Movements in Nigeria." In *Freedom's Distant Shores: American Protestants and Post-Colonial Alliances with Africa*, edited by R. Drew Smith, 155–67. Waco, TX: Baylor University Press, 2006.

Olonade, Timothy O., ed. *Battle Cry for the Nations: Rekindling the Flames of World Evangelization*. Jos, Nigeria: CAPRO Media, 1995.

Omenyo, Cephas N. "Renewal, Christian Mission, and Encounter with the Other: Pentecostal-Type Movements Meeting Islam in Ghana and Nigeria." In *Global Renewal, Religious Pluralism, and the Great Commission: Toward a Renewal Theology of Mission and Interreligious Encounter*, edited by Amos Yong and

Clifton Clarke, 137–56. Asbury Theological Seminary Series in World Christian Revitalization Movements in Pentecostal/Charismatic Studies 4. Lexington, KY: Emeth, 2011.

Outler, Albert C. "Pneumatology as an Ecumenical Frontier." *Ecumenical Review* 41:3 (1989) 363–74.

Owczarek, Christopher. *Sons of the Most High: Love of Enemies in Luke-Acts—Teaching and Practice*. Nairobi: Paulines Publications Africa, 2002.

Pagitt, Doug, and Tony Jones. *An Emergent Manifesto of Hope*. Grand Rapids: Baker, 2007.

Panikkar, Raimundo. *The Intrareligious Dialogue*. New York: Paulist, 1978.

———. *Trinity and Religious Experience of Man*. London: Darton, Longman, & Todd, 1973.

Pannenberg, Wolfhart. *Systematic Theology*. 3 vols. Translated by Geoffrey Bromiley. Grand Rapids: Eerdmans, 1991–1997.

Penney, John Michael. *The Missionary Emphasis of Lukan Pneumatology*. Journal of Pentecostal Theology Supplemental Series 12. Sheffield: Sheffield Academic Press, 1997.

Pereira, Francis. *Ephesus: Climax of Universalism in Luke-Acts—A Redaction-Critical Study of Paul's Ephesian Ministry Acts 18:23—20:1*. Anand, India: Gujarat Sahitya Prakash, 1983.

Phan, Peter, ed. *Christianity and the Wider Ecumenism*. New York: Paragon House, 1990.

Phan, Peter, and Jung Young Lee, eds. *Journeys at the Margin: Toward an Autobiographical Theology in Asian-American Perspective*. Collegeville, MN: Liturgical, 1999.

Pierce, Brian J. *We Walk the Path Together: Learning from Thich Nhat Hanh and Meister Eckhart*. Maryknoll, NY: Orbis, 2005.

Pinnock, Clark H. "Evangelism and Other Living Faiths: An Evangelical Charismatic Perspective." In *All Together in One Place: Theological Papers from the Brighton Conference on World Evangelization*, edited by Harold D. Hunter and Peter D. Hocken, 208–14. Sheffield: Sheffield Academic Press, 1993.

———. *Flame of Love: A Theology of the Holy Spirit*. Downers Grove, IL: InterVarsity, 1995.

———. *A Wideness in God's Mercy: The Finality of Jesus Christ in a World of Religions*. Grand Rapids: Zondervan, 1992.

Pittman, Don A. "Dialogical Discernment and the 'Kin-dom' of God: On Globalizing Ministries in North America." *Lexington Theological Quarterly* 28:4 (1993) 319–31.

Plunkett, Mark A. "Ethnocentricity and Salvation History in the Cornelius Episode." In *Society of Biblical Literature Seminar Papers*, edited by David J. Lull, 465–79. Atlanta: Scholars Press, 1985.

Polanyi, Michael. *Personal Knowledge: Towards a Post-Critical Philosophy*. Chicago: University of Chicago Press, 1962.

Pomerville, Paul A. "Pentecostals and Growth." In *Azusa Street and Beyond*, edited by Grant L. McClung Jr., 151–55. Gainesville, FL: Bridge-Logos, 2006.

———. *The Third Force in Missions: A Pentecostal Contribution to Contemporary Mission Theology*. Peabody, MA: Hendrickson, 1985.

Potter, Philip. "Mission as Reconciliation in the Power of the Spirit." *International Review of Mission* 80:319/320 (1991) 305–14.

Prebish, Charles S. *Luminous Passage: The Practice and Study of Buddhism in America.* Berkeley, CA: University of California Press, 1999.

Prebish, Charles S., and Kenneth K. Tanaka, eds. *The Faces of Buddhism in America.* Berkeley, CA: University of California Press, 1998.

Preece, Gordon R., and Stephen K. Pickard, eds. *Starting with the Spirit.* Hindmarsh, AU: Australian Theological Forum, 2001.

Premawardhana, Shanta. "Jamestown and the Future of Mission: Mending Creation and Claiming Full Humanity in Interreligious Partnership." In *Remembering Jamestown: Hard Questions about Christian Mission,* edited by Amos Yong and Barbara Brown Zikmund, 127–44. Eugene, OR: Pickwick, 2010.

Price, Lynne. *Theology Out of Place: A Theological Biography of Walter J. Hollenweger.* Journal of Pentecostal Theology Supplement series 23. Sheffield: Sheffield Academic Press, 2002.

Prichard, Rebecca Button. *Sensing the Spirit: The Holy Spirit in Feminist Perspective.* St. Louis: Chalice, 1999.

Prior, Michael. *Jesus the Liberator: Nazareth Liberation Theology Luke 4.16–30.* Sheffield: Sheffield Academic Press, 1995.

Queen, Christopher S., ed. *Engaged Buddhism in the West.* Boston: Wisdom, 2000.

Queen, Christopher S., et al., eds. *Action Dharma: New Studies in Engaged Buddhism.* London: RoutledgeCurzon, 2003.

Race, Alan. *Christians and Religious Pluralism: Patterns in the Theology of Religions.* Maryknoll, NY: Orbis, 1983.

Räisänen, Heikki. "The Redemption of Israel: A Salvation-Historical Problem in Luke-Acts." In *Luke-Acts: Scandinavian Perspectives,* edited by Petri Luomanen, 94–114. Publications of the Finnish Exegetical Society 54. Helsinki: The Finnish Exegetical Society and Kirjapaino Raamattutalo, 1991.

Raiser, Konrad. "The Holy Spirit in Modern Ecumenical Thought." *Ecumenical Review* 41:3 (1989) 375–87.

Rajak, Tessa. *The Jewish Dialogue with Greece and Rome: Studies in Cultural and Social Interaction.* Arbeiten zum Geschichte des ntiken Judentums und des Urchistentums 48. Leiden: Brill, 2001.

Rasmussen, Arne. "The Politics of Diaspora: Post-Christendom Theologies of Karl Barth and John Howard Yoder." In *God, Truth, and Witness: Engaging Stanley Hauerwas,* edited by L. Gregory Jones, Reinhard Hütter, and C. Rosalee Velloso Ewell, 88–111. Grand Rapids: Brazos, 2005.

———. "The Post-Christendom Theologies of Karl Barth and John Howard Yoder." In *God, Truth, and Witness: Engaging Stanley Hauerwas,* edited by L. Gregory Jones, Reinhard Hütter, and C. Rosalee Velloso Ewell, 88–111. Grand Rapids: Brazos, 2005.

Reichard, Joshua D. "Of Miracles and Metaphysics: A Pentecostal-Charismatic and Process-Relational Dialogue." *Zygon: Journal of Religion and Science* 48:2 (2013) 274–93.

———. "Relational Empowerment: A Process-Relational Theology of the Spirit-Filled Life." *Pneuma: Journal of the Society for Pentecostal Studies* 36:2 (2014) forthcoming.

———. "Toward a Pentecostal Theology of Concursus." *Journal of Pentecostal Theology* 22:1 (2013) 96–115.

Resseguie, James L. *Spiritual Landscape: Images of the Spiritual Life in the Gospel of Luke.* Peabody, MA: Hendrickson, 2004.

Rhoads, David. *The Challenge of Diversity: The Witness of Paul and the Gospels.* Minneapolis: Fortress, 1996.

Richard, Lucien. *Living the Hospitality of God.* New York: Paulist, 2000.

Richard, Pablo. "Indigenous Biblical Hermeneutics: God's Revelation in Native Religions and the Bible after 500 Years of Domination." In *Text and Experience: Towards a Cultural Exegesis of the Bible,* edited by Daniel Smith-Christopher, 260–75. Sheffield: Sheffield Academic Press, 1995.

Richie, Tony. "Azusa-Era Optimism: Bishop J. H. King's Pentecostal Theology of Religions as a Possible Paradigm for Today." *Journal of Pentecostal Theology* 14:2 (2006) 247–60.

———. "Eschatological Inclusivism: Exploring Early Pentecostal Theology of Religions in Charles Fox Parham." *Journal of the European Pentecostal Theological Association* 27:2 (2007) 138–52.

———. "God's Fairness to People of All Faiths: A Respectful Proposal to Pentecostals for Discussion Regarding World Religions." *Pneuma: The Journal of the Society for Pentecostal Studies* 28:1 (2006) 105–19.

———. "John Wesley and Mohammed: A Contemporary Inquiry Concerning Islam." *Asbury Theological Journal* 58:2 (2003) 79–99.

———. "Neither Naïve nor Narrow: A Balanced Approach to Christian Theology of Religions." *Cyberjournal of Pentecostal-Charismatic Research* 15 (February 2006). http://www.pctii.org/cyberj/cyber15.html.

———. "A Pentecostal in Sheep's Clothing: An Unlikely Participant but Hopeful Partner in Interreligious Dialogue." *Current Dialogue* 48 (2006) 9–15.

———. "Precedents and Possibilities: Pentecostal Perspectives on World Religions." *Pneuma Review* (January 2006). http://pneumafoundation.org/article.jsp?article=/article_0042.xml#note15.

———. "Revamping Pentecostal Evangelism: Appropriating Walter J. Hollenweger's Radical Proposal." *International Review of Mission* 96:382/383 (2007) 343–54.

———. *Speaking by the Spirit: A Pentecostal Model for Interreligious Encounter and Dialogue.* Asbury Theological Seminary Series in World Christian Revitalization Movements in Pentecostal/Charismatic Studies 6. Wilmore, KY: Emeth, 2011.

———. "The Spirit of Truth as Guide into All Truth: A Response to R. A. James Merrick, 'The Spirit of Truth as Agent in False Religions? A Critique of Amos Yong's Pneumatological Theology of Religions with Reference to Current Trends.'" *Cyberjournal for Pentecostal-Charismatic Research* 19 (2010). http://pctii.org/cyberj/cyber19.html.

———. *Toward a Pentecostal Theology of Religions: Encountering Cornelius Today.* Cleveland, TN: CPT, 2013.

———. "The Unity of the Spirit." *Journal of the European Pentecostal Theological Association* 26 (2006) 21–35.

———. "The Wide Reach of the Spirit: A Renewal Theology of Mission and Interreligious Encounter in Dialogue with Yves Congar." In *Global Renewal, Religious Pluralism, and the Great Commission: Toward a Renewal Theology of Mission and Interreligious Encounter,* edited by Amos Yong and Clifton Clarke, 43–70. Asbury Theological Seminary Series in World Christian Revitalization Movements in Pentecostal/Charismatic Studies 4. Lexington, KY: Emeth, 2011.

Ringe, Sharon H. *Jesus, Liberation, and the Biblical Jubilee: Images for Ethics and Christology.* Philadelphia: Fortress, 1985.

Robbins, Vernon K. "The Sensory-Aesthetic Texture of the Compassionate Samaritan Parable in Luke 10." In *Literary Encounters with the Reign of God,* edited by Sharon H. Ringe and H. C. Paul Kim, 247–64. New York: T & T Clark, 2004.

Robeck, Cecil M., Jr. *The Azusa Street Mission and Revival: The Birth of the Global Pentecostal Movement.* Nashville: Nelson, 2006.

Robert, Dana L., ed. *Converting Colonialism: Visions and Realities in Mission History, 1706–1914.* Grand Rapids: Eerdmans, 2008.

Robinson, Bob. Review of *Discerning the Spirits: A Pentecostal-Charismatic Contribution to Christian Theology of Religions,* by Amos Yong. *Pacifica: Australian Theological Studies* 17 (2004) 106–9.

Rowe, Stephen C. "A Zen Presence in America: Dialogue as Religious Practice." In *Masao Abe: A Zen Life of Dialogue,* edited by Donald W. Mitchell, 354–60. Boston: Charles E. Tuttle, 1998.

Rowlison, Bruce. *Creative Hospitality as a Means of Evangelism.* Alhambra, CA: Green Leaf, 1981.

Ruthven, Jon R. *The Cessation of the Charismata: The Protestant Polemic on Postbiblical Miracles.* Journal of Pentecostal Theology Supplement series 3. Sheffield: Sheffield Academic Press, 1993.

Saeki, P. Y. *The Nestorian Monument in China.* London: SPCK, 1916.

Salisbury, Neal. "'I Love the Place of My Dwelling': Puritan Missionaries and Native Americans in Seventeenth-Century Southern New England." In *Inequality in Early America,* edited by Carla Gardina Pestana and Sharon V. Salinger, 111–33. Encounters with Colonialism: New Perspectives on the Americas series. Hanover, NH: Dartmouth College/University Press of New England, 1999.

Samartha, Stanley J. *Courage for Dialogue: Ecumenical Issues in Inter-Religious Relationships.* Maryknoll, NY: Orbis, 1982.

Sanders, John. *No Other Name: An Investigation into the Destiny of the Unevangelized.* Grand Rapids: Eerdmans, 1992.

Sanneh, Lamin. "Christian Experience of Islamic Da'wah." In *Christian Mission and Islamic Da'wah: Proceedings of the Chambésy Dialogue Consultation,* edited by Emilio Castro, Khurshid Ahmad, and David Kerr, 52–65. Leicester, UK: The Islamic Foundation, 1982.

———. *Translating the Message: The Missionary Impact on Culture.* Maryknoll, NY: Orbis, 1989.

Satyavrata, Ivan. *God Has Not Left Himself without Witness.* Oxford: Regnum International, 2011.

Sawyer, John F. A., J. M. Y. Simpson, and R. E. Asher, eds. *Concise Encyclopedia of Language and Religion.* Amsterdam: Elsevier, 2001.

Sawyerr, Henry. *The Practice of Presence: Shorter Writings of Harry Sawyerr.* Edited by John Parratt. Grand Rapids: Eerdmans, 1994.

Schreiter, Robert J. *Constructing Local Theologies.* Maryknoll, NY: Orbis, 1985.

———. *The New Catholicity: Theology between the Global and the Local.* Maryknoll, NY: Orbis, 1997.

Scott, David. "Medieval Christian Responses to Buddhism." *The Journal of Religious History* 15:2 (1988) 165–84.

Scott, James M. "Acts 2:9–11—As an Anticipation of the Mission to the Nations." In *The Mission of the Early Church to Jews and Gentiles*, edited by Jostein Ådna and Hans Kvalbein, 87–123. Wissenschaftliche Untersuchungen zum Neuen Testament 127. Tübingen: Mohr Siebeck, 2000.

Scott, J. Julius, Jr. "Stephen's Defense and the World Mission of the People of God." *Journal of the Evangelical Theological Society* 21:2 (1978) 131–41.

Seager, Richard Hughes. *Buddhism in America*. New York: Columbia University Press, 1999.

———. *The World's Parliament of Religions: The East/West Encounter, Chicago 1893*. Bloomington, IN: Indiana University Press, 1995.

Seager, Richard Hughes, ed. *The Dawn of Religious Pluralism: Voices from the World's Parliament of Religions, 1893*. La Salle, IL: Open Court, 1993.

Seamands, Stephen A. *Ministry in the Image of God: The Trinitarian Shape of Christian Service*. Downers Grove, IL: InterVarsity, 2005.

Segovia, Fernando F. "'And They Began to Speak in Other Tongues': Competing Modes of Discourse in Contemporary Biblical Criticism." In *Reading From This Place*, vol. 1: *Social Location and Biblical Interpretation in the United States*, edited by Fernando F. Segovia and Mary Ann Tolbert, 1–32. Minneapolis: Fortress, 1995.

Sherman, Robert. *King, Priest, and Prophet: A Trinitarian Theology of Atonement*. New York: T & T Clark, 2004.

Skreslet, Stanley H. *Comprehending Mission: The Questions, Methods, Themes, Problems, and Prospects of Missiology*. Maryknoll, NY: Orbis, 2012.

Smidt, Kobus de. "Hermeneutical Perspectives on the Spirit in the Book of Revelation." *Journal of Pentecostal Theology* 14 (1999) 27–47.

Smith, David. *Mission after Christendom*. London: Darton, Longman, & Todd, 2003.

Smith, James K. A. *Desiring the Kingdom: Worship, Worldview, and Cultural Formation*. Grand Rapids: Baker Academic, 2009.

———. *Imagining the Kingdom: How Worship Works*. Grand Rapids: Baker Academic, 2013.

———. *Thinking in Tongues: Pentecostal Contributions to Christian Philosophy*. Grand Rapids: Eerdmans, 2010.

———. *Who's Afraid of Postmodernism? Taking Derrida, Lyotard, and Foucault to Church*. Grand Rapids: Baker Academic, 2006.

Smith, Wilfred Cantwell. *The Meaning and End of Religion*. New York: Macmillan, 1962.

Snook, Lee. *What in the World is God Doing? Re-Imagining Spirit and Power*. Minneapolis: Fortress, 1999.

Spencer, F. Scott. *Journeying through Acts: A Literary-Cultural Reading*. Peabody, MA: Hendrickson, 2004.

Spradley, James P. *Participant Observation*. Fort Worth, TX.: Harcourt Brace Jovanovich College Publications, 1980.

Stackhouse, John G., Jr., ed. *No Other Gods Before Me? Evangelicals and the Challenge of World Religions*. Grand Rapids: Baker, 2001.

Stenschke, Christoph W. *Luke's Portrait of Gentiles Prior to Their Coming to Faith*. Wissenschaftliche Untersuchungen zum Neuen Testament, reihe 2:108. Tübingen: Mohr Siebeck, 1999.

Stoll, David. *Is Latin America Turning Protestant? The Politics of Evangelical Growth*. Berkeley, CA: University of California Press, 1990.

Stone, Bryan P. *Evangelism after Christendom: The Theology and Practice of Christian Witness.* Grand Rapids: Brazos, 2007.

Strelan, Rick. *Strange Acts: Studies in the Cultural World of the Acts of the Apostles.* Beihafte zue Zeitschrift für die neutestamentliche Wissenschaft und die Kunde der älteren Kirche 126. Berlin: Walter de Gruyter, 2004.

Studebaker, Steven M. "Christian Mission and the Religions as Participation in the Spirit of Pentecost." In *Global Renewal, Religious Pluralism, and the Great Commission: Toward a Renewal Theology of Mission and Interreligious Encounter,* edited by Amos Yong and Clifton Clarke, 71–94. Asbury Theological Seminary Series in World Christian Revitalization Movements in Pentecostal/Charismatic Studies 4. Lexington, KY: Emeth, 2011.

———. *From Pentecost to the Triune God: A Pentecostal Trinitarian Theology.* Grand Rapids: Eerdmans, 2012.

Sunquist, Scott W. *Understanding Christian Mission: Participating in Suffering and Glory.* Grand Rapids, Baker Academic, 2013.

Sutherland, Martin, ed. *Mission without Christendom: Exploring the Site—Essays for Brian Smith.* Auckland, NZ: Carey Bible College, 2000.

Suurmond, Jean-Jacques. *Word and Spirit at Play: Towards a Charismatic Theology.* Translated by John Bowden. 1994. Reprint, Grand Rapids: Eerdmans, 1995.

Tai, Hyun Chung. "A Study of the Spirituality of Korean Christians: Focused on the Holy Spirit Movement and Shamanism." DMin thesis, School of Theology at the Claremont Graduate School, 1988.

Tanabe, George J., Jr. "Grafting identity: The Hawaiian branches of the Bodhi Tree." In *Buddhist Missionaries in the Era of Globalization,* edited by Linda Learman, 77–100. Honolulu: University of Hawai'i Press, 2005.

Tanaka, Kenneth K. *Ocean: An Introduction to Jodo-Shinshu Buddhism in America.* Berkeley, CA: Wisdom Ocean, 1997.

Tang, Li. *A Study of the History of Nestorian Christianity in China and Its Literature in Chinese: Together with a New English Translation of the Dunhuang Nestorian Documents.* European University Studies, Series XXVII, Asian and African Studies 87. Frankfurt: Peter Lang, 2002.

Tannehill, Robert C. "Paul Outside the Christian Ghetto: Stories of Intercultural Conflict and Cooperation in Acts." In *Text and Logos: The Humanistic Interpretation of the New Testament,* edited by Theodore W. Jennings, Jr., 247–63. Atlanta: Scholars Press, 1990.

Task Force on Christian Witness within a Buddhist Context, Board of the Division for World Mission and Inter-Church Cooperation of the American Lutheran Church. *Suffering and Redemption: Exploring Christian Witness within a Buddhist Context.* Chicago: Division for Global Mission of the Evangelical Lutheran Church in America, 1988.

Taylor, John V. *The Go-Between God: The Holy Spirit and the Christian Mission.* Philadelphia: Fortress 1973. Reprint London: SCM, 2004.

Tennent, Timothy C. *Invitation to World Missions: A Trinitarian Missiology for the Twenty-First Century.* Grand Rapids: Kregel, 2010.

———. "Review of *Beyond the Impasse: Toward a Pneumatological Theology of Religions,* by Amos Yong." *International Bulletin of Missionary Research* 27:4 (2003) 180–81.

Thomas, John Christopher. *The Spirit of the New Testament.* Leiderdorp, Netherlands: Deo, 2005.

Thompson, Joseph. "Rising from the Mediocre to the Miraculous." In *Out of Africa: How the Spiritual Explosion among Nigerians is Impacting the World*, edited by C. Peter Wagner and Joseph Thompson, 19–36. Ventura, CA: Regal, 2004.

Thomsen, Mark. "Confessing Jesus Christ within the World of Religious Pluralism." *International Bulletin of Missionary Research* 14:3 (1990) 115–19.

Thurman, Robert A. F. "Toward an American Buddhism." In *Buddhism in America*, edited by Al Rapaport and Brian D. Hotchkiss, 450–68. Rutland, VT: Charles E. Tuttle, 1998.

Tiessen, Terrance L. *Who Can Be Saved? Reassessing Salvation in Christ and World Religions*. Downers Grove, IL: IVP Academic, 2004.

Tinker, George E. *American Indian Liberation: A Theology of Sovereignty*. Maryknoll, NY: Orbis, 2008.

———. *Missionary Conquest: The Gospel and Native American Cultural Genocide*. Minneapolis: Fortress, 1993.

———. "The Romance and Tragedy of Christian Mission among American Indians." In *Remembering Jamestown: Hard Questions about Christian Mission*, edited by Amos Yong and Barbara Brown Zikmund, 13–28. Eugene, OR: Pickwick, 2010.

Tracy, David. *The Analogical Imagination: Christian Theology and the Culture of Pluralism*. New York: Crossroad, 1981.

Triebel, Armin, ed. *Roswith Gerloff—Auf grenzen: Ein Leben im Dazwischen von Kulturen*. Berlin: Weissensee-Verlag, 2014.

Turner, Max. *Power from on High: The Spirit in Israel's Restoration and Witness in Luke-Acts*. Journal of Pentecostal Theology Supplement series 9. Sheffield: Sheffield Academic Press, 1996.

Tweed, Thomas A. *The American Encounter with Buddhism 1844–1912: Victorian Culture and the Limits of Dissent*. Bloomington, IN: Indiana University Press, 1992.

Twiss, Richard. "Living in Transition, Embracing Community, and Envisioning God's Mission as Trinitarian Mutuality: Reflections from a Native-American Follower of Jesus." In *Remembering Jamestown: Hard Questions about Christian Mission*, edited by Amos Yong and Barbara Brown Zikmund, 93–108. Eugene, OR: Pickwick, 2010.

Tworkov, Helen. *Zen in America: Five Teachers and the Search for an American Buddhism*. 2nd ed. New York: Kodansha International, 1994.

Tyson, Joseph B. *Luke, Judaism, and the Scholars: Critical Approaches to Luke-Acts*. Columbia, SC: University of South Carolina Press, 1999.

Tyson, Joseph B., ed. *Luke-Acts and the Jewish People: Eight Critical Perspectives*. Minneapolis: Augsburg, 1988.

Udho, Enyi Ben. *Guest Christology: An Interpretative View of the Christological Problem in Africa*. Frankfurt: Peter Lang, 1988.

Victorin-Vangerud, Nancy. *The Raging Hearth: Spirit in the Household of God*. St. Louis: Chalice, 2000.

Vilaça, Aparecida, and Robin M. Wright, eds. *Native Christians: Modes and Effects of Christianity among Indigenous Peoples of the Americas*. Vitality of Indigenous Religions series. Burlington, VT: Ashgate, 2009.

Volf, Miroslav, and Dorothy C. Bass, eds. *Practicing Theology: Beliefs and Practices in Christian Life*. Grand Rapids: Eerdmans, 2002.

Vondey, Wolfgang. *Beyond Pentecostalism: The Crisis of Global Christianity and the Renewal of the Theological Agenda.* Grand Rapids: Eerdmans, 2010.

Vyver, J. D. Van de, ed. *The Problem of Proselytism in Southern Africa: Legal and Theological Dimensions.* Atlanta: Emory University School of Law, 2000.

Waldrop, Richard E., and J. L. Corky Alexander Jr. "Salvation History and the Mission of God: Implications for the Mission of the Church among Native Americans." In *Remembering Jamestown: Hard Questions about Christian Mission,* edited by Amos Yong and Barbara Brown Zikmund, 109–24. Eugene, OR: Pickwick, 2010.

Wallace, Mark I. *Fragments of the Spirit: Nature, Violence, and the Renewal of Creation.* New York: Continuum, 1996.

Walls, Andrew F. *The Cross-Cultural Process in Christian History.* Maryknoll, NY: Orbis, and Edinburgh: T & T Clark, 2002.

Warrington, Keith. *Pentecostal Theology: A Theology of Encounter.* London: T & T Clark, 2008.

Warrior, Robert Allen. "A Native American Perspective: Canaanites, Cowboys, and Indians." *Christianity and Crisis* 49 (1989) 261–65. Reprinted in *Voices from the Margins: Interpreting the Bible in the Third World,* edited by R. S. Sugitharajah, 277–85. Maryknoll, NY: Orbis.

Welker, Michael. *God the Spirit.* Translated by John Hoffmeyer. Minneapolis: Fortress, 1994.

———. "Spirit Topics: Trinity, Personhood, Mystery and Tongues." *Journal of Pentecostal Theology* 10 (1997) 29–34.

Williams, Don. *Signs, Wonders, and the Kingdom of God: A Biblical Guide for the Reluctant Skeptic.* Ann Arbor, MI: Vine, 1989.

Wimber, John, and Kevin Springer. *Power Evangelism.* San Francisco: Harper & Row, 1986.

———. *Power Healing.* San Francisco: Harper & Row, 1986.

———. *Power Points.* San Francisco: Harper San Francisco 1991.

Wink, Walter. *Engaging the Powers: Discernment and Resistance in a World of Domination.* Philadelphia: Fortress, 1992.

———. *Naming the Powers: The Language of Power in the New Testament.* 1984. Reprint, Philadelphia: Fortress, 1992.

———. *The Powers that Be: Theology for a New Millennium.* New York: Doubleday, 1998.

———. *Unmasking the Powers: The Invisible Forces that Determine Human Existence.* Philadelphia: Fortress, 1986.

Witte, John, and Richard C. Martin, eds. *Sharing the Book: Religious Perspectives on the Rights and Wrongs of Proselytism.* Maryknoll, NY: Orbis, 1999.

Woodberry, J. Dudley, Charles van Engen, and Edgar J. Elliston, eds. *Missiological Education for the Twenty-First Century: The Book, the Circle, and the Sandals— Essays in Honor of Paul E. Pierson.* Maryknoll, NY: Orbis, 1992.

Wordelman, Amy L. "Cultural Divides and Dual Realities: A Graeco-Roman Context for Acts 14." In *Contextualizing Acts: Lukan Narrative and Greco-Roman Discourse,* edited by Todd Penner and Caroline Vander Stichele, 205–32. SBL Symposium Series 20. Leiden: Brill, 2004.

Yoder, John H. *For the Nations: Essays Public and Evangelical.* Grand Rapids: Eerdmans, 1997.

———. *He Came Preaching Peace.* Scottdale, PA: Herald, 1985.

————. *The Jewish-Christian Schism Revisited.* Edited by Michael G. Cartwright and Peter Ochs. Grand Rapids: Eerdmans, 2003.

————. *The Politics of Jesus.* Grand Rapids: Eerdmans, 1972.

————. *The Priestly Kingdom: Social Ethics as Gospel.* Notre Dame, IN: University of Notre Dame Press, 1984.

————. *The Royal Priesthood: Essays Ecclesiological and Ecumenical.* Edited by Michael G. Cartwright. 1994. Reprint, Scottdale, PA: Herald, 1998.

Yoder, Perry B. *Shalom: The Bible's Word for Salvation, Justice, and Peace.* Newton, KS: Faith & Life Press, 1987.

Yong, Amos. "'As the Spirit Gives Utterance . . . ': Pentecost, Intra-Christian Ecumenism, and the Wider *Oekumene*." *International Review of Mission* 92:366 (2003) 299–314.

————. "Between the Local and the Global: Autobiographical Reflections on the Emergence of the Global Theological Mind." In *Shaping a Global Theological Mind*, edited by Darren C. Marks, 187–94. Aldershot, UK: Ashgate, 2008.

————. *Beyond the Impasse: Toward a Pneumatological Theology of Religions.* Grand Rapids: Baker Academic, 2002.

————. *The Bible, Disability, and the Church: A New Vision of the People of God.* Grand Rapids: Eerdmans, 2011.

————. "The Buddhist-Christian Encounter in the USA: Reflections on Christian Practices." In *Border Crossings: Explorations of an Interdisciplinary Historian—Festschrift for Irving Hexham,* edited by Ulrich van der Heyden and Andreas Feldtkeller, 457–72. Stuttgart: Franz Steiner Verlag, 2008.

————. "Can We Get 'Beyond the Paradigm' in Christian Theology of Religions? A Response to Terry Muck." *Interpretation* 61:1 (2007) 28–32.

————. "Christian and Buddhist Perspectives on Neuropsychology and the Human Person: *Pneuma* and *Pratityasamutpada*." *Zygon: Journal of Religion and Science* 40:1 (2005) 143–65.

————. "Christological Constants in Shifting Contexts: Jesus Christ, Prophetic Dialogue, and the *Missio Spiritus* in a Pluralistic World." In *Mission as Prophetic Dialogue: Contemporary Theological Reflections on Christian Mission,* edited by Steve Bevans and Cathy Ross. London: SCM, forthcoming.

————. "The Church and Mission Theology in a Post-Constantinian Era: Soundings from the Anglo-American Frontier." In *A New Day: Essays on World Christianity in Honor of Lamin Sanneh,* edited by Akintunde Akinade, 49–61. New York: Peter Lang, 2010.

————. *The Cosmic Breath: Spirit and Nature in the Christianity-Buddhism-Science Trialogue.* Philosophical Studies in Science & Religion 4. Leiden: Brill, 2012.

————. "Culture." In *Dictionary of Mission Theology: Evangelical Foundations,* edited by John Corrie, 82–87. Downers Grove, IL: InterVarsity, 2007.

————. "The Demise of Foundationalism and the Retention of Truth." *Christian Scholar's Review* 29 (2000) 563–89.

————. "The Demonic in Pentecostal-Charismatic Christianity and in the Religious Consciousness of Asia." In *Asian and Pentecostal: The Charismatic Face of Christianity in Asia,* edited by Allan Anderson and Edmond Tang, 93–127. London: Regnum International, 2005.

————. *The Dialogical Spirit: Christian Reason and Theological Method for the Third Millennium.* Eugene, OR: Cascade, 2014.

————. *Discerning the Spirit(s): A Pentecostal-Charismatic Contribution to Christian Theology of Religions*. Journal of Pentecostal Theology Supplement Series 20. Sheffield: Sheffield Academic Press, 2000.

————. "Francis X. Clooney's 'Dual Religious Belonging' and the Comparative Theological Enterprise: Engaging Hindu Traditions." *Dharma Deepika: A South Asian Journal of Missiological Research* 16:1 (2012) 6–26.

————. "From Azusa Street to the Bo Tree and Back: Strange Babblings and Interreligious Interpretations in the Pentecostal Encounter with Buddhism." In *The Spirit in the World: Emerging Pentecostal Theologies in Global Contexts,* edited by Veli-Matti Kärkkäinen, 203–26. Grand Rapids: Eerdmans, 2009.

————. *The Future of Evangelical Theology: Soundings from the Asian American Diaspora*. Downers Grove, IL: InterVarsity, 2014.

————. "Globalizing Christology: Anglo-American Perspectives in World Religious Context." *Religious Studies Review* 30:4 (2004) 259–66.

————. "Guests, Hosts, and the Holy Ghost: Pneumatological Theology and Christian Practices in a World of Many Faiths." In *Lord and Giver of Life: A Constructive Pneumatology,* edited by David Jensen, 71–86. Louisville: Westminster John Knox, 2008.

————. "A Heart Strangely Warmed on the Middle Way? The Wesleyan Witness in a Pluralistic World." *Wesleyan Theological Journal* 48:1 (2013) 7–26.

————. "The Holy Spirit and the World Religions: On the Christian Discernment of Spirits 'after' Buddhism." *Buddhist-Christian Studies* 24 (2004) 191–207.

————. *Hospitality and the Other: Pentecost, Christian Practices, and the Neighbor*. Faith Meets Faith series. Maryknoll, NY: Orbis, 2008.

————. "How Does God Do What God Does? Pentecostal-Charismatic Perspectives on Divine Action in Dialogue with Modern Science." In *Science and the Spirit: A Pentecostal Engagement with the Sciences,* edited by Amos Yong and James K. A. Smith, 50–71. Bloomington, IN: Indiana University Press, 2010.

————. *In the Days of Caesar: Pentecostalism and Political Theology—The Cadbury Lectures 2009*. Sacra Doctrina: Christian Theology for a Postmodern Age series. Grand Rapids: Eerdmans, 2010.

————. "The Inviting Spirit: Pentecostal Beliefs and Practices regarding the Religions Today." In *Defining Issues in Pentecostalism: Classical and Emergent,* edited by Steven Studebaker, 29–44. Eugene, OR: Wipf & Stock, 2008.

————. "Jesus, Pentecostalism, and the Encounter with Religious Others: Pentecostal Christology and the Wider Ecumenism in North America." In *North American Pentecostalism,* edited by Dale Coulter and Kenneth Archer. Global Pentecostal & Charismatic Studies series. Leiden: Brill, forthcoming.

————. "'The Light Shines in the Darkness': Johannine Dualism and the Challenge of Christian Theology of Religions Today." *Journal of Religion* 89:1 (2009) 31–56.

————. "Many Tongues, Many Practices: Pentecost and Theology of Mission at 2010." In *Mission after Christendom: Emergent Themes in Contemporary Mission,* edited by Ogbu U. Kalu, Edmund Kee-Fook Chia, and Peter Vethanayagamony, 43–58. Louisville, KY: Westminster John Knox, 2010.

————. "Mind and Life, Religion and Science: The Dalai Lama and the Buddhist-Christian-Science Trilogue." *Buddhist-Christian Studies* 28 (2008) 43–63.

————. "The Missiology of Jamestown: 1607–2007 and Beyond—Toward a Postcolonial Theology of Mission in North America." In *Remembering Jamestown:*

Hard Questions about Christian Mission, edited by Amos Yong and Barbara Brown Zikmund, 157–67. Eugene, OR: Pickwick, 2010.

———. "'Not Knowing Where the Spirit Blows . . . ': On Envisioning a Pentecostal-Charismatic Theology of Religions." *Journal of Pentecostal Theology* 14 (1999) 81–112.

———. "On Divine Presence and Divine Agency: Toward a Foundational Pneumatology." *Asian Journal of Pentecostal Studies* 3:2 (2000) 167–88.

———. "Pentecostalism and the Theological Academy." *Theology Today* 64:2 (2007) 244–50.

———. *Pneumatology and the Christian-Buddhist Dialogue: Does the Spirit Blow through the Middle Way?* Studies in Systematic Theology 11. Leiden: Brill, 2012.

———. "A P(new)matological Paradigm for Christian Mission in a Religiously Plural World." *Missiology: An International Review* 33:2 (2005) 175–91.

———. "Poured Out on All Flesh: The Spirit, World Pentecostalism, and the Performance of Renewal Theology." *PentecoStudies: An Interdisciplinary Journal for Research on the Pentecostal and Charismatic Movements* 6:1 (2007) 16–46. http://www.glopent.net/pentecostudies.

———. "Primed for the Spirit: Creation, Redemption, and the *Missio Spiritus.*" *International Review of Mission* 100:2 (2011) 355–66.

———. "Review of *Journeys at the Margins: Toward an Autobiographical Theology in Asian-American Perspective,* by Peter Phan and Jung Young Lee, eds." *Asian Journal of Pentecostal Studies* 3:2 (2000) 327–31.

———. "*Ruach,* the Primordial Waters, and the Breath of Life: Emergence Theory and the Creation Narratives in Pneumatological Perspective." In *The Work of the Spirit: Pneumatology and Pentecostalism,* edited by Michael Welker, 183–204. Grand Rapids: Eerdmans, 2006.

———. "Salvation, Society, and the Spirit: Pentecostal Contextualization and Political Theology from Cleveland to Birmingham, from Springfield to Seoul." *Pax Pneuma: The Journal of Pentecostals & Charismatics for Peace & Justice* 5:2 (2009) 22–34.

———. Sanctification, Science, and the Spirit: Salvaging Holiness in the Late Modern World." *Wesleyan Theological Journal* 47:2 (2012) 36–52.

———. "The Spirit Bears Witness: Pneumatology, Truth and the Religions." *Scottish Journal of Theology* 57:1 (2004) 14–38.

———. "The Spirit, Christian Practices, and the Religions: Theology of Religions in Pentecostal and Pneumatological Perspective." *Asbury Journal* 62:2 (2007) 5–31.

———. *The Spirit of Creation: Modern Science and Divine Action in the Pentecostal-Charismatic Imagination.* Pentecostal Manifestos 4. Grand Rapids: Eerdmans, 2011.

———. "The Spirit of Hospitality: Pentecostal Perspectives toward a Performative Theology of the Interreligious Encounter." *Missiology: An International Review* 35:1 (2007) 55–73.

———. *Spirit of Love: A Trinitarian Theology of Grace.* Waco, TX: Baylor University Press, 2012.

———. "Spirit Possession, the Living, and the Dead: A Review Essay and Response from a Pentecostal Perspective." *Dharma Deepika: A South Asian Journal of Missiological Research* 8:2 (2004) 77–88.

———. *The Spirit Poured Out on All Flesh: Pentecostalism and the Possibility of Global Theology.* Grand Rapids: Baker Academic, 2005.

————. "The Spirit, Vocation, and the Life of the Mind: A Pentecostal Testimony." In *Pentecostals in the Academy: Testimonies of Call*, edited by Steven M. Fettke and Robby Waddell, 203–20. Cleveland, TN: CPT, 2012.

————. "Spiritual Discernment: A Biblical-Theological Reconsideration." In *The Spirit and Spirituality: Essays in Honor of Russell P. Spittler*, edited by Wonsuk Ma and Robert P. Menzies, 83–104. London: T & T Clark, 2004.

————. *Spirit-Word-Community: Theological Hermeneutics in Trinitarian Perspective.* New Critical Thinking in Religion, Theology and Biblical Studies Series. Burlington, VT: Ashgate, 2002.

————. "Syncretism." In *Dictionary of Mission Theology: Evangelical Foundations*, edited by John Corrie, 373–76. Downers Grove, IL: InterVarsity, 2007.

————. "Technologies of Liberation: A Comparative Soteriology of Eastern Orthodoxy and Theravada Buddhism." *Dharma Deepika: A South Indian Journal of Missiological Studies* 7:1 (2003) 17–60.

————. *Theology and Down Syndrome: Reimagining Disability in Late Modernity.* Waco, TX: Baylor University Press, 2007.

————. "Trinh Thuan and the Intersection of Science and Buddhism: A Review Essay." *Zygon: Journal of Religion and Science* 42:3 (2007) 677–84.

————. "The Virtues and Intellectual Disability: Explorations in the Cognitive Sciences of Moral Formation." In *Theology and the Science of Moral Action: Virtue Ethics, Exemplarity, and Cognitive Neuroscience*, edited by James Van Slyke, Gregory R. Peterson, Kevin S. Reimer, Michael L. Spezio, and Warren S. Brown, 191–208. Routledge Studies in Religion 21. New York: Routledge, 2013.

————. "Wesley and Fletcher—Dayton and Wood: Appreciating Wesleyan-Holiness Tongues, Essaying Pentecostal-Charismatic Interpretations." In *From the Margins: A Celebration of the Theological Work of Donald W. Dayton*, edited by Christian T. Collins Winn, 179–90. Eugene, OR: Pickwick, 2007.

————. "Whither Evangelical Theology? The Work of Veli-Matti Kärkkäinen as a Case Study of Contemporary Trajectories." *Evangelical Review of Theology* 30:1 (2006) 60–85.

————. "Whither Systematic Theology? A Systematician Chimes in on a Scandalous Conversation." *Pneuma: The Journal of the Society for Pentecostal Studies* 20:1 (1998) 85–93.

————. "Whither Theological Inclusivism? The Development and Critique of an Evangelical Theology of Religions." *The Evangelical Quarterly* 71:4 (1999) 327–48.

————. *Who is the Holy Spirit?: A Walk with the Apostles.* Brewster, MA: Paraclete, 2011.

Yong, Amos, and Barbara Brown Zikmund, eds. *Remembering Jamestown: Hard Questions about Christian Mission.* Eugene, OR: Pickwick, 2010.

Yong, Amos, and Clifton Clarke, eds. *Global Renewal, Religious Pluralism, and the Great Commission: Toward a Renewal Theology of Mission and Interreligious Encounter.* Asbury Theological Seminary Series in World Christian Revitalization Movements in Pentecostal/Charismatic Studies 4. Lexington, KY: Emeth, 2011.

Yong, Amos, with Jonathan A. Anderson. *Renewing Christian Theology: Systematics for a Global Christianity.* Waco, TX: Baylor University Press, 2014.

Yong, Amos, Frank D. Macchia, Ralph Del Colle, and Dale T. Irvin. "Christ and Spirit: Dogma, Discernment and Dialogical Theology in a Religiously Plural World." *Journal of Pentecostal Theology* 12:1 (2003) 15–83.

Yoo, Boo-Woong. "Response to Korean Shamanism by the Pentecostal Church." *International Review of Mission* 75 (1986) 70–74.

York, John V. *Mission in the Age of the Spirit.* Springfield, MO: Logion, 2000.

Young, Richard Fox. "*Deus Unus* or *Dei Plures Sunt*? The Function of Inclusivism in the Buddhist Defense of Mongol Folk Religion against William of Rubruck 1254." *Journal of Ecumenical Studies* 26:1 (1989) 100–37.

Scripture Index

Subject Index

Abe, Masao, 153n9, 154, 155n14
Abraham, 47, 73, 123, 186, 189,
    193n25, 212
adaptation, 157
Adeney, Frances S., 2n2, 148
accommodation, 159
affect, 229
African independent Churches, 23
afterlife, 21
Akinade, Akintunde E., 168n2
Albrecht, Daniel, 24n10
Alcott, Amos Bronson, 152
Alexander, J. L. Corky, Jr., 145–47
Alexander, Loveday, 81n11
Alexander, Paul, 122n7
al-Faruqi, Isma'il, 223n3
alienation, 218
Allen, Roland, 38n4, 52
Alonso, Pablo, 207n24
American Academy of Religion, 45
American Society of Missiology, 8,
    95n55
Anabaptists, 169, 171, 178
ancestor spirits, 29, 32–33
ancestors, 24–25, 28, 200
Anderson, Allan H., 2n3, 102, 104,
    189n17
Anderson, Gerald H., 39n6
Anderson, James B., 48n25
animism, 23n8, 33–34
anonymous Christianity, 226n7
anthropology, 50, 130
anti-Semitism, 67, 94n53
apatheia, 131
apocalypse, 125

Apollinarianism, 198
apologetics, 81, 93, 155–56, 164, 171,
    209
  evangelical, 161, 164–65
  interreligious, 164
  medieval, 151n3
apostolic succession, 225
Areopagus, 129, 137, 216
Arianism, 198
Aristotle, 67
Arnold, Edwin, 152
Arterbury, Andrew E., 88n33
Asian American theology, 10
Assemblies of God, 19–20, 26, 28
assimilation, 157, 159, 179
Ateek, Naim, 90n40
atheism, 152
atonement, 107, 205
Azusa Street, 98, 100

Babel, Tower of, 41, 57, 213, 230
Baird, Robert D., 73n25
Baker, James T., 142n6
Balthasar, Hans Urs von, 185n7
baptism, water, 171n12, 226
Barclay, John M. G., 41n9
Barnhart, Bruno, 155n17
Barreto, Eric Daniel, 83n19
Barrows, John Henry, 153n8
Bartchy, S. Scott, 91n48
Barth, Karl, 49n28, 184, 212
Bartleman, Frank, 90n38
Batchelor, Stephen, 159n24
Bayer, Charles H., 176n30
Bays, J. Daniel, 90n39